FRANCE AND NORTH AMERICA
THE REVOLUTIONARY EXPERIENCE

FRANCE AND NORTH AMERICA
THE REVOLUTIONARY EXPERIENCE

Proceedings of the
SECOND SYMPOSIUM OF FRENCH-AMERICAN STUDIES
March 26-30, 1973

Edited by
MATHÉ ALLAIN AND GLENN R. CONRAD

The USL Press
Lafayette, Louisiana
1974

IN MEMORIAM

Beatrice Fry Hyslop

Beatrice Fry Hyslop, whom the French nicknamed "Béatrice de France," and her colleagues, "Mademoiselle Cahiers," was born in New York City on April 10, 1899. After being graduated from Mount Holyoke College in 1919, she entered Columbia University where she was awarded a Master's degree in 1924 and a Ph.D. in 1934. In 1936 she joined the faculty of Hunter College with which she remained associated until her death in 1973.

An indefatigable scholar, physically as well as intellectually, Miss Hyslop attended the meetings of many learned societies. She addressed the International Congress of Historical Sciences in 1950 (Paris), 1955 (Rome) and 1960 (Stockholm); and the Congress of Learned Societies in 1952 (Grenoble) and 1955 (Rouen).

Beatrice Hyslop made the study of the 1789 cahiers her own private preserve. In 1933 she published her monumental Répertoire critique des Cahiers de Doléance which she followed with a no less monumental Supplément in 1952. Her French Nationalism According to the General Cahiers appeared in 1934 and her Guide to the General Cahiers in 1936. Her life devotion to the Duke of Orleans resulted in a study L'apanage de Philipe-Egalité Duc d'Orléans (1785-1791), published in 1965.

The French government recognized her services to French historical studies by making her an Officier d'académie in 1952 and a chevalier of the Legion of Honour in 1961.

French Revolution scholars in particular and historians in general will sorely miss this warm and gracious lady. Her colleagues at the University of Southwestern Louisiana and the symposium participants are particularly grateful to have had the opportunity of spending a week with her and of experiencing her formidable curiosity, unflagging energy and incisive questioning.

The editors respectfully dedicate this volume to the memory of Beatrice Fry Hyslop.

FOREWORD

The United States and modern France were born of revolution, almost simultaneously. In the two hundred years which have passed since their revolutionary births, both France and the United States have undergone smaller revolutions--political, social, intellectual--and each country has influenced the course of revolutionary developments in the other. Thus, looking forward to the bicentennial of the American Declaration of Independence, eighteen scholars spent a week in 1973 exploring the many facets of the revolutionary experience, from the very concept of revolution, to the future of revolutions.

As might be expected from a gathering of scholars, there was an enormous variety of views. Robert Holtman predicted this diversity in his keynote address and, as Amos Simpson commented in his summation, the audience was not disappointed. Professor Holtman also introduced, prophetically, a theme which was to recur throughout the week, that is from Robert Caponigri's subtle and complex study of constitutions to Henry Ehrmann's discussion of the May 1968 upheaval in France. Quoting Pierre Renouvin's statement "For it is always necessary to come back to power," Professor Holtman points out that a revolution cannot take place without leadership and power among revolutionaries or without its concomittant, lack of power and leadership among those in authority. Robert Caponigri similarly underlines the role of power: "The basic constitutive element of the social order is power," he states, and then defines constitution as "the flow of social power through the structure of right obligation and authority." Of course, power in Professor Caponigri's paper is not the same power Father Padberg refers to when he quotes the graffito "L'imagination prend le pouvoir," nor is it what Henry Ehrmann has in mind when he counters that "Power has to be taken by something more than imagination." Power, for Professor Caponigri, is the common good mediated "at the level of right and obligation, of the basic constitution," not the physical might involved in the power politics Marie Donaghay describes. But a definition of power such as Caponigri's entails a certain definition of revolution. Albert Soboul insists that revolution is short, violent, and total; Mario Fratti sees revolution as any change which is constructive; Bernard Harvey gives a mathematical formula for revolution; but Robert Caponigri defines revolution as an alteration of the legitimizing principle which establishes this "flow of social power."

Historians often are not comfortable with power as an abstraction. They prefer an incarnate power, imbedded in people, and leaders. Richard Bienvenu, speaking as an historian, insists that "Ideas do not live, men do." Power for historians means powerful leaders, and the need for such people in revolutions was illustrated again and again by the assembled scholars. Revolutions can occur only if constituted authority fails to act, a point illustrated by Professor Laurent's description of the division existing among those in authority in Santo Domingo and by Henry Ehrmann's analysis of the French government's failure of nerve in May 1968.

No revolution is possible in any field without strong towering figures to unify and clarify the movement. Without an ideology, says George Rudé, there is no revolution; a revolution "needs an ideology or Weltanschauung to give some degree of unity and coherence to an otherwise diversified movement." This ideology, Professor Rudé states, is composed of two elements, the inherent ideology one is born with and the derived ideas one learns. The derived ideas, according to Richard Bienvenu, are those of the intellectual leaders, and the impact of these ideas in no way depends on a correct understanding of them by revolutionaries.

What holds true in the domain of ideas also prevails in the arts and sciences. As Albert Griffith points out, "the taste of the society influences the artist in what he is capable of doing," but in turn "the artist can have a counter-influence on the tastes of that same society." Professor Griffith emphasizes that Susan Sontag's statement "Art today is an instrument for modifying consciousness and organizing new modes of sensibility" was as true in the eighteenth century as it is in the twentieth. Gita May proves the point in her discussion of Rousseau's impact on eighteenth-century sensibility. It may be simplistic to say that the French Revolution

was "la faute à Rousseau, la faute à Voltaire,"--Professor Bienvenu discusses at some length this elusive cause-and-effect rela-
tionship--but no one can deny that Romanticism would have had a
different cast had La Nouvelle Héloïse and Emile never been published.

The impact of leaders on the arts can also be seen in architecture and painting. Marie Antoinette's hameau, Roy Graham
tells us, made the pittoresque fashionable, and the architects whose
taste was formed during the years immediately preceding the
French Revolution spread the style in the New World.

In the arts, just as in politics, the much quoted remark
"There goes the crowd. I am their leader. I must follow" often
holds true. The social and intellectual climate of the revolutionary
years shaped the sensibility of the artistic leaders. Jean-Louis
David, Keith Marshall tells us, painted "the manifesto of the neoclassical school" with his Oath of the Horatii, a painting which
crystallizes the scattered elements of the new sensibility. A similar development took place in landscape architecture when Hogarth's
serpentine line became the organizing principle. *

Transfer of power--political, economic, social, intellectual,
aesthetic--is therefore at the very heart of revolution. It is the
mainspring of revolution, whether one speaks of a revolution of
rising expectation as does Holtman; of an anti-feudal reaction, as
does Soboul; of the frustrations of petits-blancs and affranchis as
does Laurent; or whether one wishes to treat the revolutions in
taste which take place in painting, architecture, landscaping,
literature or theatre. Transfer of power is also at the heart of
revolutionary consequences. The new principle of legitimization,
to borrow Caponigri's phrase, transfers political power to a new
class or group but by so doing affects people and through them both
thought and sensibility. Such transfers will always take place for
power is, in its essence, fluid and not static.

Today, old-style political revolutions may be no longer
necessary, may even be impossible--as Amos Simpson states
when summing up that exciting week--the old-type revolution may

---

*David Chase's lecture "American Landscape: Stylistic
Influences in the Revolutionary Age" was delivered from notes and
unfortunately could not be readied in time for inclusion in this
volume.

ix

only survive as an "exhilarating" memory as the French Revolution still is according to Soboul. Yet revolution, in one form or another will continue. The awareness which, according to Mario Fratti, "will save the world" is as revolutionary as life itself, and life as Caponigri quotes, is change so that "to be perfect is to have changed often." We may well conclude with Professor Holtman "The Revolution is dead; long live the Revolution."

The papers included in this volume were first presented at a symposium of French-American studies held at the University of Southwestern Louisiana on March 26-30, 1973. The Institute of French Studies, organizer of the symposium, dedicated the event to the Honorable James Domengeaux, Chairman of the Council for the Development of French in Louisiana, in gratitude for his tireless effort to perpetuate le fait française in the state.

The Institute wishes to express its sincere appreciation for the generous support of the University and the gracious cooperation of its many branches and departments. The School of Art and Architecture designed the poster used here as jacket design and erected the Revolutionary Pavilion; the School of Music organized an evening of opera and ballet as well as a recital of French and Acadian piano music performed by Edgar Davis; Mrs. John Love, at the Art Center for Southwestern Louisiana, assembled an exhibit of French paintings from 1812 to 1972, and the USL Union provided excellent daily luncheons in its pleasant facilities.

Many people helped in making the week memorable. The Institute particularly wishes to thank Mrs. Larry Baker who coordinated the social activities, Professor William Moreland, who acted as liaison with the School of Art and Architecture, and Professor Edgar Davis who performed the same function with the School of Music. President Clyde Rougeou and Vice-President Ray Authement are owed special thanks for their help during the week and for their unfailing support of the project.

Mathé Allain and Glenn Conrad
University of Southwestern Louisiana
Lafayette, Louisiana
1974

Robert B. Holtman holds the Ph. D. from the University of Wisconsin. An active member of the Southern Historical Association and French Historical Studies, Dr. Holtman is the author of many studies on French history including Napoleonic Propaganda and The Napoleonic Revolution as well as numerous articles. Professor Holtman is presently lecturing at Louisiana State University.

Robert Caponigri, professor of philosophy at Notre Dame University, is the author of Time and Idea: The Theory of History in Giambattista Vico, History and Liberty: The Historical Writing of Benedetto Croce, Modern Catholic Thinkers, History of Western Philosophy (5 volumes), Major Trends in Mexican Philosophy, Contemporary Spanish Philosophy, as well as innumerable articles.

Richard T. Bienvenu, who teaches history at the University of Missouri in Columbia, is a specialist of European intellectual history, with emphasis on the history of social thought. His publications include The Ninth of Thermidor: The Fall of Robespierre; and The Utopian Vision of Charles Fourier which he coedited with Jonathan Beecher. He is presently at work on the long-term project "Work In Western Thought and Culture, 1600 to the Present."

Marie Martenis Donaghay teaches history at Radford College. A specialist of early European history, Professor Donaghay is a graduate of the University of Delaware. She holds the Ph. D. from the University of Virginia, having been awarded a three-year P. F. DuPont Fellowship, a French government grant, and a Woodrow Wilson Dissertation Fellowship.

Albert Marius Soboul, who holds the chair of French Revolution at the Sorbonne, is a pupil of Georges Lefebvre. Director of the Institute of French Revolution, president of the Société des Etudes Robespierristes, and editor of the Annales historiques de la Révolution Française, Professor Soboul is a prolific writer. Besides his monumental Les Sans-Culottes parisiens en l'an II, he has published 1789. "L'an I de la Liberté"; Saint-Just. Discours et Rapports; Les campagnes montpelliéraines à la fin de l'Ancien Régime; Les Soldats de l'an II; Précis d'histoire de la Révolution française; Le procès de Louis XVI; La France à la veille de la Révolution; Le Directoire et le Consulat; Les Sans-Culottes; La première République, 1792-1804; La civilisation et la Révolution française I: La crise de l'Ancien Régime.

Gérard M. Laurent, curator of the Musée National of Haiti, has written numerous studies on Haiti, including Coup d'Oeil sur la politique de Toussaint L'Ouverture, Six études sur J. J. Dessalines, T. L'Ouverture à travers sa correspondence, Documentation historique pour nos étudiants, Pages d'histoire d'Haiti, Le Comissaire Sonthonax à Saint-Domingue, A Brief History of Haiti for Foreigners, and Contribution à l'histoire de Saint-Domingue.

Albert J. Griffith is interested in Southern fiction, American romanticism, and the literature of the mixed media. He contributed the volume on Peter Taylor to the Twayne United States Authors Series. His articles have appeared in journals such as the Explicator, America, Emerson Society Quarterly, Studies in Short Fiction, Georgia Review, and Commonweal. He teaches English at Our Lady of the Lake, in San Antonio.

Keith Cooper Marshall is still writing his doctoral thesis on Ruskin for Oxford University, but has firmly established himself in New Orleans as lecturer, opera chronicler, and gallery director. He has lectured extensively in England, France and New Orleans. His publications include John McCrady; Divergent Delicacies: French Decorative Arts of the Early Twentieth Century, and many articles on art and drama.

Roy E. Graham, now Resident Architect at Williamsburg, Virginia, was teaching architecture and architectural history at the University of Texas, Austin, when he delivered the paper published below. His publications include Texas Historic Forts, a five-volume study, and Progressive Preservations. He is presently working on an architectural biography of Joseph Jacques Ramée and on a history of Texas courthouses.

George Rudé, who is currently teaching at Sir George Williams University in Montreal, has been contributing articles on revolutionary history since 1955 to journals such as History Today, Annales historiques de la Révolution française, The Historical Journal, The Guildhall Miscellany, English Historical Review, and the Flinders Journal of History and Politics. His books include the seminal The Crowd in the French Revolution, The Crowd in History, Wilkes and Liberty, Revolutionary Europe, The Eighteenth Century, and Paris and London in the Eighteenth Century.

Bernard George Harvey, who holds the Ph.D. from Oxford, is a specialist of nuclear research and spectroscopy as well as of the nuclear and chemical properties of transuranium elements which he has researched for the British Ministry of Supply. Presently working in the Lawrence Berkeley Laboratory of the University of California at Berkeley, Bernard Harvey has published numerous papers in scientific periodicals.

Mario Fratti, a native of Aquila, Italy, had a European reputation when he came to the United States in 1964. This visit was originally intended for the purpose of reviewing the New York stage for European publications, but Dr. Fratti joined the faculty of Hunter College and remained in New York which he finds an exhilarating city. The author of some fifty plays, Mario Fratti has had his work performed in Europe, South America, Asia, and Canada. In New York his plays have had off-Broadway productions, though one play, The Victim, is being readied for a Broadway run after a successful Toronto tryout.

Gita May was born in Brussels where she studied art at the Académie Royale des Beaux-Arts. She holds the Ph.D. from Columbia University where she is the first woman to have held a full-time position. A specialist of Pre-Romanticism, Mrs. May is the author of Diderot et Baudelaire, Critiques d'art; De Jean-Jacques Rousseau à Madame Roland: Essai sur la sensibilité préromantique et révolutionnaire; and Madame Roland and the Age of Revolution. Her articles have appeared in PMLA, Symposium, The Romance Review, The French Review, French Studies, L'Esprit créateur and Revue d'Histoire Littéraire de la France.

John William Padberg, S.J., is a specialist of modern intellectual history and historical theology. Father Padberg is currently serving as Acting Executive Vice President of St. Louis University. He is the author of Colleges in Controversy: The Jesuit College in France from Revival to Suppression, 1815-1880 and many articles in professional journals.

Henry W. Ehrmann was born in Berlin but left Germany in 1933, being among the first Hitler exiles. He served as research associate at the New School of Social Research from 1940-1943, and as educational specialist for the United States government from 1943 to 1947. Now retired, Professor Ehrmann has been associated with Dartmouth College since 1961. A specialist of comparative government, international law, and legal philosophy, Professor Ehrmann is the author of French Labor from Popular Front to Liberation, Organized Business in France, and Politics in France.

Amos E. Simpson, professor of history at the University of Southwestern Louisiana, is a specialist of modern European history as evidenced by his publications: Hjalmar Schacht in Perspective; Why Hitler?; Death of an Old World: Europe, 1914-1945; Genesis of a New World: Europe, 1945 to the Present. His interest in state and local history is manifested by his coauthored biography of Henry Watkins Allen of Louisiana, and many articles in Louisiana and Arkansas journals.

CONTENTS

FRANCE AND NORTH AMERICA
THE REVOLUTIONARY EXPERIENCE

PLUS ÇA CHANGE

Robert B. Holtman

Probably one should not begin a week-long symposium, whether on revolution or any other topic, with an X-rated talk. Yet that is what this is going to be. Not because it will be lurid-- if there are any lurid details, they will have to come in the papers that follow. The program does not reveal the fact, but Professor Conrad wrote that he wanted a keynote speech, and to me, at least, a keynote address at a scholarly gathering is an unknown quantity. (For that matter, you are an X-rated audience. As I was pre- paring this talk, I had little idea just what kind of audience would be here this morning.) Before Professor Conrad asked whether I would undertake this function, and I accepted, I had thought of key- note addresses only in a political sense. And, like Artemus Ward,[1] "I am not a politician, and my other habits are also good."

It was another humorist, though of quite a different kind, Robert Louis Stevenson, who said that man does not live by bread alone; he needs catchwords.[2] One catchword which has done yeo- man duty is "Plus ça change, plus c'est la même chose" (the more it changes, the more it is the same thing). Although Profes- sor Conrad once intimated that he was trying to persuade Professor

---

[1]Pen name of Charles Farrar Browne.

[2]"Man is a creature who lives not upon bread alone, but principally by catchwords." Virginibus Puerisque, I, Ch. 2.

1

Simpson to change the title of his summation to "Plus c'est la même chose," I am glad he did not succeed in doing so. Had he succeeded, it would have revealed a "communications gap," to bring in another catchword, as this week--starting with this very paper-- will show that things are not the same after a period of change.

As we shall be approaching our topic for the week from basically an historical point of view, before we proceed further a word is in order on the nature of history. What I am about to say is not, of course, the final word; it merely conveys some of my own thoughts and convictions on historical study and the historical approach. Historians do not agree among themselves as to just what distinguishes their discipline. Pieter Geyl, the outstanding Dutch historian who died in 1966, put it very well by saying that history was "argument without end."[3] That is one reason it is often frustrating to students who are seeking answers. You can well imagine that it is not very satisfying to a student who asks his professor what the answer is (in Officers' Candidate School we referred to this as the 'school solution') to be told, "The answer is--that there is no answer."

The most obvious feature of history is that it deals with the past. Not all the past, for then there would be no prehistory, but that part of the past for which man has left written records. Because these records are never complete, even when none of them has been lost or destroyed, the historian can never be completely sure that he has the right answer.

In our discussions this week, I am sure that we are going to have disagreement. Professors Cobb, Rudé, and Soboul have all specialized, to a greater or lesser degree, in the role of the common man in the French Revolution. Yet their interests are diverse. Professor Soboul is interested in the matters of lower-class political action and possible class consciousness. Professor Cobb himself describes what he writes as impressionistic history. Professor Rudé has been interested in destroying myths as to the composition of the crowd in the French Revolution.

Another extremely important characteristic of history is that it deals, or should deal, with the concrete. When we speak of the American Revolution, or the French Revolution, we are talking about a concrete development which occurred in a specific place at a specific time--and it matters that it was then and there! We try to study it in the round, not to extract one aspect to see how it fits into an abstract concept.

---

[3]Pieter Geyl, <u>Napoleon</u>, <u>For</u> <u>and</u> <u>Against</u> (New Haven, 1949), 16.

For history, whatever else it may be, is not a social science. (The debate is still continuing as to whether history is a humanity or a social study; one leading university has hedged by permitting each member of its history department to decide whether his courses will count as humanities or social studies credit toward a degree requirement.) It is not a social science because it is not interested in establishing laws. Mr. Cobb is quite right in his desire, expressed in the introduction to The Police and the People, not to want to establish general laws or to be accused of writing scientific history.[4] And after my remarks today, I trust you will not say, along with Mr. Cobb in his warning against comparative study, "So-and-so, who attempted to write an Anatomy of Revolution, disappeared here without a trace."[5]

In not seeking to establish laws, history differs from such disciplines as economics, political science (a misnomer if there ever was one, for politics is obviously more an art than a science), and sociology. Historians are of course interested in trends, and in making useful associations of the concrete facts with which they must begin. But a trend and a law are quite different. A trend is subject to reversal at any time; a law is immutable, something on the basis of which accurate predictions can be made. If there is one thing above all of which the historian is wary, it is making predictions. I learned my own lesson many years ago, almost thirty-three to be exact. I was at that time a doctoral student in a department whose chairman, a specialist in British history, was an immigrant from Norway who always retained a delightful accent. (I might mention parenthetically that one night when a social snob, looking down her nose, told him that her ancestors had come over on the Mayflower, he responded: "Really? I came when there was restricted immigration.") When the Germans invaded Norway during World War II, this British history specialist predicted that the English would drive the Nazis out in two weeks. It took two weeks, plus five years.

Another respect in which history differs from other social studies is that it deals only with change. We often hear that a country, or some other area, does not have any history during a certain period of time. This is merely another way of stating that there has not been any meaningful change. The sociologist, or the political scientist, or the economist, is willing to deal with still pictures;

---

[4]R. C. Cobb, The Police and the People: French Popular Protests, 1789-1820 (Oxford, 1970), xix.

[5]Ibid.

the historian demands movies. The social scientist, for purposes
of study, is willing to stop the world, or the revolution--not to get
off, but to analyze it at one moment or analyze one aspect of it.
History, then, is a much more dynamic type of study than the
others about which we have been talking--unless they adopt a historical approach. And that is another reason students find history
difficult; unlike a foreign language or mathematics, where one
builds by repeating, it keeps moving on from one thing to the next.

The changes with which history concerns itself may be
more or less fast or slow, more or less partial or complete. If
the changes come rapidly enough and are sufficiently far-reaching,
we speak of a revolution--without any consensus as to just when
change changes from evolution to revolution. We are starting our
considerations with the American and French revolutions. In one
of his books, Professor R. R. Palmer uses these terms in speaking
of the American Revolution: "The upheaval in America was a revolution as well as a war of independence."[6] In his thinking, therefore, simply winning independence from the mother country was
insufficient for the events in America to be called revolutionary;
other changes had to accompany that development. Although I
personally believe that the impact of the colonies' wrenching themselves from British control was sufficiently great that their doing
so was not just a palace revolt, it is true that we talk about the
ideals as well as the actions of the revolutionaries.

Without trying to delimit evolution and revolution (any
attempt to do so would probably be no more soundly based than the
Papal Line of Demarcation of 1492, between the Spanish and Portuguese realms of colonial exploitation), let us turn our attention
for a few minutes to the problem of when revolutions occur. For
they are not inevitable.

The whole concept of the lack of inevitability in history
inspired some forty years ago a book entitled If, or History
Rewritten. A group of scholars and writers each contributed an
essay on how later developments would have been different, "if."
In the introduction the editor states, "There is no action or event,
great or small,...which might not have happened differently, and
happening differently, have perhaps modified the world's history for
all time."[7] If there are any devotees of science fiction in the

---

[6]R. R. Palmer and Joel Colton, A History of the Modern
World, 4th ed. (New York, 1971), 368.

[7]J. C. Squire, ed., If, or History Rewritten (New York,
1931), v.

audience, they especially will appreciate this line of thought. André Maurois, in his essay on "If Louis XVI Had Had an Atom of Firmness," says: "There is no privileged Past....There is an infinitude of Pasts, all equally valid....At each and every instant of Time, however brief you suppose it, the line of events forks like the stem of a tree putting forth twin branches....One of these branches represents the sequence of facts as you, poor mortal, know it; and the other represents what History would have become if one single detail had been other than it was."[8]

George Kennan has said much the same thing in other, less extreme terms in his volume on The Marquis de Custine and His Russia in 1839: "It is a reasonable view...that the Russian Revolution was fortuitous, insofar as it was the product of a number of factors in the sudden coming-together of which no logical pattern can be discerned. One can think of a number of individual circumstances any one of which might very easily, but for the hand of chance, have been quite different than it actually was--and different in such a way as to obviate the second Russian Revolution of 1917, if not the first....This, I reiterate, might have happened. It was a possibility. And...it was only by action of the hand of chance that it did not happen."[9]

If revolutions, then, are not inevitable, when and why and how do they come? Before answering these questions, at least in part, we must note that there is a wide variety of revolutions. There are revolutions which are political, economic, social, intellectual, liberal, reactionary--or a combination.

The diversity is revealed in the topics which are going to be discussed this week. When we talk about the American and French revolutions, we are thinking, probably, mainly in political terms. But look in your programs at some of the other topics to be discussed. (I want to emphasize that I have not seen any of the papers and do not know what themes the speakers are going to develop.) Professor Caponigri deals with the matter of social change. The sessions on Wednesday are devoted to cultural affairs--art, architecture, and a consideration of changes in likes and dislikes. Thursday we move into the areas of science and the theatre. Friday the question of religion and morals, and their relationship to revolution, is on the docket. Finally, a paper on

---

[8]Squire, If, or History Rewritten, 112.

[9]George F. Kennan, The Marquis de Custine and His Russia in 1839 (Princeton, N. J., 1971), 130-131.

the outburst of May, 1968, in which the students played a large role, keeps us from forgetting that revolution is still with us; and Professor Simpson reminds us that it <u>will</u> be with us, and offers some thoughts as to its direction.

But to return to some of the factors which help bring on revolution. An obvious one, if we speak of political revolution, is war. War can so upset the domestic relationships in a country that a revolution becomes not only desirable, but feasible. Particularly is this true if the country is on the losing side. Mussolini even went so far as to state that no government ever fell for domestic reasons alone. This is, of course an exaggeration--we do not have to look further than the French Revolution to see its error (unless we go back some distance for the wars)--but it does serve to illustrate the importance foreign war may play.

If I were to hazard a statement as to the most important factor making for the liberal type of revolution we have in mind with the American and French revolutions, I should say that it is a sudden, even though possibly temporary, halt brought to an improvement in conditions. France had long been one of the most prosperous of European countries. But near the end of the eighteenth century the prosperity of the majority of the people began to suffer. In large part this was caused by a rapid increase in the population, with no corresponding increase in output. Prices therefore rose, bringing with them all the kinds of disgruntlement which you can either imagine or call to mind from experience. Added to this general situation we have the more devastating one of poor harvests in the years immediately preceding the revolution, so that prices rose even more, there was increased unemployment, and even hunger.

We should emphasize, however, that misery is not <u>the</u> cause of revolution. If it were, instead of talking about the French Revolution we would be discussing the German Revolution, or the Spanish, or the Polish, or the Russian.

If we look briefly at the background of two other revolutions, we find a situation similar to that in France. Russia under Witte and Stolypin[10] had been gaining ground economically, and it had got at least a reasonable facsimile of a legislature after the revolution of 1905. (We might reflect for a moment on the fact that the name of the Russian legislature, <u>duma</u>, comes from the word <u>to think</u>, while the French and English word "parliament" comes

---

[10]Count Sergei Witte served as minister of finance from 1893 to 1903, and Count Peter Stolypin served as minister of the interior from 1906 to 1911.

from the word to speak!) Then came World War I to disrupt the gains, a war in the midst of which came the two revolutions of 1917.

In America it was more a feeling of being hedged in than of actual hardship. The story of how Britain, after the French and Indian War, decided to make the colonies actually pay toward the support of the government--earlier it had cost more to collect the taxes than the imposts yielded--and to contribute to their defense is too well known to all of us to need much stress here. But the American situation does reveal at least one other very important factor.

Assuming that all the conditions are ripe for a revolution-- and we shall say more about these conditions in a moment--no revolution would occur unless there was leadership. The Americans who felt the pinch of the new British policy were the potential leaders: the merchants, the editors, the lawyers. (I might mention that these last two are also among the most vocal groups.) In France, likewise, though for different reasons, men in the upper social brackets assumed the leadership.

This brings us to a realization that those in positions of authority play a predominant role. This was epitomized, I believe, in a colloquium organized by Professor Soboul in honor of the bicentennial of Napoleon's birth. Although the announced intention was to have the colloquium deal with history seen from below, to treat the history of men rather than of a man, Professor Pierre Renouvin, who had the final word of the conference, said: "Have we met men very much?...We have always met first and foremost 'power.' For it is always necessary to come back to power."[11] The difficulty of making the history of men meaningful is not difficult to comprehend: history is the story of change, and it is generally the men at the top who, in either a positive or a negative sense, make the meaningful decisions which bring on change. Although he concentrates on the common people, Professor Cobb has stated that the most astonishing fact about the history of the French Revolution is that a popular movement ever emerged, not that it failed.[12] The presence of leadership is a necessity, perhaps even more important for what might be considered a reactionary revolution (for example, fascism or nazism) than for the kind we more commonly think of.

---

[11]La France à l'Epoque napoléonienne, special issue of the Revue d'histoire moderne et contemporaine, Vol. 17 (July-Sept., 1970), 920.

[12]Cobb, Police and the People, xiv.

It should not surprise us that a minority, the leaders, is so important. Even though there is a tendency in this country to sneer at the Soviet Union because only ten percent of the people are Communists (card-carrying, that is), a mere four percent of the people in the United States contribute either time or money to the Democratic or Republican parties. Only five percent of the French people were involved in or with the maquis in World War II. Activists are always in the minority.

Still another factor making revolutions possible is the weakness of those in authority. Their weakness may be merely that of being unable to initiate or accept change which would avert what to them will be a catastrophe. Such was the weakness of Louis XVI, a ruler of good intentions without the backbone necessary to put his good intentions into effect or to back them when they caused discontent. Similarly weak was Nicholas II of Russia, even though not quite so weak as the movie Nicholas and Alexandra made him appear. Louis Gottschalk has said, and I agree, that the weakness of the ruling class is an absolute prerequisite for a revolution. [13] Perhaps this is an application of the dictum of Herbert Spencer that "motion universally takes place along the line of least resistance."[14]

No revolution could be put through if the government were able to maintain effective control of its troops, and to use them effectively. In the American Revolution, Britain was handicapped by the vast distances and the hostility of European rivals. In the French Revolution, for many reasons, the king did not and could not use his armed forces well to maintain his position.

Gottschalk has also rather firmly stated that without the American Revolution there would have been no French Revolution. [15] (Probably we shall hear some more on this from Professor

---

[13]Louis R. Gottschalk, "The Place of the American Revolution in the Causal Pattern of the French Revolution," as quoted in Herman Ausubel, The Making of Modern Europe (New York, 1951), 501.

[14]Herbert Spencer, Principles of Psychology, quoted in Richard L. Schoenwald, ed., Nineteenth-Century Thought: The Discovery of Change (Englewood Cliffs, N. J., 1965), 146.

[15]Gottschalk, "The Place of the American Revolution," especially page 501: "The French Revolution could hardly have come about without the American Revolution."

Donaghay.) The cost to France of the American Revolution completely ruined its finances, given the atmosphere of the times; and it was the financial plight of the French government which served as the immediate, precipitating cause of the Revolution. Gottschalk also ascribes other causal influences to the American Revolution: it gave experience to men who became important leaders in the initial phases of the French Revolution; French censorship had to be relaxed because the American Revolution, which France was backing, was influenced by the ideas which were being censored. And the mere fact that the new state proved to be viable served as an inspiration, just as the mere existence of the Soviet Union long inspired communists elsewhere. There is no question but that revolution tends to breed revolution. A revolution in one place will tend to inspire people elsewhere who have pent-up antagonisms to undertake a similar movement. One place to which the idea of revolution may spread is the colonies, as M. Laurent will explain.

It has become somewhat of a historical cliché to say "no ideas, no revolution." Although the statement is true to a large extent, one is impressed, time and again, by the fact that the revolutionaries did not plan to be revolutionaries, that they tried to call a halt to revolution as soon as possible. An article by George Taylor on "Revolutionary and Nonrevolutionary Content in the Cahiers of 1789" in the Fall, 1972, French Historical Studies reveals very clearly that a revolution tends to sneak up on people, that--contrary to the claim of de Tocqueville--there was no revolutionary mentality in eighteenth-century France. Mr. Taylor makes the point that the revolutionary state of mind was a result and not a cause of the crisis starting in 1787.[16] He also points out, as did M. Louis Trenard in a talk to the Interuniversity Consortium on Revolutionary Europe last month, that not only did the intellectuals not think of themselves as revolutionary, but they found themselves in opposition to the more radical phases of the revolution.

If there had been a revolutionary mentality developed by the thinkers of the eighteenth century, the philosophes, it would have been a result of the Enlightenment. But historians have now become wary of speaking of "the Enlightenment." They hedge by using such terms as "mature Enlightenment" and "high Enlightenment." We can look forward to a presentation on this very matter of the Enlightenment and the revolutionary mentality this afternoon. To Professor Bienvenu, we say "Welcome."

---

[16]George V. Taylor, "Revolutionary and Nonrevolutionary Content in the Cahiers of 1789," French Historical Studies, Vol. VII, No. 4 (Fall, 1972), 479-502.

The plight of the intellectuals during the revolution, mentioned a moment ago, results from the tendency of revolutions to become more radical as they progress. One element which pushes a revolution further and deeper is becoming embroiled in a war. The Reign of Terror in France and the period of War Communism in Russia are good examples. Professor Trenard used a phrase I liked--he called the men for whom the revolution became too radical "Sorcerer's Apprentices," men unable to sweep back the tide.

The opposition of the intellectuals also illustrates the historical truism that what men want, what they design, is not always what occurs. In fact, the results of their deliberate actions to obtain a certain desired result might be just the opposite of what they intended. Conversely, we cannot reason that because a revolution took place, it was the goal men sought.

After a time there may take place what has come to be known, because of the French Revolution, as a Thermidorian Reaction; the moderates gain control. But it should be noted that this is much less likely in a reactionary revolution than in a liberal or democratic one.

Although we have stressed that only a minority can be expected to be activists, it is equally true that this minority must have at least the passive support of the majority. Peasants and proletarians do not engineer revolutions, but without their backing the minority cannot succeed.

We have heard of politicians being pushed or pulled, kicking and screaming, into the twentieth century. Many a man or woman has been similarly pulled into an economic or social revolution. At least passively, they have gone along with political change. But if political revolutions are made by minorities, how much more true that statement must be for an intellectual revolution. Although Newton said that all he had done was stand on the shoulders of those who had preceded him, that position--as at a Mardi Gras parade--gave him an eminence permitting him to see further than any man before him, and further than all but a few after him. There has been only one Isaac Newton, only one Albert Einstein, only one Max Planck. One of the outstanding differences, it seems to me, between an intellectual revolution and any other kind is the relative smallness of the number who accomplish the former. The change from neoclassical art to romantic art was a true revolution in its field, about which we shall hear from Mr. Marshall and Ms. May. The number of leaders in this change was infinitesimal.

For the French, contemporary history begins in 1789--somewhat further back than most of us have in mind when we use the term "contemporary." The reason, of course, is the conviction that whether for better or worse (and there still exists a schism with respect to the French Revolution) the changes effected by the Revolution separate the world we know from what prevailed earlier. Without even attempting to list, far less to detail, these changes, we might mention such items as the increased importance of that amorphous thing, the bourgeoisie; a revamped administrative and judicial system; popular participation in government; the opening of careers to talent, talent abetted by a national system of education; the idea of civil liberty.

Much the same thing may be said of the American Revolution, which in its early phases led Turgot, the first and one true reform minister of Louis XVI, to say, "This people is the hope of the human race."[17] He made the statement because of our idealism, the belief in individual rights, in government by the people. For a long time the United States remained a symbol of idealism to the world.

There is, however, another side to having had a revolution. We Americans, for instance, tend to feel that our revolution eliminated a bad situation, replacing it with a desirable one which will last permanently. We fail to realize that static institutions cannot last. Although we give lip service to our great documents of liberty, we tend to be ignorant of and to fear their statements. Some years ago a reporter gained at least fleeting fame by taking some of the statements from the Declaration of Independence and asking people on July 4 whether they subscribed to them. He had to ask a hundred to find the first one. This attitude led Professor Herbert J. Muller to conclude his book The Children of Frankenstein by writing "There is also a real possibility that America... may go down as the greatest failure in history,"[18] because of the advantages we enjoyed in a new land of immense resources. He went on to say, somewhat more optimistically (or less pessimistically) in a later book: "A study of the whole recorded history of man is finally always a study of failure.... It is also a study of great achievement that survives the failures and the deaths, and that may still inspire. So we may hope that America too will be remembered for its dreams and its ideal achievements, not merely

---

[17]In a letter to Dr. Price, March 22, 1778, as found in his Oeuvres, 2:809. This volume is volume IV of Collection des principaux économistes, ed. by Eugène Daire and Hippolyte Dussard (Paris, 1844).

[18]Herbert J. Muller, The Children of Frankenstein (Bloomington, Ind., 1970), 416.

its failures. "[19]

At the colloquium on Napoleon to which I referred earlier, Professor Soboul said, "We shall never finish with Napoleon. His history will never be totally finished, nor ever totally written."[20] The same may be said of the French Revolution, the American Revolution, of revolutions. It, and they, are too diverse, too profound, ever to have "the truth" written about them. New problems relating to them are constantly being posed. Historians will continue to debate about them and, again in Geyl's terms, perhaps to use and abuse their history. But one thing is certain: the revolutions effected change. And that is good. As Jacob Burckhardt, best known for his writing on art history, said in his essay "On Fortune and Misfortune in History," "Only the fairy tale equates changelessness with happiness."[21] Without change there is no history; without change there is no happiness.

The Revolution is dead; long live the Revolution.

---

[19]Herbert J. Muller, In Pursuit of Relevance (Bloomington, Ind., 1971), 35-36. The quotation is taken from the essay, "The Seamy Side of American History."

[20]France à l'époque napoléonienne, 338.

[21]Jacob Burckhardt, Force and Freedom: An Interpretation of History, ed. by James Hastings Nichols (New York, 1955), 318.

PHILOSOPHY, REVOLUTION AND SOCIAL CHANGE

A. Robert Caponigri

Introduction

Philosophy, revolution, social change: this would surely seem a casual conjunction of concerns. Yet, on reflection, that is not the case. Historically, in the order of events, and in theory in the order of ideas, a real continuity has obtained between these notions and the realities they denote. For has not philosophy been proclaimed the great fomentor of revolution, not in an abstract manner, but historically, as a true efficient cause? This was surely the case with the French Revolution, in the minds both of the great Edmund Burke and in the major figures of the traditionalist movement; both saw the historical principle of that revolution in the philosophy of the Enlightenment and especially in its ideas concerning the abstract basis of right and the manner in which the constitutions of nations can be adjudicated and re-created. And was not Ferrari among the first to say that not historically only, but in the order of logical necessity, philosophy, as a human activity, must have an effect, in every order, which can only be called revolutionary? And surely to suggest that revolution, in its most inclusive sense, must be recognized to be a form of social change must seem the acme of understatement. Revolution, as Plato said of the polis and man, especially in its more violent forms, is social change writ large. No, amid this trinity of terms a definite unity obtains, though one which is by no means immediately apparent. The task, then, is to trace this inner relation which must, when clarified, cast reflective illumination on all the component terms.

To undertake this task, in even the most modest way, with any hope of success, an order of inquiry must be established; for every inquiry (as Aristotle said, in the Poetics, of every whole) must have a beginning, a middle and an end. In the present inquiry, the end would seem to be more readily apparent than the beginning, for what we would like the inquiry to produce is a clearer notion of what revolution is in its essence and what role it can and possibly must play in modern social life. Our point of departure, however, is much less clear and must, in any event, be somewhat arbitrary. We must choose, and hope that the choice will be a happy one and lead us to that middle which in turn will lead us to our desired end. Or, with Hegel (in his animadversions on the Kantian criticism, as to the point of departure of philosophy) we must not lay too heavy burdens on ourselves. We must begin where we are. And what can be more certain than that we, like mankind at every juncture of his history, stand knee-deep in social change. The burden of choice, then, is lightened for us. Our point of departure is given us as Ortega would say, by our circumstance.

Revolution and Social Change

The most striking, and at the same time the most disconcerting, feature of social change in our time is the language in which men speak of it. More particularly, it is the ease, and the tone of approbation, with which the idiom of revolution is applied to social change in all its aspects and dimensions. Contemporary man adopts this idiom spontaneously, it would seem, to express his response to change in every area of life from the most trivial to the most weighty. Alterations in fashions of dress, in literary style, in artistic taste, in politics, education, art, yes even in religion, are all depicted in the language of revolution. And, of course, we can all remember when the great revolution in philosophy was officially announced on the BBC network and thus, we assume, made official. Moreover, this idiom is applied in the most approbative manner. The highest accolade that can be bestowed on any thing: a scientific discovery, a fresh departure in architecture, a new policy in government or education, is to call it revolutionary; and, needless to say, new deans are expected to bring only revolutionary ideas to their office. When all change is revolutionary, however, no change exists at all, but simply chaos and his Miltonic companion, Old Night; for significant, indeed merely recognizable, change occurs only relative to some principle of order. Some clarification, consequently, seems mandatory. We must find a canon by which to distinguish, within the total welter of social change, a particular event of change, or process of change, that which demands to be recognized as revolutionary.

Change, then, to be significant, indeed to be change at all, implies order. Without order, there is no change but only chaos, that unspeakable condition which embarrassed even Satan, a most order-conscious creature if ever there was one, when, in his flight from Hell to Eden, he encountered the old Anarch face to face. If true in general, this fact is eminently true, in social change. Every social structure exhibits two facets: there are, on the one hand, the principle or principles which constitute it and order it, and, on the other, the transactions, relations, oppositions in unity, etc., which transpire or have their <u>locus</u> in that order. The principles of that order stabilize the transactions which are possible within the order, assign the <u>loci</u> and the functions of components, distribute their efficiency-differential and define the ambit of the whole. But the actuality of the order consists in the reality of those transactions, of those components, of those relations and efficiencies. In saying this, of course, we do no more than reiterate Aristotle; in this day, however, no small feat. It follows, then, that changes or alterations, within such a totality, can be of two kinds. They may be changes within the system, or they may be changes of the system, that is, of the principle or principles which establish the order which, in turn, constitutes the system. But at once it must be said that, while the distinction between the two kinds of change may seem facile abstractly, it is by no means so in actuality. There, in fact, the greatest acumen is necessary to distinguish the one from the other. For events may corrode principles, while false principles may corrupt not events only, but with greater disaster, persons as well. In social change, as in the spiritual life, discernment is the axial function, <u>phronesis</u>, no science, but an art, and hence only dubiously teachable.

But a further distinction seems necessary to our purpose. Every social system or order is dynamic; that is to say, it provides the conditions of and the energy for change within itself, for changes which are according to the system, and hence are integral to the system, constitutive of the system. These provisions for change within the system, in turn, may touch either the transactions and relations within the system or, conceivably, the principles of the system itself. I say conceivably, because, as we shall see, the possibility of this kind of provision is a key issue in the notion of revolution. Changes within the system, but not according to the provisions of the system for changes within the system, are productive of deviations or monstrosities within the system and to its principles; they are absolute only if it can be shown that one and only one system is allowable and normative. Changes at this level, whether according to the system, or deviate, cannot be called revolutionary in any strict sense, but only, as Burke says, by a philosophy of analogy. The analogue, to which he is making reference, is the order of principles. With the question of change in the order of principles, we enter the realm of the revolutionary; but only problematically, for as we shall see, certain distinctions and clarifications will be necessary before the notion of revolution may emerge in anything like its full light. Before this is possible, however, another concept must be drawn into the arena of discourse, to be discretely veronicaed, like a lusty bull by a reluctant matador. This is the concept of constitution.

Constitution and Revolution

The concept of constitution represents a refinement upon the concept of system, a refinement necessary, we believe, for the penetration of the notion of revolution. In its substantial aspect, the constitution is the social system, but it is the social system in the distinction and interrelation of its components and processes rather than simply in its structure. Constitution contains within itself the elements, not only of the structure of the system, but of its constituting processes, its coming to be, and hence, since whatever comes to be is liable, in principle at least, to pass away, its possible passing away, through any process whatever, including revolution. What we must essay, consequently, in brief and modest form, is some comprehension of this concept of constitution.

The basic constitutive element of the social order is power. The power here in question is strictly human power, that is, the capacity of human persons to act and interact. This power must be carefully distinguished from other forms of power with which it is sometimes, too frequently perhaps, identified or confused, "physical" force. This confusion leads, on the other hand, to a misprision of the role of coercion in processes of social control and in the constitution and, on the other, to a misunderstanding of the type of science which it is possible to have about constitutional processes. Physical force, coercion, is always an instrumental component in the constitution, never a truly constitutive element; as a consequence, it becomes clear that the study of constitution must always be conceived as a strictly humanistic discipline. There can never be more than a loose and, not infrequently, deceptive analogy between human energy and physical power, a fact which renders a physics of politics essentially implausible.

The play of action and reaction between human agents, that is the flow of social power, is essentially free, spontaneous, and unstructured. That is to say, it contains within itself no inherent morphological principle which determines it to assume one structure rather than another. Nevertheless, it does, like any free play of power, tend to assume diverse patterns spontaneously; these, however, cannot be determined with any certainty a priori. An interesting example of what is meant by this free play is provided by the romantic theory of love. Love in romantic theory is just such a free play of forces, and its course can only be fortuitous. But since the outcome of such free play is unpredictable, it is as readily conceivable as fate. Hence also the dubious character of that philosophy which would make romantic love the basis of so rigid a social institution as marriage.

The structures of human action and interaction achieved through the operation of spontaneous casual principles are effective but not necessitating. That is to say, many forms of spontaneous human association are not only possible, but effective in the sense that they render human communication possible and achieve identifiable human goals with reasonable consistency and efficiency. It is necessary to place some emphasis on this point because it has not infrequently been taught that the principles of social order ought to be of this spontaneous and nonnecessitating character. We would agree that such structures will always flourish and will, to a great extent, form a substantial proportion of the associations into which human persons enter. But two points concerning such associations would seem to need emphasis. First, effective though they may be, they never exhibit that particular kind of structure called constitution; second, so long as the structuring principle of association is spontaneous and nonnecessitating, there can be change, but not revolution.

In any association spontaneously engendered and maintained and structure by a nonnecessitating principle, e.g., romantic love, there is invocation and response which is either unilateral or mutual and involves some good, material or otherwise, which is transferred or conferred. There is present, therefore, in such associations, the rudiments of constitutions, i.e., embryonic rights and obligations. But these rights and obligations are only embryonic, because their exchange rests on no necessitating principle; they remain essentially gifts and their exchange is subject to conditions to which the concept of revolution cannot apply. The pattern of exchange of gifts is transmuted into a structure of rights and obligations (whether mutual or unilateral is not here at question) only when established on the basis of a necessitating principle.

The relationship betwen simple community and constitution rests on the continuity of this structure of invocation and response (which involves the further elements of presence and recognition). The essential structure of constitution is that of invocation and response transformed into a situation of right and obligation by being reestablished on the basis of a necessitating principle. (The question of whether the principle is necessitating because recognized as such by those enacting the pattern of right and obligation, or is antecedently necessitating, independently of such recognition, is a very important one but one which we cannot enter into here at any length.) We noted earlier that invocation and response are mediated by a good. At the level of right and obligation, of the basic constitution, the common good mediated is power itself. For a right is constituted of effective power to make a claim; claim is that into which invocation is transmuted by being established on a necessitating principle; and claim is answered in terms of power, the expenditure of power by the respondent, his response transmuted into obligation by being in its turn established on a necessitating principle. Within this structure the _matter_ (i. e. , the good which is transferred, etc.) of right and _obligation_ is a variable.

The emergence of the system of right and obligation, the rudimentary and essential constitution, through the process of reestablishment of invocation and response on necessitating principles, generates a third dimension of constitution, authority. The origin of authority lies in the fact that once invocation and response are no longer spontaneous, have been transmuted into right and obligation, the right and obligation must in turn be necessitated; or, more precisely, the flow of social power through the pattern of right and obligation must be specified. The specification of the flow of power through right and obligation is the essential nature and function of authority. The fundamental structure of constitution, consequently, is that of the golden triangle: authority, right, and obligation.

Authority itself, however, can be either spontaneous or necessitated. Or, more accurately, the function of identifying or generating right and obligation, and directing the flow of social power through its pattern itself remains merely spontaneous and, hence, only embryonically authority so long as it is not in turn established on a necessitating principle. So long as this function remains spontaneous, its principle of change cannot be revolution. The constitution is completed only when the authority is also established on a principle of necessity. It is through the function of authority, through its mediating principle, through it as necessitating principle, that the necessity of the pattern of right and obligation is established.

The process by which right, obligation, and authority are translated from the merely spontaneous state to the necessitated

state, from the de facto to the de jure condition, is the process of
legitimization.   Legitimization is, consequently, the most central
process of the social genesis of constitution.   Through legitimization, the constitution is established in its entirety and its integrity.
We are now, consequently, in a position to identify constitution with
a certain unambiguity: constitution is the establishment of the pattern
of flow of social power through the structure of authority, right and
obligation.

At this point a number of questions arise which we shall only
mention and enumerate, not because they are unimportant and not
deserving of careful analysis, but because within the limited span
of this paper we are concerned to get on to the more central question,
that is, the relation between constitution and revolution· Among these
questions are the possible bases of legitimization, the possible forms
it may take, the precise mechanisms by which it generates civil
obedience.   Despite the term, law is but one legitimizing principle;
others range from "divine right," by the grace of God, to popular
consensus.   What all have in common, however, is their effect;
i. e., whatever the principle invoked, legitimization always has the
effect of translating the structure of invocation and response into the
golden triangle of authority, right, and obligation. The same is true
of the forms of legitimization: diverse in kind, they are one in their
effect, they express the relation authority, right, and obligation;
whether it be the anointment of an emperor or king by a pontifex
maximus or the casting of votes in the local polling place.   Equally
various are the contents of legitimization: the credenda, the tre-
menda, the miranda which it enshrines; but equally single is their
effect.

Legitimization, then, is the basic establishing principle of
constitution. In its material aspect, constitution is the flow of social
power through the structure of right obligation and authority; its
formal aspect is the legitimizing principle which establishes that
flow and gives it its obligating force. Recognition of this fact en-
ables us to take a further step toward the recognition of the essential character of revolution. Revolution is a transaction at the constitutional level: it is change at the constitutional level. Furthermore, revolution is change at this level, directed toward the status
of the legitimizing principle of the constitutional order. It is the
alteration of the legitimizing principle of the constitutional order
and, hence, of the constitutional order itself.   This and only this
kind of social change is revolutionary.

Legitimization, the Closed Constitution,
and the Viability of Revolution

Legitimization is, then, the central establishing process of constitution. Through it, the constitution comes into being as de juré and not merely de facto and from it the constitution achieves its primary characteristic: its obligatory character. Nevertheless, essential as the process of legitimization is, it is also ambiguous in its effect. It tends, of its own dynamism, to the generation of the closed constitution and through this process to affect profoundly the possibility and viability of revolution conceived as social change at the constitutional level and directed specifically at the status of the legitimizing principle of the constitution. What, then, is the closed constitution?

The closed constitution is that constitution in which any tentative alteration of the status of the legitimizing principle of the constitution is adjudicable by the system of norms and subject to penal action under the system of sanctions erected by the process of legitimization for the perpetuation and the stability of the constitution. Intimate to the structure of any constitution, and sustained by the principle of legitimization on which that constitution rests, is the system of controls by which that constitution renders itself effective and self-perpetuating. Within any constitution, two forms of the expenditure of the social synergism may be distinguished, both of which are validated by the legitimizing principle. The first is the expenditure of social synergism in the pursuit of the substantive goals of the constituted society. In the case of our own country, it will be remembered these were defined as life, liberty, and the pursuit of happiness, and, more specifically, justice, the common defense, etc. The second form of the expenditure of social synergism is a replicative movement directed toward securing the conditions which will insure the pursuit of the substantive goals. It is this second form of the expenditure of social energy which is essential to the notion of the closed constitution. This second form of the expenditure of social energy generates its own institutional structures: systems of norms, adjudicative processes, sanctions concerning not the pursuit of the substantive goals of the society directly, but the conditions which secure the pursuit of these substantive goals aginst impediment or deviation. The aim of this expenditure of social energy and the rationale of the institutions it calls into existence is the constitution itself, its preservation and perpetuation against any change except such as might be specifically provided for within and by the constitution itself, and legitimized by the constitution. The constitution thus forms a completely closed system, protected against alien change and especially against tentatives toward the alteration of its basis of legitimacy by this inner mechanism of self-perpetuation.

The closed constitution gives rise to an anomalous situation with respect to revolution. Revolution, it will be recalled, was identified as a tentative of social change directed against the status of the legitimizing principle of the constitution itself. The anomalous situation which arises is that any such tentative within the structure of the closed constitution must be adjudicated according to the very principle the status of which it is calling into question. Hence arises the notion of lèse majesté, ultimately of treason, and hence arises, too, what has been called the juridical theory of revolution. According to this conception, revolution as defined, that is as a tentative social change directed against the status of the legitimizing principle of the constitution, is by definition intolerable within the constitution. Against such a tentative, all of the defensive mechanism of the constitution is immediately aroused to repel it, to isolate and destroy it, and to bring to bear upon it all the punitive forces which the constitution can muster. The force of the closed constitution is to abort revolution by the rejection mechanism of the constitution itself.

More than one jurisprudentialist has recognized the essential analogous character of this situation. Some have censured it simply in terms of the sterility it engenders in any such constitution. Others have castigated it as a situation of essential injustice, in which the plantiff, i. e. , in this case, the constitution, is also judge and executioner over the adjudication and the rectification of the alleged delict, i. e. , the tentative of social change aimed at the status of the legitimizing principle of the constitution. The only palliative of this anomalous situation is that offered by those jurisprudentialists, like Cotta, who point out that it is entirely possible for a revolution, which has succeeded, to be assimilated into the constitution under attack and thus in its turn to become legitimized. That this is not a genuine resolution of the anomaly, but a mere palliative seems very clear.

The history of revolutions bears out this picture. In every case of revolution in history, the constitution has exhibited the tendency to treat the revolutionary effort as a basic lèse of the constitution itself and to bring to bear upon it and its perpetrators the full force of its juridical and penal resources. And when it has proved less than successful in aborting the effort and in expelling the center of that revolutionary movement from its center, the constitution, when strong, has ended up, as Cotta has noted, in assimilating the revolution to itself; or, when it is weak, simply disappearing from history.

The theorist who has placed this tendency of the process of legitimization to generate the closed constitution in greatest relief is Hobbes. And he looked upon the process with complete complacency although the specific theory by which he explained this process and justified its consequences, namely his form of the contract theory, does not recommend itself universally. The true force of the Hobbesian theory of contract, dubious as it is in itself, serves to call attention to the deeper question whether there can be an absolute legitimizing principle or whether, in fact, every legitimizing principle sustaining a closed constitution does not degenerate into tyranny and coercion; into tyranny, because that constitution, in the process of defending itself, transfers its concern from the common good to a particular good, its own, or identifies the common good with its own interest, the classical definition of tyranny; into force or coercion because, in the adjudication of any tentative toward constitutional change at the level of the legitimizing principle, the constitution becomes involved in a situation which can be resolved only by recourse to a self-legitimized application of that ultimate sanction. Hobbes, it may be repeated, seems to look upon these consequences with complete complacency. But most others in the areas of thought and action alike, do not, giving rise to that view shared alike by activists and theoreticians which we may call, in contrast to the juridical, the ethical theory of revolution.

The Ethical Theory of Revolution

The ethical theory of revolution takes its point of departure precisely in this question, namely whether any principle of legitimization can be absolute and the closed constitution thus justified. In response, it holds that no <u>de juré</u> structure of power is definitive; that every such structure is adjudicable and that a constitution which is self-adjudicating and self-rectifying as to its principle of legitimization inevitably conceals an elemental injustice. This, however, is only the negative aspect of the ethical theory of revolution. The positive aspect is that, for every legitimizing principle and for every constitution there must be a higher principle (higher in this employment is a purely dialectical term) from the ground of which that constitution may be judged, not merely in respect to its particular propositions, but as to the principle of legitimization on which it rests. The ethical theory of revolution is thus itself seen to be a revolutionary principle; <u>i.e.</u>, a principle of social change which touches the legitimizing principle of constitutions. And, historically, all revolutions have been ethical in this sense, that is they have without exception appealed to such a higher principle against the immunity from criticism and change of the legitimizing principle of the constitution.   Transformations short of this, that is, transformations which touch only the particular enactments within a constitution, no matter how far-reaching they may be, cannot be called revolutionary in this radical sense, although in their cumulative force they may generate a revolutionary situation.

This limitation on the immunity of the principle of legitimization of constitutions from transcendent (if not transcendental) adjudication may be taken in two ways. It may be taken, first, in a limited and so to say empirical sense. This is the sense in which Aristotle took it, apparently, in the study which he made of the constitutions of ancient Greece, the sole example of which in our possession is the Constitution of Athens. It was perhaps his purpose to formulate, by a comparative study of these constitutions, some principle which might be employed precisely for the purpose of adjudicating them transcendentally with respect to their legitimizing basis; but this conclusion cannot, of course, be reached with certainty simply on the basis of this single document.   Any given constitution is limited; it can be comprehended from within in terms of its own grounding principle. It can also be evaluated and judged from a transcendent point of view, and this not with respect only to its substantive enactments within the framework of its legitimizing principle, but with respect to the legitimizing principle itself. This empirical view is valid and historically has been used as the particular ethical ground of given revolutionary movements.

It is, however, clearly a limited ground and creates only a limited casuistic situation. Beyond it lies a deeper question of greater theoretical interest and of wider practical implication. Is there a principle in virtue of which every constitution, every de juré systemization of power, can be adjudicated as to its legitimizing principle?   If there is not, why not?   And, if there is, what is it? This is the ethical problem of revolution in its lapidary form. For if there is such a principle, revolution as a principle of social change is removed from the shadow of the sanction and penal structure of every constitution bent on vindicating its own validity and becomes an ethical concept of far greater range.

The ethical problem of revolution, consequently, is recognized to be the quest for this higher principle. This quest, in turn, involves at least three subsidiary inquiries, namely, what may be the form of this ethical principle, what may be its seat, the existential subjectivity in which it has its locus, and finally, what is its vindicating or effectuating force.

Three avenues seem to be open toward the response to this question. The first is the avenue of personal witness. The second is the avenue of the transcendental principle. The third is the way of history.

Personal Witness
As the Ethical Principle of Revolution

The ethical concept of revolution as personal witness may be reduced to three propositions: one, the form of the higher law in virtue of which the legitimizing principle of any constitution may be adjudicated is that of a personal existential intuition. Its seat, consequently, is the person. (The person here may be taken in two senses, i. e., in the charismatic sense, the elect individual, or in the diffused charismatic sense, as in equalitarian democracy in which the charismatic discernment of the principle is diffused numerically, in a group charisma, a revolutionary elite, or a party.) Its vindicating force differs in each of these cases. In the case of the charismatic personal witness it is death; in the elite revolutionary class, it is a collective futuristic martyrdom; in revolutionary democracy, history.

The examples of personal charismatic witness which inevitably come to mind are Socrates and Christ. Socrates, in his struggle with the Athenian polis, exhibits personal witness to the ethical principle of revolution in a classical form. Although his opposition to the polis took concrete form in a diversity of issues, the one object of his concern was the legitimizing principle of power. His personal intuition into the higher ethical principle was a skepsis: the know thyself; and this skepsis he addressed both to the individual citizen and to the state. But the force of his argument in either case was strictly analogous: the only legitimizing principle was virtue, the virtue, on the one hand, of the good man, the virtue, on the other, of the polis itself, which must be justice. But neither to the virtue of the individual nor to the virtue of the state did Socrates offer an apodictic and transcendental form. The one and the other remained for him a skepsis: a quest. The individual must embark on the endless quest of his true self-knowledge which could, of course, never be the knowledge of an object; the state must be committed to the equally endless quest of its true principle in every instance, must be a continual process of self-discovery and self-recovery. But what was the vindicating force, the effectuating force of Socrates' witness? It could be only one thing: his death. It is tempting to pause here and meditate on the death of Socrates as so many have done before us; for no matter how many comment on it, it remains an unexhausted fount of human wisdom. For many see in his death, a failure of his witness; for he seems to have succumbed to the self-vindicating force of the state, and his distinction between that state as his nourishing mother and those who held temporary power in her name does not seem persuasive to everyone. Others, however, see in his death the ultimate form of his witness to that higher law, for his death is the ultimate utterance of his skepsis. Whatever the interpretation favored, the death of Socrates is the death which every personal witness to the higher law must die or be prepared to die as the last and unanswerable word of his witness.

The instance of Christ as witness to the higher principle in virtue of which systems of power may be adjudicated is far more difficult to interpret. The gravest error of interpretation would be to limit his witness to the temporal forms of polity. His witness is directed to a far more basic object: the condition of man. The principle he invokes is charity. The force of charity is not merely the transformation of temporal human societies. It is the creation of that one society in which all mankind is united, the Church. As a result, a certain ambiguity invests Christ's attitude toward the limited structures of temporal power and toward injustice as it infects those forms. He counsels patience in the form of suffering. But this does not in any way weaken his witness; it only complicates it, for he prayed that the kingdom of charity of the Father's love come on earth as it is in heaven. And his witness, too, is sealed by the ultimate effectuating force of all personal witness: his death.

The Revolutionary Minority

The second locus of the higher principle in virtue of which the pretensions of systems of power may be adjudged in their legitimizing principle may be the revolutionary minority. This is a constant phenomenon of history. The form of the higher principle to which a revolutionary minority witness is usually ideological. Its effectuating force is in its outward manifestation, the mastery of the forms of revolutionary technique. Its inner form, however, resides in a state of consciousness which may be described as collective martyrdom which is futuristic in the sense that they are ready to endure present suffering in the name of a future good in which they will not share.

The diffusion of the charismatic vision of the higher principle in virtue of which the legitimizing principle of a constitution may be adjudicated through the numerical plurality of persons is an elusive phenomenon. Its terminus seems to be anarchy, rather than a new principle of legitimization, the eschewing of power rather than its transformation into right. The classical anarchist theories exhibit its major traits which can be studied with most instructiveness, perhaps, in the case of Lamennais and his theory of the people in his middle writings, such as the Livre du peuple and the Paroles d'un croyant.

The Transcendental Ethical Basis of Revolution

The transcendental form of the ethical theory of revolution has taken a number of forms. The classical form is, of course, classical natural law theory. Kantian formalism exhibits a similar structure, though it involves mankind in a dualism of inner freedom and outward conformity through its distinction between law and morality, which largely nullifies its force as a principle. The characteristic of transcendental principles is their appeal to reason as an open process. Their limitation lies in their lack of effectuating force. They demand the ethical will, but cannot command it.

Historical-Dialectic and Ethical Revolution

The historical-dialectical forms are the most sophisticated. The best examples are Hegel of the Philosophy of History (not of the Philosophy of Right) and Vico. Marx was not an original theorist in this area; he gave only a specific content, revolutionary and utopian, to a preexisting schema. The limitations of these theories are numerous. They hypostatize an historical intelligence and will, the existential locus of which is indeterminable. Providence, Weltgeist, proletariat, all share in this flaw. Moreover, all these forms postulate a philosophy of history. The philosophy of history as a theoretical enterprise has, however, shown itself exceedingly vulnerable to criticism and, hence, a labile basis for an ethical conception of revolution. These theories do, however, serve a very important function: they point the way to the positive concept of revolution as the form of man's historical freedom and to that of the institutionalization of revolution as a normative form of social change.

Revolution as the Form of Man's Historical Freedom

Revolution thus exhibits a rude dialectical form, historically and theoretically--the tension between the thrust of the process of legitimization of power toward the closed constitution and the ethical quest both for a higher principle in virtue of which all the pretensions of legitimacy to absolute status may be adjudged and for a form of power which may effectuate this ethical vision historically. Like most dialectical tensions, this one, too, is not definitive. It points rather to the need of a synthesis in which the elements of tension may be brought into constructive, instead of mutually destructive, relation. This synthesis, in the present case, we would suggest, might take the form of the idea of revolution as the form of man's historical freedom.

We might seek an abstract formulation of this idea, by contrasting it with other ideas of man's freedom: the classical doctrine of free will, which moves historically under the shadow of the free will-determinism controversy, the existential views of man's freedom, etc. But a more instructive path would be to have recourse to a concrete exemplification, if such can be found. A utilizable example is at hand, I believe, in Burke's exposition and defense of the British constitution in his letter on the French Revolution. Some critics have characterized Burke's views as merely an enlightened conservatism; it certainly is that. There is, however, a deeper level to his thought. Cutting through his wealth of detail (while protesting, however, that it constitutes a most valuable dimension of the essay) we may try to enucleate his basic idea. This is the idea that the forms of power, in which freedom effectively consists, are won through an unending historical struggle, the inner form of which is a constant questioning and reassessment of the legitimizing ground of the deployment of power through authority, right, and obligation. This questioning may, at many points, seem to be directed only at the particular provisions of the constitution. Actually, however, in every instance what is being adjudicated, within the context of some particular issue, is the principle of the legitimization of power itself. What Burke maintains concerning the British constitution, the principles of which he identifies through the analysis of its historical workings, is that a constitution which is self-rectifying at the level of its legitimizing principle is not only possible in idea but, in his view, actually exemplified in that constitution. His, consequently, is a conservatism which is, at the same time, liberating; for through the process of continual historical criticism effective forms of human freedom are generated, on the basis of already achieved historical freedoms, through the constant rectification of the legitimizing principle of the deployment of power. This movement, not a movement within the constitution alone, but of the constitution itself, is essentially revolutionary in the sense we have sought to define. It is an unending process of social change directed at the principle of legitimization of the constitution in and through the constant reassessment and transformation of its particular provisions. This is a thoroughly immanent revolutionary movement, a fact which explains Burke's reluctance to define the legitimizing principle of the British constitution and his preference, instead, for exhibiting it in its historical workings. From this exhibition there emerges the only positive concept of revolution to be encountered, namely, that it is the form of man's historical freedom.

The Institutionalization of Revolution

The instructive, though to some no doubt paradoxical, conclusion to be drawn from this conception of revolution, not as the
spastic reaction of liberty against the constraining bond of legitimacy, but as the form of man's freedom in history, is the institutionalization of revolution.   This idea means that the most viable
form of constitution must be thought to be that which provides within its own structure and dynamic, the effective conditions for the
constant reevaluation and adjudication of its own legitimizing principle in the concrete form of the constant testing of the range of
effective freedom which that constitution generates and guarantees.
Such a constitution, clearly, will have neither an ideological nor a
purely operative character. It will resist reduction to a set of abstract credenda or to a set of rules of procedure. It will appear
only in history, as an historical process and its vigency and actuality will be attested, not by any abstract argument, but precisely
by the kind of exhibition which Burke attempts with respect to the
British constitution. The only absolute condition for such a constitution, which would institutionalize revolution within itself as its
own constitutive dynamic, would seem to be the effective cultivation
of the historical consciousness: the mentality which accepts history
seriously.   Such a constitution must appear, not as a static structure, but as a process of continuous self-generated change throughout the fabric of the constitution itself. The vision of such change
may, perhaps, appear vertiginous. Some consolation for this muta-
bility is surely to be found, however, in Newman's wise remark:
to live is to change and to be perfect is to have changed often.

THE ENLIGHTENMENT AND THE SPIRIT OF REVOLUTION

Richard T. Bienvenu

The debate on the relationship between the Enlightenment and the French Revolution was probably the first of that long and interminable line of historical controversies engendered by the revolution. Unlike many of the issues raised in historical debates over the revolution, however, certain questions about the Enlightenment and the revolution seem to have been settled rather quickly.

I am not referring, obviously, to the primeval controversy which has inspired so much impassioned prose from the era of Burke and Paine into our own day: was the revolution the fault--or the crowning achievement--of the philosophes? Nor do I refer to the great metahistorical question: was the revolution in some ultimate sense the result or the material expression of the ideas of the Enlightenment? Questions such as these are likely never to be settled. Many of us would insist, moreover, that these are not questions that historians can or properly should ask. The Enlightenment's moral culpability is no longer considered to be a matter for scholarly discussion; and most historians are in practice content to leave the problem of the ultimate nature of the historical process to philosophers or ideologists. Instead they have addressed themselves to investigating problems such as the role played by Enlightenment thought and propaganda in the outbreak of revolution in 1789; or they have attempted to measure the extent to which the achievements of the revolution were based on or inspired by philosophe political theory. Although there was never any sort of unanimity among historians on these questions, there did exist until recently a kind of consensus, if only at the level of university textbooks. That consensus may be summarized in this way: the actual outbreak of revolution in 1789 was the result of an interlocking series of political and economic crises which had very little or nothing at all to do with the ideas and aspirations, values and programs of the Enlightenment. As Mounier, one of the participants in the revolution, put it: the revolution was produced by circumstances that were utterly foreign to the philosophes; their ideas did not bring about the crisis of 1788 or 1789.[1]

The problem of the connection between the ideals of the Enlightenment and the accomplishments of the revolution is considerably more complex, but even on this issue historians had arrived at a general interpretation that was widely accepted. That interpretation consisted essentially of the view that the revolution, at least in its early pre-republican phases, achieved many of the Enlightenment's goals and that its leaders were quite consciously implementing a program which the philosophes had developed. This program, drawn in part from English liberal thought and reflecting the values and aspirations of a rising social class, was based on what Diderot (and many others) had termed the "sacred and inviolable" right of private property. The philosophes believed that the right to own, increase, and dispose of the fruits of one's labor, or, as it was understood, one's property, constituted the foundation of a free and prosperous society; they demanded, consequently, the end of state intervention in economic matters and denounced the parasitism of an unproductive aristocracy and clergy. By the 1780s, moreover, most Frenchmen who considered themselves "enlightened" had come to insist as a matter of course that royal absolutism, the arbitrary exercise of force and governmental control of the expression of thought were all incompatible with the natural, inalienable rights of men. Governments, they concluded, must rule by laws promulgated and known; citizens could not be deprived of their freedom save by due legal process; and both state and church must refrain from censoring the expression of unorthodox ideas.

This program of economic, civil, and intellectual freedom can be extracted, it has been argued, from the writings of the philosophes who may have disagreed, argued and quarreled but were nevertheless in accord in their demand for liberty. This

---

[1]Quoted by G. Weill, "Les causes de la Révolution française d'après un témoin," Revue de synthèse, LIX (1939), 131.

libertarian program can also be found stated formally in terms that are both explicit and universal in the Declaration of the Rights of Man and the Citizen, a document which provides us with an epitome of eighteenth-century enlightened thought and also seems to establish the closest kind of link between the Enlightenment and the early revolution.

The consensus which I have just described has begun to break up, apparently yet another victim of the scholarly altercations and sometimes bitter feuding which presently disturb French revolutionary studies. Recent historical writing, much of it based on the exploitation of new sources and some of it on the reexamination of old evidence, has thrown new light on the relationship between the Enlightenment and the revolution. Unfortunately, the light shed so far has been either too dim or too blinding and it is difficult to know where we stand. It often appears, in fact, that we have entered what the Saint-Simonians would have called a critical epoch in eighteenth-century and revolutionary historiography, a period in which most scholarly energy seems directed at the dissolution of old assumptions and the introduction of new complexities which cannot, on the one hand, be assimilated into the older explanations and, on the other hand, refuse to fall into any sensible new pattern of their own. What was once thought to have been a fairly clear progression from the ideas of the Enlightenment to the thought of at least the moderate revolutionaries has been called into question and, indeed, no longer seems tenable.

For in the rather complicated and perplexing picture of the eighteenth century that has been taking shape recently, the Enlightenment, and especially Enlightenment political theory, appears as a "disordered and moderate body of thought." The last phrase is George V. Taylor's, but it is probably not incorrect to suggest that those adjectives summarize the emerging new view of the Enlightenment. Taylor's stimulating and impressive "Interim Report..." on a comprehensive analysis of the cahiers, Robert Darnton's lively observations on literary low life in the 1780s and the earlier essays of Alfred Cobban as well as Joan McDonald's monograph on Rousseau's influence, all expose the dangers of viewing the Enlightenment through the radicalizing prism of the revolutionary experience.[2] We are not surprised to find that the experi-

---

[2]The debate and the the temporary consensus in which it resulted may be followed conveniently in William F. Church, ed., The Influence of the Enlightenment on the French Revolution, 2nd ed., (Boston, 1973). This anthology contains Cobban's essay, "The Enlightenment and the French Revolution," as well as an excerpt

ence of revolution distorted the historical vision of the revolutionaries themselves, most of whom claimed descent from one or
more of the philosophes; but even today the revolution's shock continues to distort historical perspective by leading historians to
assume that the .major portion of the revolutionary program was
prefigured in and prepared by the Enlightenment.

It is precisely the interpretation of the Enlightenment as a
movement essentially radical and revolutionary in intent and in
effect which is, we are now told, false. Neither the revolution nor
the Declaration of the Rights of Man, Professor Taylor has argued,
could have been "predicted from the corpus of French Enlightenment thought." Even the continuity of purpose and of theory which
was once supposed to have linked the Enlightenment and the Declaration seems threatened. Professor Taylor, for example, has
advanced the provocative contention that the drafters of the Declaration were not writing an epitome of Enlightened political and
social principles but were in fact breaking new ground by (oddly
enough) returning to the a prioristic rationalism of the seventeenth
century, the very sort of deductive rationalism which the philosophes had abandoned in favor of empiricism by the time the great
Encyclopedia had begun to appear. By drawing up in the Declaration a formal statement of general principles from which specific
laws were to be thereafter derived, Professor Taylor concludes,
the men of 1789 were in a sense creating a new, radicalized Enlightenment under the intense pressure of the revolutionary
struggle.[3]

Other historians have recently advanced in various ways
the thesis that the Enlightenment was essentially moderate. Their
arguments also imply that we should focus our attention on the
revolutionary crisis itself for it was this unprecedented stimulus
that generated a new and distinctive set of political ideas which
were truly radical. Robert Darnton argues in his essay in the
social history of Enlightenment thought that whatever revolutionary

---

from Joan McDonald's Rousseau and the French Revolution.
George Taylor's characterization of the Enlightenment as a "disordered and moderate body of thought" appears in "The Cahiers of
1789: An Interim Report," French Historical Studies, VII (1971-
1972), 488. Robert Darnton's exploration of the relationship between the "high" and "low" Enlightenments is entitled "The High
Enlightenment and the Low-Life of Literature in Pre-Revolutionary
France," Past and Present, No. 51 (1971), pp. 81-115.

[3]Taylor, "The Cahiers of 1789," p. 488.

potential the Enlightenment once had, the cutting edge of _philosophe_ radicalism was quite effectively blunted by the emergence of a generation of successfully established and domesticated _philosophes_ who "argued over Gluck and Piccini, . . . chanted the old litanies about legal reform and _l'infâme_, and collected their pensions. "[4] Even the heroic generation of the _philosophes_ did not, we are reminded, make political demands that could in the least be called radical. On the contrary, all of them from Voltaire to Rousseau often expressed a dread of social disorder and they repeatedly warned against the dangers of even tinkering with society. Thus Rousseau could describe himself as a "man who is more averse to revolution than anyone else in the world," a man "who has always insisted upon the maintenance of existing institutions" because "their destruction would only take away the palliative while leaving their faults. . . . "[5] The great _philosophes_ were in fact often timid enough in writing and in deed to tempt us to assume that had Voltaire, Diderot and Rousseau lived to witness the debates on the Declaration of the Rights of Man they would have stood dumbly by at a loss for words or ideas, if indeed they had not already fled the country with the first _émigrés_.

The relationship between the thought of the Enlightenment and the revolution has been called into question in yet another way by the late Alfred Cobban who years ago insisted that "the political content of the French Enlightenment must not be exaggerated. "[6] The fact that Rousseau's _Social Contract_ became one of the revolution's sacred books must not mislead us, Cobban and others have warned. _The Social Contract_ belongs to the body of Enlightenment political theory only in a very special sense: the treatise was pure theory, a speculative exercise which Rousseau in no way offered as a viable political alternative. In fact, the book was not taken seriously by Rousseau's contemporaries for it was generally assumed to be utopian, irrelevant to French politics and, hence, harmless. Rousseau himself, moreover, did not believe that the kind of democracy he described in _The Social Contract_ could ever

---

[4]Darnton, "The High-Enlightenment," p. 115.

[5]Quoted by Henry Peyre, "The Influence of Eighteenth Century Ideas on the French Revolution," _Journal of the History of Ideas_, X (1949), 79.

[6]Alfred Cobban, "The Enlightenment and the French Revolution," _Aspects of the Eighteenth Century_, Earl R. Wasserman, ed. (Baltimore, 1965), p. 309.

work in any setting but that of a small city state.   The book was, at any rate, not too widely read before 1792, according to Joan McDonald who also further discounts the influence of Rousseau on the revolution because she has found that he was just as often cited by counterrevolutionaries as by revolutionaries.[7]

After reviewing these arguments can we escape the conclusion that the Enlightenment's influence on the revolution must be judged to have been relatively slight and that the revolution really constitutes a new departure in the history of political and social thought?   That the Enlightenment did not cause any of the events of 1789 and beyond has always been clear enough.   Yet it now appears necessary to add that since the Enlightenment was a moderate, disordered and even basically nonpolitical body of thought, it neither helped to generate a revolutionary mentality nor provided a program of what was to be done once the revolution had gotten underway.

But here, I feel, some caution is necessary. Despite the excellence and importance of these and other recent studies we have not really come much closer to settling the problem of the relationship between Enlightenment and the spirit of revolution. The real value of much of the recent work is that it restores the integrity and individuality of Enlightenment and revolutionary thought by reminding us once again that we distort both the En-lightenment and the revolution by interpreting either solely in terms of the other.   Beyond that not inconsiderable accomplish-ment, however, these reevaluations do not take us too far. And the problem, I want now to suggest, lies not in the answers which historians like Taylor, Cobban or McDonald have offered but in the questions they have asked and the assumptions with which they approach the subject.

Let me begin with one striking but rather commonplace characteristic of the approach taken by scholars who have tried to examine the influence of philosophe political thought on revolu-tionary politics and political theory, I mean the singularly narrow way in which "political thought" is defined. For it seems to me that we can accept Alfred Cobban's contention that the Enlighten-ment was poor in political thought only if we define "political thought" so narrowly that it includes only formal considerations on the nature, source or limits of political power or technical analy-ses of the structure and functioning of political institutions; at the same time we exclude those ethical values and aspirations which

---

[7]Joan McDonald,   Rousseau and the French Revolution (London, 1965), p. 155.

underlie and inform formal political ideas. It is this very con-
striction of what political thought is, I suspect, that led Joan
McDonald to believe that she could satisfactorily assess Rousseau's
influence on the thought of the revolutionaries by examining the
reception of Rousseau's only formal political work, The Social
Contract. (It is, I might add parenthetically, an equally misleading approach that prompts many other historians to belittle the influence of Rousseau on the ground that he explicitly stated that
France was too large and socially disparate to become the kind of
democratic state he described in The Social Contract.)

It is especially surprising that, of all of the writers of the
Enlightenment, Rousseau should be so treated. Rousseau's vehement condemnation of inequality, his celebration of Spartan and
Roman civic virtue, and his moving evocations of social solidarity
or fraternity may not be, strictly speaking, political ideas or
theory, but they were political passions which sounded responsive
chords in the hearts of many of his readers who came into their
intellectual and political maturity during the 1780s and 1790s.

Rousseau's widespread and profound influence as an effective writer, a man whose books were commonly able to evoke in
their readers what seem to us to be the most excessive kinds of
responses is too well established for us to insist upon it any
length. Yet his case is simply the most notable of many; there are
other examples of common and deeply felt values, embodied and
propagated in the most varied kinds of works, which also contributed to the political mentality of the revolutionary generation, if
not to its formal political theory. Take, for example, the widespread admiration and affection for the virtue of the ancients,
particularly for the republican virtue of the ancient Romans. In
certain respects this was a literary cult, the common possession
of all individuals with a certain degree of education. Consequently,
no one would wish to claim that the Enlightenment's admiration for
the republican virtues of the ancient Romans in any real sense
caused the emergence of republicanism as a political force during
the early years of the revolution. But can we also deny that the
cult of antique republicanism facilitated the transition to republicanism by providing Frenchmen with heroic republican exemplars,
a republican iconography and symbolism (even if it now seems so
inauthentic) and in this way helped to shape the mentality and self-
image of the first French republicans?

The philosophes' admiration for Roman virtue had as a
corollary a hatred of despotism which they often defined as the
arbitrary exercise of force. Again, this is not an idea or a sentiment which caused events; but it is the sort of idea which shaped
perceptions and the ways in which events were interpreted. Con-

sequently, although the hatred of despotism made no immediate difference--Diderot's often quite-veiled and allusive attacks on despotism drove neither him nor anyone else into action against Bourbon despotism--that same sentiment in a situation which provided scope for its expression could shape events such as the drafting of the Declaration of the Rights of Man. As Paul Bastid has pointed out, a good part of the Declaration may be seen as an attempt to establish barriers against the kinds of despotism which the philosophes had so roundly and consistently denounced.[8] The list of such "non-political" ideas and values could be extended, but I hope that my point has been made sufficiently clear to allow me to turn to another rather curious habit of some of the historians who deal with the problem of intellectual influence.

As I pointed out a few minutes ago, some historians seem to wish to discount the importance of the Enlightenment's foremost democratic political philosopher--Rousseau--on the ground that Rousseau insisted that democracy was not suitable for large states. Now this is incontrovertibly true and obvious to any attentive reader of Rousseau. But I would like to suggest that when we are investigating the problem of the influence of one man's writings on another man's thought, the intentions, desires, and even the qualifications of the theorist are somewhat irrelevant. Does it really make any difference that Rousseau never intended his democratic theory to be applied to the French solution? Apparently some historians think so. McDonald, to take a slightly different example, thinks it significant (significant of a lack of influence) that anti-revolutionaries commonly understood Rousseau better than did the revolutionaries who cited Rousseau to support their position.[9] Professor Taylor, to take another example, does not think it sufficient to establish that the framers of the Declaration were sincerely convinced that they were in some fundamental sense heirs of the Enlightenment; he must point out that in this the revolutionaries were mistaken. They were not truly heirs of the Enlightenment because they were radical, deductive, ideological rationalists while the real philosophes were moderate empiricists. I must confess a certain perplexity at this attitude as well as a suspicion of the methodological assumption which it implies. It does not seem correct to assume that certain political ideas can be said to have had an influence only when they have been correctly interpreted. If the framers of the Declaration actually believed that they

---

[8]Paul Bastid, Sieyès et sa pensée (Paris, 1939), p. 350.

[9]McDonald, Rousseau and the French Revolution, p. 155.

were heirs of the Enlightenment, we must conclude that they had been influenced by the Enlightenment in an historically significant way. The accuracy, the objective basis of their self-perception is not in this case a legitimate historical question.

Let me add very hastily that I do not recommend that we suspend all critical judgment in such matters. I recognize that we ourselves must make the greatest effort to understand and to present accurately and faithfully the thought of (in this instance) the philosophes themselves. No one who is interested in understanding Rousseau would read Robespierre or the proceedings of the Jacobin Club, just as no student of Nietzsche would turn to the Nazi propagandists who quite deliberately deformed his thought. On the other hand, our first task when we seek to trace the influence of ideas is to ascertain what the men we are studying felt was of crucial importance in their intellectual development. We are not doing anything very significant when we examine whether Sieyès, Mirabeau, or Robespierre really understood the nuances, subtleties or even the major arguments of the books and thinkers by whom they claim to have been influenced. Perhaps we are confronting here a minor occupational hazard of no real historiographical significance--a kind of misdirected pedagogical zeal: because we are all of us teachers in one way or another we insist on proving not only that the revolutionaries read the philosophes, but that they understood them correctly; that, in a word, they got it right. But while this may merely be a bad habit, I suggest that it can lead to serious distortions in our accounts of the past.

The difficulties--or what I take to be difficulties--in current attempts to analyze the role played by the Enlightenment in the preparation of a spirit of revolution seem to me to stem from a set of unconscious assumptions and habits of analysis with which historians approach problems of intellectual or ideological influence. Perhaps the common denominator of what appears to me to be fallacious approaches to the issue we have been considering here is that we have often looked rather too steadily and even exclusively at relationships between ideas, books, and bodies of thought and not enough at the actual human beings on whom these ideas are assumed to have exerted (or not exerted) an influence.

Let me illustrate how this displacement can lead us astray by examining somewhat more closely one of the arguments I mentioned earlier. The question of whether we might have predicted either the revolution or the Declaration of the Rights of Man from the Enlightenment would seem to be rather easy to resolve now that we have stopped reading the Enlightenment through the radicalizing prism of the revolution. Professor Taylor argues quite convincingly that we cannot have predicted the Declaration from the "corpus of French Enlightenment thought as it stood on December 31, 1786."[10]   But to agree that we cannot predict even the most moderate revolutionary theory (or practice) from the corpus of Enlightenment thought does not really diminish the contribution of the Enlightenment to the revolutionary spirit, nor does it call into question--as it is apparently meant to do--the basic continuity of Enlightenment thought and the principles of 1789. I belabor this point because it seems to me important that we realize that the answer to the question--could the Declaration have been predicted?--is essentially without significance. Given our historical vantage point (which is by no means without its disadvantages) the question of predictability irresistibly poses itself, but even a correct answer tells us little and usually misleads us.

Indeed, if we use the criterion of predictability to establish a nexus between one body of ideas and principles and a subsequent body of thought, we will be able to establish such bonds only when we are dealing with the institutionalized transmission of a body of formal thought or with the doctrinal history of religious or political sects. In most instances, in the important instances, however, the search for predictability must be profitless. I imagine that few of us would expect an historian of Christian thought to be concerned with whether the Nicene Creed might have been predicted from the words of Jesus; nor would we wish to deny that Karl Marx influenced Leninism or Stalinism on the grounds that the mutations Marxism underwent after the death of Marx could not have been predicted from his writings.

Historians would do well--when they investigate the transmission and development of ideas in the past--to ponder the methodological modesty of that preeminently historical school of psychology, psychoanalysis. Psychoanalysis sets for itself the same goal historians seek to reach: by a variety of means the psychoanalyst and his patient seek to discover the mental history of a person, of an individual psyche, by establishing a chain of effects and their causes, working backward from the known to the unknown. Yet psychoanalytical theory does not, as far as I know, concern itself with _predicting_ the direction an individual mind might take, even though its basic assumption is that there exists in the psychological biography of each of us a fundamental and even tyrannical continuity. If we were to apply the criterion of predictability to a person's intellectual development (rather than to the development of a somewhat disembodied corpus of thought such as the Enlightenment) we would often be unable to explain major

---

[10]Taylor, "The _Cahiers_ of 1789," p. 488.

changes or fundamental mutations other than by assuming ruptures and discontinuities that do not seem to occur in other aspects of an individual's mental life.

Here, perhaps, is a clue to the real source of our difficulties: we all too often do forget that even intellectual history is primarily concerned with the ideas of men, whether we consider them as individuals, as members of a party or faction or even members of a social class. Ideas do not live, men do, and I believe that we cannot come to any sound conclusions on the role played by enlightened thought without refocusing our attention precisely on the men of the 1770s and 1780s. Unfortunately, there seems to exist a relentless tendency to move in the opposite direction: we disembody ideas and reify movements of ideas. Perhaps reification is not the correct word, for we commonly transform the "Enlightenment" not into an object but into an active, acting subject. What else are we to make of the phrases which all of us use: "The Enlightenment believed," or "The Enlightenment sought" or "The Enlightenment demanded..."? Of course, it may be objected that such phrases are not to be taken as meaningful in any real sense; they are convenient, short-hand symbols for a more complex phenomenon which would be tedious in the extreme to describe fully. But we pay too high a price for these conveniences when we end by believing that the symbols are real.

Even when such general characterizations are unavoidable and accurate they remain dangerous. The Enlightenment was, we must agree with Professor Taylor, disordered and moderate. But can we follow him when he implies that, though disordered and moderate, it stood as a kind of monolith which the generation of men who came into their own intellectual maturity after 1780 had consciously to accept, modify, or reject? I find it hard to believe that anything of this sort occurred or that Sieyès, Mirabeau or even Robespierre would have described his intellectual development and his philosophical choices in this fashion. What, for example, might Sieyès have replied to our assertion that the Enlightenment had become empirical after 1751 and that he was obliged, in the heat of the crisis of 1789, to reach back to the seventeenth century for the rationalism which the philosophes had rejected? We know, with a fair degree of certainty, that Sieyès had never abandoned the rationalism of the seventeenth century; that he was indebted to both Locke and Descartes, and that his rationalism had indeed become "totalitarian," in the sense that his political theory was rigidly, geometrically rational. We also know that Sieyès' real objection to Montesquieu was not that Montesquieu collected and analyzed empirical data, but that he did not carry his analysis far enough or high enough to reach the fundamental general principles which the empirical data merely expressed.[11] Now, we may wish to argue that Siéyès was atypical (along with Condorcet), or that he was not really a member of the Enlightenment, or at the very least, that he was not a philosophe of the stature of Voltaire, Diderot or Montesquieu.

Siéyès' stature and the question of his membership in the Enlightenment are debatable questions. What is not debatable is that Voltaire, Montesquieu and Diderot (and the rest of the philosophes commonly acknowledged as great) were all dead by 1785. If their thought lived on and exercised an influence during the 1780s and 1790s, consequently, it did so not because "great ideas live" or even because their books were in print. To put this another way: the Enlightenment became in the 1780s, at least in part, what subsequent thinkers made of it. If the Enlightenment had real meaning for the 1780s, its meaning resided in what the men who lived into the revolutionary decade thought, felt, and did. In a very real sense it does not matter at all what Rousseau, Diderot or Voltaire thought or would have thought about the kinds of changes wrought by the men of 1789; the ideas of the philosophes were in the public domain by the beginning of the 1780s and had become important elements in the minds of men who were to face new problems and a revolutionary opportunity. These ideas did not create that opportunity, and certainly did not in every case transform themselves into a revolutionary spirit. Yet until we make another effort to follow as minutely as we can the development of Enlightened ideas and values we will be saddled with a view of the Enlightenment which conceives of it not as a way of thinking (as Diderot defined it) but as a corpse (albeit moderate and disordered) whose dead hand the revolutionaries had to cast off in order to frame a document listing rights and principles which few if any of the philosophes would have rejected.

What I am suggesting is simply that we do no more than re-embody the Enlightenment in the men who composed it, that we re-unify men and ideas. I must admit that such an approach will probably not result in a new synthesis; indeed it may even prove futile simply because the problem of intellectual influence pursued in this way is fundamentally intractable. And such an approach will certainly not appeal to those of us who wish to make certain kinds of general statements about the past--statements that can or must be expressed in tables, figures and graphs. I am not unwilling to abandon the search for that kind of statement because I believe that the closer we get to them the farther we stray from that

---

[11]Bastid, Siéyès, pp. 293-305, 308.

investigation of human concreteness and specificity which was once
thought to be the special domain of the historian.

This remark exposes me, I am afraid, as something of a
methodological retrograde, the sort of historian who reduces history to biography, or, in this case, to intellectual biography. If
my critical observations on what seem to me the distortions inherent in the very questions historians are asking about Enlightenment and the revolution suggest an alternative approach, that
approach must be the rather traditional one of detailed and intensive study of the intellectual or philosophical (and, when possible,
psychological) biographies of the men who carried Enlightenment
thought into the revolution.

This is why Robert Darnton is in a way right to advise us to
descend from the Parnassus of the High Enlightenment and direct
our gaze upon the lesser and later figures of the philosophe movement. It is not so much, as he seems to wish to suggest, that the
angry, embittered and really revolutionary down-and-outers of the
Parisian Grub Street were the true and legitimate heirs of Voltaire
and Rousseau, but rather that these writers--as well as many not
so alienated and unsuccessful--in fact represented what the Enlightenment had become or was in the process of becoming: one of
the philosophical or theoretical components of an emerging revolutionary spirit.

THE AMERICAN REVOLUTION, VERGENNES' ENGLISH POLICY AND THE COMING OF THE FRENCH REVOLUTION

M. Donaghay

The Peace of Versailles of 1783 which formally ended the Anglo-French phase of the American Revolution also called for a new commercial treaty between France and Great Britain by January 1786. Following the signature of the peace, the British professed satisfaction with the status quo so that the French had to maneuver them into serious commercial negotiations. Once involved, however, the British quickly worked out an apparently favorable agreement which significantly reduced duties and restrictions on Anglo-French trade. Signed on September 26, 1786, and executed the following May, the Anglo-French commercial treaty, popularly known as The Eden Treaty, regulated trade between the two countries until denounced by France in January 1793, just before Great Britain declared war on revolutionary France.

Almost from the date of signature the commercial treaty provoked heated debate concerning the French role in the negotiations and the ruinous effects of the resultant agreement on the French economy. Why, then, did the French negotiate such an agreement? Because the Anglo-French commercial treaty of 1786 was conceived in political terms as a means of bringing Great Britain under French influence. It was a desperate effort; the financial legacy of the American Revolution precluded French participation in another way, and Europe after 1782 presented many war possibilities. It was an unsuccessful effort; the commercial treaty and Vergennes' attempted Anglo-French rapprochement fell

43

victim to the rivalry which he had sought largely to negate; to the French financial situation which became public knowledge with the Assembly of Notables; and to the confusion in the French government which followed the death of the old foreign minister in February 1787. [1]

Charles Gravier, comte de Vergennes, had become minister of foreign affairs in 1774, at which time he carefully examined the situation of France vis-a-vis other states. This study resulted in a series of mémoires which explored possible courses of action and in a series of conclusions which helped shape French foreign policy during the next thirteen years. In one such mémoire Vergennes studied the possibility of an Anglo-French alliance or commercial treaty and concluded that British interests precluded either. France could only view Great Britain as a dangerous rival, and Vergennes therefore pursued the same course as his predecessors Fleury and Choiseul: he worked to keep the peace, to maintain the status quo on the Continent, and to preserve British isolation. To restore French prestige, so badly damaged during the Seven Years' War, he intended to take advantage of the first opportunity to reduce British power. That opportunity came with the outbreak of the American Revolution. [2]

---

[1]Studies of the Anglo-French Commercial Treaty of 1786 include: C. A. Butenval, Précis Historique et Economique du Traité de Commerce signé à Versailles, le 26 Septembre 1786 (Paris, 1869); Camille Bloch, Etudes sur l'Histoire Economique de la France (1760-1786) (Paris, 1900), pp. 239-269; François Dumas, Etude sur le Traité de Commerce de 1786 (Toulouse, 1904), is the standard work; Léon Cahen, "Une Nouvelle Interprétation du Traité Franco-Anglais de 1786-1787," Revue Historique, CLXXXV (1939), 257-285; Oscar Browning, "The Treaty of Commerce between England and France in 1786," Transactions of the Royal Historical Society, ns II (1885), 349-364; J. Holland Rose, "The Franco-British Commercial Treaty of 1786," The English Historical Review, XXIII (1908), 709-724; W. O. Henderson, "The Anglo-French Commercial Treaty of 1786," Economic History Review, 2nd series, X (1957-1958), 104-112; and John Ehrman, The British Government and Commercial Negotiations with Europe, 1783-1793 (Cambridge, 1962), pp. 28-69. Much of the following has been drawn from my dissertation, "The Anglo-French Negotiations of 1786-1787" (University of Virginia, 1970).

[2]France, Ministère des Affaires Etrangères, "Considérations sur la possibilité d'une alliance entre la France et l'Angle-

As a war the American Revolution was something of a mixed success for France. On the diplomatic front, the French outmaneuvered the British at every turn, thus maintaining peace and the status quo on the Continent despite some passing crises and minor territorial exchanges. By the end of the war, therefore, all Europe was set against Great Britain which was set in the light of disregarding the rights of other nations. Then, the rapid succession of British ministries after the fall of Lord North in early 1782 reduced Great Britain's prestige still further, while, conversely, French "credit" and "consideration" in Europe were reestablished.

In military affairs, however, French activity after 1781 fell short of expectations. At first the French war effort was largely diplomatic, but in late 1780 Louis XVI brought into his cabinet two generals who thought in military terms. The new minister of the marine, Charles de Castries, and his comrade in arms Philippe de Ségur, the new minister of war, were determined to settle the question of American independence by force. Vergennes preferred diplomatic solutions and opposed a war of "conquest" which might revive memories of an aggressive France as well as destroy Great Britain as a possible counterweight to Russian ambitions in the eastern Mediterranean. But Castries and Ségur wanted to crush Great Britain so that France could, as Castries phrased it, "dictate" the law in Europe.

Mitigated military successes and unmitigated financial distress prevented Castries and Ségur from carrying out their plans. The Franco-American operation assured American independence by forcing Cornwallis' surrender at Yorktown, but plans for a Franco-Spanish invasion of Jamaica were upset by the British naval victory at the Saints Passage. The British also checked the Franco-Spanish siege of Gibraltar and captured Trincomali. France's allies grew restless for peace, and Russia and Austria prepared to finish off the Ottoman Empire--a change in the balance of power which would bring other alterations in the map of Europe. At home, the financial situation, never really bright, worsened as the deficits mounted and loans proved ever more difficult to obtain. By the time peace negotiations got underway, France seemed on the verge of bankruptcy. Thus, in late 1782, when Castries complained about proposed concessions, Vergennes rather testily asked who would provide the money to continue the war. Moreover, restriction of trade during the war and poor grain harvests depressed France's major industry, wines. As a result, the

---

terre," 1774, Mémoires et Documents, Angleterre, 56, 116-112vo.

French government had to contend with a growing economic crisis in addition to its financial difficulties. So, while the British had been somewhat reduced from their "arrogant" posture of 1763 and the relative situation had been equalized in European eyes, France, just as Great Britain, was in desperate need of peace. Under these circumstances, Vergennes negotiated a moderate peace with Great Britain during the fall and winter of 1782-1783.[3]

Following the American Revolution it was essential that France have a long peace in which to reorganize her finances and reform her military whose performance had been marred by a marked lack of discipline at critical junctures. Vergennes, moreover, thought the European situation explosive and believed that Great Britain was ready to provide the spark in the form of subsidies. Unable to sustain another war, France had to prevent the British from igniting the European powder keg. Vergennes, therefore, returned to the alternatives rejected in 1774, an Anglo-French rapprochement and a commercial treaty.

In 1774 Vergennes had observed that

> ...the [British] nation feels generally that it suits it absolutely to aim all its views towards commerce and even to make political interests yield to those of trade....[4]

If economic considerations influenced British policy to that degree, an Anglo-French commercial agreement, by implication, would give a clever foreign minister a powerful instrument for restraining England. A commercial treaty conceivably would enable France to draw Great Britain into her system for maintaining the balance of power and peace on the Continent while weakening a once-dreaded rival--or so Vergennes thought. It would, moreover, increase the volume of legitimate trade between the two countries, thus stimulating the sagging French economy, especially the wine industry, and raise needed revenue. An Anglo-French commercial treaty could thus provide economic as well as political advantages.

The British were aware, however, of the political dangers inherent in such an agreement, and Vergennes feared they might

---

[3]On the French economic crisis, especially in the wine industry, see C. E. Labrousse, _La Crise de l'Economie Française à la Fin de l'Ancien Régime_ (Paris, 1944), I.

[4]"Considérations sur la possibilité d'une alliance," p. 121.

resist a commercial treaty with France. Even if he managed to conclude an agreement with Great Britain, the foreign minister realized that it might well be rejected by Parliament, just like the commercial clauses of the Commercial Convention of Utrecht (1713). Indeed, Vergennes had ruled out a commercial treaty in 1774 because the difficulties seemed insurmountable. But, in 1782, the situation was more critical and the foreign minister had fewer options so that he decided to seek either a new commercial treaty with Great Britain or full execution of the Utrecht agreement. Vergennes set to work with great care and persistence to secure the desired treaty while maintaining British isolation. As he predicted, the British proved very reluctant to engage in commercial negotiations.[5]

Work towards an Anglo-French rapprochement and a commercial treaty began simultaneously in the fall of 1782, during the peace negotiations. The French negotiator, Rayneval, discussed Vergennes' system for maintaining the peace and status quo in Europe in detail with the British prime minister, the Earl of Shelburne. Vergennes stressed the need for Anglo-French cooperation to forestall trouble in Europe and indicated an area of immediate concern, the Levant. There Great Britain and France had a mutual interest in preventing the partition of the Ottoman Empire and Russian acquisition of Constantinople. The foreign minister spoke of rapprochement and then argued that trade need not be the source of friction between Great Britain and France; indeed, new commercial arrangements would help cement good relations between the two nations. While Shelburne professed to be impressed by Vergennes' "pacific system," he balked at the idea of commercial negotiations. Such discussions should be postponed until after the conclusion of the peace agreement; besides, proposed reform of British trade policy would render a new commercial treaty unnecessary. As a result, the Preliminary Peace only provided for the appointment of commissioners to discuss a new commercial agreement. Negotiations with the Fox-North coalition which replaced the Shelburne administration in the spring of 1783 were no more successful. Article Eighteen of the Definitive Peace specified that the commissioners were to negotiate new commercial arrangements by January 1, 1786. Despite his efforts, Vergennes failed to secure an explicit statement which provided for either the

[5] "Considérations sur la possibilité d'une alliance," pp. 116-122vo. Vergennes, "Articles proposé à la Cour de Londres...," September 6, 1782, Archives des Affaires Etrangères, Correspondance Politique, Angleterre 538, p. 109.

full execution or termination of the Utrecht agreement. Sadly, he noted, "I had to choose between two parts: that of arguing and finishing nothing (i. e.: the Definitive Peace), or that of ceding on the objects which...are of no consequence." The formation of the Pitt administration in late 1783 raised hopes of cooperation, but the new prime minister concentrated on domestic policy and left the conduct of commercial negotiations in the hands of Foreign Secretary Carmarthen who distrusted the French and sought an alliance with Russia and Austria.[6]

Vergennes, however, as early as 1783 had moved to insure France against the possibility of British resistance to a new commercial treaty. Following the fall of the Shelburne government, he asked the controller-general to lift wartime restrictions placed on British trade. True, this action allowed British goods to flow into France on a pre-war basis, but it also gave the foreign minister some leverage. Then, when the British wasted the first year of the period fixed in the Definitive Treaty (despite French warnings that they would regard the Utrecht agreement as abolished once the period was spent), Vergennes implemented his plan. During 1785 he selectively struck one major British industry after another in a series of well-spaced, restrictive decrees. When the British protested the decrees against carriages, textiles and hardware, the foreign minister reminded them that decrees were not irrevocable. Moreover, he noted, France had to protect itself from the flood of British goods especially when, it seemed, Britain wanted so little in return. Throughout this maneuver, Vergennes and his chargé d'affaires in London compared notes on the results and considered additional measures designed to wreak havoc on the British economy until the pressure on the British government proved irresistible. Concurrent with these treaties, the French accelerated construction activity on fortifications at Dunkirk while Vergennes successfully mediated the dispute between Austria and the Dutch Republic over the closure of the Scheldt in such a way as to maintain the French connection with Austria and, at the same time, secure an alliance with the Dutch Republic. In late 1785, the French chargé d'affaires noted that the British government was increasingly inclined "to facilitate the negotiations." Indeed, shortly thereafter Carmarthen announced the appointment of a new negotiator and asked for an extension of the deadline. Ver-

---

[6]Vergennes to Adhemar, "Instructions," April 25, 1783, Archives des Affaires Etrangères, Correspondance Politique, Angleterre 14, supplement, pp. 362, 367.

gennes granted the British request, now confirmed in his belief regarding the influence of economic matters on British policy.

During this unproductive phase of the commercial negotiations, the French indicated that they had no particular plan concerning the discussions, and that, indeed, it was "impossible" to form any program without knowledge of British intentions. In fact, Vergennes and his undersecretary, Rayneval, were busily collecting information and drafting strategy for serious commercial negotiations with the help of the controller general, Charles de Calonne. After studying the French protectionist system and the free-trade system recommended by all the "modern economists," Vergennes rejected both and decided upon a mixed system which would destroy illicit trade, increase revenue, encourage domestic manufacturers to improve quality and lower prices, and give France some commercial advantages. Such a mixed system could be achieved through a combination of special arrangements for the major items of Anglo-French trade and "most favored nation" treatment for the rest. Major French products included wines, brandies, silks, woolens, cloths and fashions, while Great Britain offered such goods as beer, cheese, coal, lead, tin, cottons, woolens and hardware. Various bargains involving these articles were considered. For example, the British had a decided advantage in hardware which could not be kept out of France so that it would be wise to admit hardware in return for concessions on wine. British textiles cost less than French textiles, but Vergennes hoped to secure agreement on a duty which would permit improvement of French cottons, that is a duty low enough so that French manufacturers would have to mechanize as their British competitors had or go out of business. All in all, Vergennes thought that France had much to gain under such a mixed system. [7]

In the winter of 1786, the British feverishly prepared for the commercial negotiations they could no longer avoid, heartened by reports from Paris that the French were mired in their own research. When the British negotiator, William Eden, arrived in France at the end of March 1786, this British misconception was strengthened by the French approach to the negotiations. During his first conference with Vergennes, Eden tried to enter into specifics, but the foreign minister purposely spoke in general terms. In subsequent meetings Vergennes discussed his desire for an Anglo-French rapprochement and his system for maintaining peace

---

[7]By "modern economists," Vergennes meant the physiocrats such as Du Pont de Nemours who advised the government concerning trade policy.

and the <u>status</u> <u>quo</u> on the Continent until Eden got the impression that outside of laying the foundations of a pacific and commercial system, "I do not believe that France gains any other material advantage except a reduction in wines..." And Vergennes indicated that one way to improve Anglo-French relations was through commercial arrangements, for better regulated trade would remove a source of much ill-feeling between the two countries. Early conferences with Rayneval, the French negotiator, reinforced the impression that the French were not too well informed on the details of trade relations and thus would prefer to stick to generalities. Of course, this was precisely the impression Vergennes intended to convey. [8]

By keeping the initial conversations confined to quite general discussions, Vergennes was able to sound out the British negotiator's sympathies, win his confidence, and establish the rapport necessary for later hard bargaining. While the foreign minister was much less successful in winning the confidence of Pitt and Carmarthen, he did manage to deceive them about French preparedness. This deception was designed to lure the British into negotiating seriously and into feeling the deal they were making was so good that they would not consider backing out when the French started to press their demands at the end of the negotiations. The French chargé d'affaires in London intimated this approach when he stated the commercial discussions would probably deteriorate into a battle between British "greed" and French "justice." Vergennes, more directly, stated after the conclusion of the negotiations that he preferred the British to believe that they had made an excellent bargain rather than that they had been entrapped by the French. He added that he hoped the British euphoria would last long enough to see the treaty through Parliament. Always there was the fear that the new treaty would suffer the fate of the Utrecht agreement, and this fear made Vergennes cautious, too cautious perhaps. Finally, by pretending to be unprepared, the French forced the British negotiator to agree on general principles before fixing specific duties. When declarations were finally exchanged in June 1786, Vergennes had obtained the mixed system of "most favored nation" and a special tariff, the very system he had outlined between 1784 and 1785. [9]

---

[8] Eden to Carmarthen, April 17, June 6, 1786. Public Records Office, 27/19, pp. 11-13.

[9] Barthélemy to Vergennes, January 1, 1786, Archives des Affaires Etrangères, Correspondance Politique, Angleterre 555, p. 3-3vo; Carmarthen, "Declaration," May 31, 1786, Public Records Office, 27/19, pp. 11-13.

Concerning specific items of trade the French were careful to mention only their major items first, such as wines and cambrics. At the same time, they offered the British considerable concessions on goods such as hardware and cottons, while all the time convincing the British that they were getting everything for nothing--a suggestion which Eden reported to his superiors with amazing regularity. Once the British had been promised most of what they wanted, Calonne and Vergennes began negotiations for lower duties on French products. Calonne threatened to raise some of the favorable duties already conceded and to exclude other goods if the British failed to admit certain French articles to the special tariff. While this last minute campaign was not always successful, it did secure the admission of fashions and plate glass on a duty of twelve per cent. To be sure, the British were then under such pressure to conclude the treaty that concessions were extracted with ease and there was no risk of British withdrawal from the negotiations, as Vergennes feared. Although they failed to secure the admission of silks, the French negotiators seem to have obtained more or less what they wanted with regard to the special tariff. Adding silks would have encouraged the Opposition in Great Britain, and Vergennes remembered only too well the fate of the Utrecht Commercial Convention. Much to Eden's relief, the completed commercial treaty was signed on September 26, 1786. In January 1787 an additional convention settled or clarified several points left vague in the September agreement.

Much of Vergennes' efforts in 1786 were devoted to bridge building between France and Great Britain. But the cultivation of trust, confidence, and understanding, after so many years of rivalry and national hatred, was a long, tedious and often difficult process involving more than just talk. French influence over anti-British movements in India and the Dutch Republic did not make the task any easier. The conclusion of the September and January accords, however, showed that the two nations could negotiate in good faith where their interests were involved. Vergennes was prompt to point this out.

I hope we have demonstrated that when two great powers discuss their interests with frankness and precision the difficulties disappear and one works the greatest weal possible by the simplest means. . . .10

10Vergennes to Eden, January 15, 1787, Archives des Affaires Etrangères, Correspondance Politique, Angleterre 559, p. 39vo.

Only trade was involved in the September and January treaties, but the implication was plain: other Anglo-French difficulties could be resolved in a similar manner. Thus, the seeds of rapprochement were carefully sown and nurtured. By the end of September 1786, some signs of growth were apparent, for the British were impressed both by the talk of rapprochement and the way the negotiations were conducted. Pitt was struck by the fairness of the French proceedings while Eden praised the sincerity and good faith with which the French sought a rapprochement with Great Britain. Even the British ambassador, who was not as close to Vergennes as Eden, came to a similar conclusion and urged his government to do everything possible to further the trend. Carmarthen suspected ulterior motives, especially political ones, and instructed the equally suspicious embassy secretary, Hailes, to ferret out the truth, but Hailes found that economic reasons, such as revenue, seemed to be paramount French considerations.[11]

Both the rapprochement and the new commercial treaty received a series of unexpected blows in early 1787. Vergennes, whose health had been failing for several months, died soon after the signature of the Additional Convention. His policies and plans for transforming the Anglo-French commercial treaty of 1786 into an effective instrument died with him. His successor, the comte de Montmorin, a childhood companion of the king, was only forty. He had been ambassador to Spain during the American Revolution, but, aside from that, had little diplomatic experience and his ineptitude would quickly become manifest.

The second blow came with the Assembly of Notables and the dismissal of Calonne, the other architect of the Anglo-French commercial treaty of 1786. Ever since he had become controller general in 1783, Calonne had actively sought to revive the ailing French economy and make France competitive with Great Britain. By 1786 Calonne believed that piecemeal measures were not sufficient to cure the financial and economic ills which resulted, in part, from the American Revolution. Thus, the controller general drafted a comprehensive program of financial, economic and governmental reform. Because the tax and governmental reforms were extensive and deleterious to privilege, Calonne recommended an assembly of notables to give them a seal of approval. Such an assembly, it was hoped, would prove reasonably manage-

---

[11]Eden to Carmarthen, September 27, October 10, 1786, Public Records Office, 27/20, pp. 172, 247-247vo.

able, and calling the assembly would be less risky than forcing the Parlement of Paris to register the royal edicts immediately or summoning the Estates General, a tacit admission of bankruptcy. The worsening financial situation finally persuaded Louis XVI to support Calonne's proposals. The controller general failed to gain the support of other ministers who openly or covertly opposed the project as too grand and dangerous. (Castries commented that Calonne's fall would be "brilliant.") The illness of both Vergennes and Calonne delayed the opening of the assembly until the end of February 1787, a fact which heightened public anxiety and gave the Notables an opportunity to meet and intrigue among themselves.

The Assembly of Notables proved infinitely more independent and troublesome than anticipated. Angered by Calonne's uncompromising attack on privilege, the Notables moved from criticism to obstruction to revolt. Little by little, they harried the controller general into revealing the amount of the current deficit and making other concessions he had hoped to avoid. Undermined by blunders and charges of corruption, Calonne was dismissed in early April 1787. Thus, the one man with sufficient knowledge to resolve the financial disarray, if that was possible, was gone. With him went all the measures, such as the abolition of internal tariffs, which might have mitigated the effects of the new Franco-British commercial agreement. The Assembly of Notables was dissolved in May 1787, after it insisted that fiscal proposals be laid before the Parlement of Paris or the Estates General. During the summer, the battle was carried to the Parlement of Paris which balked at registering the tax proposals and called upon the king to summon the Estates General. When the Parlement of Paris declared enforced registration of the tax decrees unconstitutional and inaugurated malpractice proceedings against Calonne, the government exiled it to Troyes in mid-August 1787. By the end of summer, then, the fiscal problem was no closer to solution than it had been in January. The behavior of the Assembly of Notables and its subsequent repercussions damaged enormously the prestige and stability of the French government. The privileged orders had discovered the effectiveness of combined opposition, and Europe now knew the seriousness of the French fiscal problem. As bankruptcy signified an inability to make war in eighteenth-century Europe, previously meek states took notice and suddenly became brave.

It was against this background that the French and English conducted negotiations regarding the execution of the commercial agreements, the Dutch crisis and other matters. Like the French government's confrontation with privilege, these discussions were marked by miscalculation, futility and humiliation. As Vergennes had indicated on many occasions, more was at stake in these negotiations than the issues under consideration. In February 1787 Rayneval warned Montmorin that peace with Great Britain was likely to endure as a result of the commercial treaty, British isolation, and the disarray of British finances which was likened to that of France. But he reminded his superior that Great Britain required careful surveillance. Despite this warning the French seemed intent on destroying as soon as possible the favorable impressions of France which the late foreign minister had labored so hard to create. The deterioration was caused in part by Montmorin's inexperience and in part divergent ministerial views concerning the negotiations: from the beginning Vergennes had seen the negotiations in political terms as a means to bring Great Britain under French influence; Calonne had seen them in purely economic terms as a way to expand French trade and make French industry more competitive; while Castries, whose heart was never in the negotiations, had sought to protect and extend French interests even if the discussions collapsed as a result. While Vergennes lived, he acted as a mediator between Calonne and Eden to negotiate duties and between Castries and Eden to negotiate a consular treaty. Neither Calonne nor Castries seem to have understood or appreciated the real purpose of the negotiations. It was, perhaps, a grave error not to have educated the other ministers better, but Vergennes was most eager that the British not know the full extent of his plans. Besides, the opposition of Calonne and Castries had its uses in making the British more malleable. By destroying Vergennes' nascent rapprochement, the French ministers insured British reentry on the Continent to the detriment of French interests.

Between February and April 1787, the negotiations concerning the execution of the commercial arrangements became embroiled in discussions concerning the duty on French linens entering Ireland and the extension of the reserve on Portuguese wines to those of Spain. While both disputes ended in favor of the British position, a great deal of damage was done by the manner in which the two points were handled. Despite French assurances, the conduct of these negotiations had begun to sow doubts regarding French sincerity, doubts which were enforced by formal execution of the commercial treaty. At first the French indicated that the date was finally fixed for May 10, 1787. After Calonne's dismissal, Eden began to hear disturbing rumors about French plans for putting the agreements into effect. The rumors proved only too true. Contrary to the September and January accords, British goods were restricted to fewer than a dozen French ports, duties on cloth were assessed by weight instead of value, and cottons paid an extra duty. Although the original debacle was straightened

out by the end of May 1787, other problems arose over the perception of duties and the definition of a French seaport. Meanwhile,
British customs began to enforce strictly every regulation which
would hamper or restrict French trade, and in November 1787
Montmorin warned that the French would retaliate if the British
continued those practices. In early 1788 his threat was carried
out. Thus, a year and a half later the signature of the treaty which
was to transform Anglo-French relations, the trade war between
the two countries had resumed.

Eden observed a month after the Anglo-French commercial treaty of 1786 that:

> ... the Treaty was formed under the administration
> of M. de Vergennes, M. de Calonne and M. de
> Miromesnil; ... its execution immediately devolved
> upon M. de Montmorin, M. de l'Archevêque de
> Toulouse, M. de Villedeuil, and M. de la Moignon,
> all of whom I found strangers to its contents and
> some of them perhaps adverse to its principles...[12]

Some of the difficulties encountered in enforcing the treaty sprang
from the situation Eden described, but there had always been disagreement within the French cabinet concerning the Anglo-French
negotiations. When the negotiators began work on the special
tariff, the advocates of relatively free trade and those of protec-
tionism engaged in acrimonious debate during a session of the
committee of the Council of State held on August 1, 1786. So heated
was the debate that a long mémoire was drafted to counter objections to the proposed treaty, but not until the king in council had
approved the next steps in the negotiations. The debate continued
and, in 1788, was dramatized by the public clash between Du Pont
de Nemour and the Chamber of Commerce of Normandy. When the
treaty went into effect in May 1787, protectionist officials did much
harm in their efforts to protect French interests, and the wretched
enforcement of the agreement not only antagonized the British but
also hurt French trade and industry. Difficulties over enforcement of the commercial agreement were made worse by the fact
that the proposed consular treaty had never been completed as a

---

[12]Eden to Carmarthen, June 7, 1787. Public Records
Office, 27/25, p. 13. Miromesnil and Lamoignon, his successor,
were Keepers of Seals; the Archevêque de Toulouse refers to
Loménie de Brienne, later First Minister; and M. de Villedeuil
was controller general during the summer of 1787.

result of Castries' insistence upon legal rights and reciprocity. Without consuls, all complaints had to be channeled either through the ambassador who was not in a position to investigate such minutiae properly, or directly to the respective foreign ministries where they became grounds for protest. Thus, each confiscation tended to embitter relations between the two countries. Most importantly, the commercial treaty of 1786 failed because of the very problems it sought to resolve: Anglo-French political rivalry on the Continent and the fiscal legacy of the American Revolution.

The execution of the treaty had raised grave doubts about French sincerity, but the fatal blow to Vergennes' English policy was delivered by the Dutch crisis during the summer and fall of 1787. The crisis proved that Vergennes was wrong when he believed that all Anglo-French difficulties, political as well as commercial, were negotiable. The Dutch crisis also resulted in the complete reversal of the relative positions of Great Britain and France. Until 1787 Great Britain was isolated while France appeared to be at the center of a great European system of alliances; by the end of 1787, Great Britain was allied with the Dutch Republic and Prussia while France had been effectively isolated and humiliated. The Dutch crisis arose out of the perennial struggle between the House of Orange and the republicans who represented the country's commercial and local interests. Dutch involvement in the American Revolution on the French side united those discontented with the pro-British House of Orange. Thereafter, rivalry between the pro-British Orangists and the pro-French republicans moved towards one of its periodic climaxes.

The increasing French role in Dutch politics posed a threat to the British position in India, but the Pitt administration did little more than send an able minister, James Harris, to The Hague in late 1784. Pitt particularly avoided involvement in the Dutch situation during the commercial negotiations with France. Nevertheless, Harris revived the pro-British Orangist party to such an extent that by the winter of 1787 the Dutch Republic was on the verge of civil war despite Vergennes' efforts to reconcile the two factions. Two weeks after the Anglo-French commercial treaty went into effect, the British government took a more active role in the Dutch question. Significantly, Pitt noted that French financial difficulties made war unlikely. At the same time French agents in the Dutch Republic let the situation get completely out of hand as the republicans moved to ever more extreme positions. In late June 1787 the Dutch question was internationalized when the republicans seized the Princess of Orange who was the sister of the king of Prussia. As a result, the Prussian government, with British encouragement, demanded an apology and satisfaction. During July and August Prussian troops gathered on Dutch borders;

Montmorin adopted a high tone while the French government did nothing to back it up despite the dubious credibility of French power. Anglo-French negotiations to secure an accommodation in the Dutch Republic were stalemated as each side sought to prevent intervention by the other rather than secure a lasting settlement. With the mounting crisis in the Dutch Republic and increasing tensions between Turkey and Russia, cooperation with Great Britain paled while fears and rivalry came to the fore. The Austrian ambassador confirmed this shift in August 1787 when he wrote, "As to England, M. de Montmorin does not appear to have adopted the dreams of M. de Vergennes on the possibility of a solid rapprochement between the two courts."[13]

In September the French dilemma posed by the Dutch crisis was outlined to the Council of State. While the Dutch connection held the keys to India, the British had so undermined the republican position that France had to choose between publicly deserting her allies or facing the possibility of a war she could not afford. The former would shatter French prestige and leave France isolated so that Montmorin adopted a firm tone on the premise that neither Prussia nor Great Britain was willing to risk war. It was a disastrous miscalculation. When Prussian troops entered the Dutch Republic a few days later, France declared that she would support the province of Holland, but sent no aid. The British continued to negotiate, avoiding provocative acts until the fall of Amsterdam, then terminated the matter with a public humiliation. Declarations were exchanged acknowledging that France had never intended to intervene in Holland. Too late, Montmorin realized that "our domestic affairs have contributed essentially to the demonstrations which the courts of London and Berlin have risked...." At the same time, Anglo-French negotiations on the Turkish situation emphasized the demise of Vergennes' English policy. Vergennes had hoped to use the Anglo-French rapprochement to curb Russian designs on the Ottoman Empire, but now the British and French sought to penetrate each other's plans with regard to the Russo-Turkish war which began in August 1787, while agents of each power in the courts of Europe attempted to justify its role in the affair and discredit that of the other. After all the idealistic language concerning Anglo-French cooperation, this was indeed a sordid denouement.[14]

---

[13]Alfred d'Arneth and Jules Flammermont, Correspondance secrete du Comte de Mercy-Argenteau, 2 vols. (Paris, 1889), I, 175.

[14]Montmorin to Vauguyon, October 29, 1787. Archives des Affaires Etrangeres, Correspondance Politique, Espagne 623, p. 359vo.

Transcripts of Crown-copyright records in the Public Record Office appear by permission of the Controller of H. M. Stationary Office.

LA REVOLUTION FRANÇAISE
DANS L'HISTOIRE DU MONDE CONTEMPORAIN

Albert Soboul

La Révolution de 1789-1794 a marqué l'avènement de la société moderne, bourgeoise et capitaliste, dans l'histoire de la France. Sa caractéristique essentielle est d'avoir réalisé l'unité nationale du pays sur la base de la destruction du régime seigneurial et des ordres féodaux privilégiés: la Révolution, selon Tocqueville dans L'Ancien Régime et la Révolution "dont l'object propre était d'abolir partout le reste des institutions du Moyen-Age."[1] Que la Révolution française ait abouti finalement à l'établissement d'une démocratie libérale précise encore sa signification historique. De ce double point de vue, et sous l'angle de l'histoire mondiale qui nous occupe ici, elle mérite d'être considérée comme le modèle classique de la révolution bourgeoise.

L'étude comparative de la Révolution française pose ainsi deux séries de problèmes.

Problèms d'ordre général: ceux qui concernent la loi historique de la transition du féodalisme au capitalisme moderne. A reprendre la problématique posée par Marx au livre III du Capital, cette transition s'effectue de deux façons: par la destruction totale de l'ancien système économique et social, c'est "la voie

---

[1]Alexis de Tocqueville, L'Ancien Régime et la Révolution in Oeuvres Complètes, Vol. II. Introduction par Georges Lefebvre (Paris, 1952), p. 99.

réellement révolutionnaire,"--par la sauvegarde de l'ancien mode de production au sein de la nouvelle société capitaliste, c'est la voie de compromis.[2]

Problèmes d'ordre particulier: ceux qui tiennent à la structure spécifique de la société française à la fin de l'Ancien Régime et qui rendent compte des caractères propres de la Révolution française au regard des divers types de "révolution bourgeoise."[3]

De ce double point de vue, l'histoire de la Révolution française ne saurait s'isoler de celle de l'Europe. Dans tous les pays du continent la formation de la société moderne s'est esquissée au sein même de l'ancien système économique et social à survivances féodales, puis à ses dépens. Dans tous les pays d'Europe, cette évolution s'est faite à des degrés divers au bénéfice de la bourgeoisie. La Révolution française n'a pas été la première dont la bourgeoisie profita: avant elle, la révolution de Hollande au XVIe siècle, les deux révolutions de l'Angleterre au XVIIe, la révolution américaine au XVIIIe siècle ont jallonné cette évolution. Encore s'agit-il de rendre compte du caractère exemplaire de la Révolution française.

Si la Révolution française fut la plus éclatante des révolutions bourgeoises, éclipsant par le caractère dramatique de ses luttes de classes les révolutions qui l'avaient précédée, elle le dut sans doute à l'obstination de l'aristocratie ancrée sur ses privilèges féodaux, se refusant à toute concession, et à l'acharnement contraire des masses populaires. La bourgeoisie n'avait pas souhaité la ruine de l'aristocratie; le refus du compromis et la contre-révolution l'obligèrent à poursuivre la destruction de l'ordre ancien. Mais elle n'y parvint qu'en s'alliant aux masses

---

[2]Karl Marx, "Aperçu historique sur le capital marchand," in Le Capital (Paris, Editions Sociales, 1966), Tome VI, 342. Sur le probleme de la transition du féodalisme au capitalisme, cf. The Transition from Feudalism to Capitalism: A Symposium by Paul Marlor Sweezy et al. (London, 1954); Rodney Hilton, "Y eut-il une crise générale de la féodalite?" Annales, VI (1951), 23-30; Guiliano Procacci, Georges Lefebvre et Albert Soboul, "Une discussion historique: du féodalisme au capitalisme," La Pensée, XXII (1956), 10-32.

[3]Ce sont les problèmes que pose plus particulièrement, Georges Lefebvre, "La Révolution française dans l'histoire du monde," Annales, III (1948), repris dans Etudes sur la Révolution française (Paris, 1954), 317-326.

rurales et urbaines, à qui il fallut bien donner satisfaction: la révolution populaire et la terreur firent place nette, la féodalité fut irrémédiablement détruite, la démocratie instaurée.

Du féodalisme au capitalisme, la Révolution française emprunta donc "la voie reellement révolutionnaire." En faisant table rase de toutes les survivances féodales, en affranchissant les paysans des droits seigneuriaux et des dîmes ecclésiastiques, dans une certaine mesure aussi des contraintes communautaires, en détruisant les monopoles corporatifs et en unifiant le marché national, la Révolution française marqua une étape décisive dans la voie du capitalisme. Supprimant la propriété foncière féodale, elle a par là-même libéré les petits producteurs directs et rendu possible la différenciation de la masse paysanne et sa polarisation entre le capital et le travail salarié. De là des relations de production entièrement nouvelles, le capital une fois soustrait à la sujétion féodale ayant rendu mercantiles les forces de travail. Ainsi a été assurée finalement l'autonomie de la production capitaliste, et cela aussi bien dans le domaine agricole que dans le secteur industriel. De ce passage à la société capitaliste, et à la lumière de la Révolution française, deux conditions apparaissent nécessaires: la désagrégation de la propriété foncière féodale et l'affranchissement des paysans. La question agraire occupe "une position axiale" dans la révolution bourgeoise.

L'aile marchante de cette révolution fut moins la bourgeoisie commerçante (dans la mesure où elle demeurait uniquement commerçante et intermédiaire, elle s'accommodait de l'ancienne société: de 1789 à 1793, des Monarchiens aux Feuillants, puis aux Girondins, elle tendit généralement au compromis), que la masse des petits producteurs directs dont l'aristocratie féodale accaparait le surtravail ou le surproduit, en s'appuyant sur l'appareil juridique et les moyens de contrainte de l'Etat d'Ancien Régime. L'instrument politique de la mutation fut la dictature jacobine de la petite et moyenne bourgeoisie, appuyée sur les masses populaires: catégories sociales dont l'idéal était une démocratie de petits producteurs autonomes, paysans et artisans indépendants, travaillant et échangeant librement. La révolution paysanne et populaire était au coeur de la révolution bourgeoise et la poussait en avant.[4]

---

[4] Sur les aspects théoriques de ces problèmes, voir Maurice H. Dobb, Studies in the Development of Capitalism (Londres, 1946); H. K. Takahashi, Shimin ka-kumei-no kozo [Structure de la révolution bourgeoise] (Tokyo, 1951), compte-rendu par Charles Haguenauer, Revue historique, CCXVII (1955), 345.

La victoire sur la féodalité et l'Ancien Régime n'a pas cependant signifié l'apparition simultanée de nouveaux rapports sociaux. Le passage au capitalisme ne constitue pas un processus simple par lequel les éléments capitalistes se développent au sein de l'ancienne société, jusqu'au moment où ils sont assez forts pour en briser les cadres. Il faudra longtemps encore pour que le capitalisme s'affirme définitivement en France: ses progrès furent lents pendant la période révolutionnaire, la dimension des entreprises demeurant souvent modeste, le capital commercial prépondérant.[5] La ruine de la propriété foncière féodale et du système corporatif et réglementaire, en assurant l'autonomie du mode de production capitaliste, n'en avait pas moins frayé sans compromis la voie aux rapports bourgeois de production et de circulation: transformation par excellence révolutionnaire.

Bouleversant les structures économiques et sociales, la Révolution française brisait en même temps l'armature étatique de L'Ancien Régime, balayant les vestiges des anciennes autonomies, détruisant les privilèges locaux et les particularismes provinciaux. Elle rendit ainsi possible, du Directoire à l'Empire, l'instauration d'un état nouveau répondant aux intérêts et aux exigences de la bourgeoisie moderne.

De ce double point de vue, la Révolution française fut loin de constituer un mythe comme on l'a prétendu.[6] Sans doute la féodalité au sens mediéval du mot ne répondait plus à rien en 1789: mais pour les contemporains, bourgeois et plus encore paysans, ce terme abstrait recouvrait une réalité qu'ils connaissaient fort bien (droits féodaux, autorité seigneuriale) et qui fut finalement balayée. Que d'autre part les Assemblées révolutionnaires aient été peuplées essentiellement d'hommes des professions libérales et de fonctionnaires publics, non de chefs

---

[5]Il faut cependant souligner les progrès de l'économie au cours de la période napoléonienne qui se soude si étroitement à la période révolutionnaire. Voir Ernest Labrousse, "Du bilan du monde en 1815. Elements d'un bilan économique: La croissance dans la guerre," Comité international des sciences historiques XVIIᵉ Congrès, Vienne, 1965. Rapports, I. Grands thèmes, p. 473.

[6]Alfred Cobban, The Myth of the French Revolution (Londres, 1955). Du même auteur et du même point de vue, The Social Interpretation of the French Revolution (Cambridge, 1964). Voir Georges Lefebvre, "Le mythe de la Révolution française," Annales historiques de la Révolution française, XXVII (1956), 337-345.

d'entreprises (dans la Constituante, les deux tiers des députés appartenaient aux professions libérales, 13% seulement au monde des affaires, marchands, banquiers, manufacturiers, capitalistes petits et grands; des 1539 membres de la Constituante et de la Convention, 629 détenaient des fonctions publiques, parmi lesquels 289 possédaient des offices avant la Révolution), on n'en peut tirer argument contre l'importance de la Révolution française dans l'instauration de l'ordre capitaliste: outre que manufacturiers, financiers et négociants étaient représentés par une petite minorité fort active, outre l'importance des groupes de pression (députés du commerce, club Massiac défenseur des intérêts des planteurs, des armateurs et des raffineurs),[7] le fait essentiel est que l'ancien système de production et d'échange fut détruit et que la Révolution française proclama sans restriction aucune la liberté d'entreprise et de profit, ouvrant par là la voie au capitalisme. L'histoire du XIXe siècle, en particulier celle de la classe ouvrière, démontre que ce ne fut pas là un mythe.

Etape nécessaire de la transition générale du féodalisme au capitalisme, la Révolution française n'en conserve pas moins, au regard des diverses révolutions similaires, ses caractères propres qui tiennent à la structure spécifique de la société française à la fin de l'Ancien Régime.

Ces caractères ont été niés. La Révolution française n'aurait été "qu'un aspect d'une révolution occidentale, ou plus exactement atlantique, qui a commencé dans les colonies anglaises d'Amériques, peu après 1763, s'est prolongée par les révolutions de Suisse, des Pays-Bas, d'Irlande, avant d'atteindre la France entre 1787 et 1789. De France, elle a rebondi aux Pays-Bas, a gagné l'Allemagne rhénane, la Suisse, l'Italie"[8]... La Révolu-

---

[7]Voir essentiellement J. Letaconnoux, "Le Comité des députés extraordinaires des manufactures et du commerce et l'oeuvre économique de l'Assemblée Constituante (1789-1791)", Annales révolutionnaires, VI (1913), 149-208; Gabriel Debien, Les Colons de Saint-Domingue et la Révolution. Essai sur le club Massiac, (Août 1789-août 1792) (Paris, 1953).

[8]Jacques Godechot, La Grande Nation. L'Expansion révolutionnaire de la France dans le monde (1789-1799) (Paris, 1956), I, 11. Cette conception d'une révolution "occidentale" ou "atlantique" a d'abord été avancée par Robert R. Palmer, "The World Revolution of the West," Political Science Quarterly, LXIX (1954), 1-14. Elle a été reprise et développée par Jacques Godechot et Robert R. Palmer,

tion française s'intégrerait dans "la grande révolution atlantique." Sans doute, on ne peut sousestimer l'importance de l'Océan dans la rénovation de l'économie et dans l'exploitation des pays coloniaux par l'Occident. Mais là n'est pas le propos de nos auteurs, ni de montrer que la Révolution française ne fut qu'un épisode du mouvement général de l'histoire qui, après les Révolutions hollandaise, anglaise et américaine, contribua à associer ou à porter la bourgeoisie au pouvoir. La Révolution française ne marque d'ailleurs pas le terme géographique de cette transformation, comme les qualificatifs ambigus d'atlantique ou d'occidental le donnent à entendre: au XIXe siècle, partout où s'est installée l'économie capitaliste, l'ascension de la bourgeoisie a marché de pair; la révolution bourgeoise fut de portée universelle. D'autre part, à mettre sur le même plan la Révolution française et "les révolutions de Suisse, des Pays-Bas et d'Irlande"..., on minimise étrangement la profondeur, les dimensions de la première, et la mutation brusque qu'elle constitua. Cette conception en vidant de tout contenu spécifique, économique (anti-féodal et capitaliste), social (anti-aristocratique et bourgeois) et national (un et indivisible), tiendrait pour nul un demi-siècle de l'historiographie révolutionnaire, de Jean Jaurès à Georges Lefebvre.

Tocqueville avait cependant ouvert la voie à la réflexion, lorsqu'il demandait "pourquoi des principes analogues et des théories politiques semblables n'ont mené les Etats-Unis qu'à un changement de gouvernement et la France à une subversion totale de la société." Poser le problème en ces termes, c'est dépasser l'aspect superficiel d'une histoire politique et institutionnelle, pour s'efforcer d'atteindre les réalités économiques et sociales dans leur spécificité nationale.

La Révolution française s'assigna finalement une place singulière dans l'histoire du monde contemporain.

"Le problème de l'Atlantique du XVIIIe au XXe siècle," X Congresso internazionale di scienze storiche. Relazioni (Florence, 1955), pp. 175-239; Robert R. Palmer, The Age of the Democratic Revolution. A Political History of Europe and America, 1760-1800, vol. I: The Challenge (Princeton, 1959); Jacques Godechot, Les Révolutions (1770-1799) (Paris, 1963). Exposé d'ensemble par Jacques Godechot et Robert R. Palmer, "Révolution française, occidentale ou atlantique," Bulletin de la société d'histoire moderne, Douzième série (juillet 1960),pp. 1-10. Bibliographie dans Jacques Godechot, "Révolution française ou révolution occidentale?" L'Information historique (1960), p. 6. Cette conception a été critiqué par Georges Lefebvre, Annals historiques de la Révolution française, XXIX (1957), p. 272.

Révolution de la liberté, elle se plaça, comme la Révolution américaine, sous l'invocation du droit naturel, et conféra à son oeuvre un caractère universaliste qu'avait négligé la Révolution anglaise. Mais qui pourrait nier que la déclaration de 1789 affirma ce caractère avec bien plus de force que les Déclarations américaines? Ajoutons qu'elle alla plus loin dans la voie de la liberté. Elle affirma la liberté de conscience et admit les protestants et les juifs dans la cité: mais en créant l'état civil, le 20 septembre 1792, elle reconnaissait au citoyen le droit de n'adhérer à aucune religion. Elle libéra l'homme blanc: mais, par la loi du 16 pluviose an II (4 février 1794), elle abolit "l'esclavages des nègres dans toutes les colonies."

Révolution de l'égalité, la Révolution française dépassa singulièrement les révolutions qui l'avaient précédée. En Angleterre ni aux Etats-Unis, l'accent n'avait porté sur l'égalité, l'aristocratie et la bourgeoisie s'étant associées au pouvoir. La résistance de l'aristocratie, la contre-révolution et la guerre contraignirent la bourgeoisie française à pousser l'égalité des droits au premier plan. Ainsi put-elle rallier le peuple et vaincre. Mais ainsi s'esquissa en l'an II un régime de démocratie sociale caractérisé par un compromis entre les conceptions bourgeoises et les aspirations populaires. Les masses populaires se rendaient compte du sort qui les attendaient: c'est pourquoi elles se montrèrent hostiles à la liberté économique qui ouvrait la voie à la concentration et au capitalisme. Leur idéal à la fin du XVIIIe siècle, était que chaque paysan fut propriétaire, chaque artisan indépendant, que le salarié fut protégé contre la toute-puissance du riche.

Après le 10 août 1792 et le renversement du trône, la bourgeoisie révolutionnaire ayant institué le suffrage universel et scellé son alliance avec les sans-culottes, il fallut bien dépasser l'égalité théorique des droits et progresser vers cette "égalité des jouissances" qu'ils réclamaient. De là, la direction de l'économie pour mettre les prix en harmonie avec les salaires et assurer à tous le pain quotidien: la taxation et la réglementation furent institués par la loi du maximum général du 29 septembre 1793, les fabrications de guerre et le commerce extérieur furent nationalisés. De là encore, la tentative d'un enseignement public accessible à tous par la loi du 29 frimaire an II (19 décembre 1793). De là, l'esquisse d'une sécurité sociale par la loi de bienfaisance nationale du 22 floréal an II (11 mai 1794). Cette république égalitaire de l'an II remplit la bourgeoisie possédante d'indignation et d'effroi; après le 9 thermidor, elle parut bannie à jamais. Mais demeura dès lors, dans la conscience des hommes, cette conviction que la liberté sans l'égalité n'est que le privilège de quelques-uns, que la liberté et l'égalité sont inséparables, que l'égalité

politique elle-même peut n'être qu'une vaine apparence quand
s'affirme l'inégalité sociale. "La liberté n'est qu'un vain fantôme
quand une classe d'hommes peut affamer l'autre impunément, avait
déclare l'enragé Jacques Roux, le 25 juin 1793, à la tribune de la
Convention. L'égalité n'est qu'un vain fantôme quand le riche,
par le monopole, exerce le droit de vie et de mort sur son
semblable. "[9]

 Révolution de l'unité, la Révolution française acheva la
nation devenue une et indivisible.[10] Sans doute la monarchie
capétienne avait constitué le cadre territorial et administratif de
la nation, mais sans pousser cette tâche jusqu'au bout: en 1789,
l'unité nationale demeurait imparfaite. La nation demeurait sec-
tionnée territorialement par l'incohérence des divisions administratives et la persistance du "morcellement féodal;" la diversité
des poids et mesures, les douanes intérieures s'opposaient à la
constitution d'un marché national. Bien plus: la nation était sec-
tionnée socialement, la société d'Ancien Régime était hiérarchisée
et en partie corporative; or, selon la remarque de Georges
Lefebvre, qui dit corps implique privilèges; partout régnait
l'inégalité. Et cela, alors que la nation, déjà créée par l'unite de
gouvernement, avait vu au XVIIIe siècle sa cohésion renforcée par
les multiples liens qu'avaient tissés le progrès matériel, l'expansion du français, l'essor de la culture et l'éclat des Lumières.

 Les ordres, états, corps et corporations abolies, les
Français sont libres et égaux en droits, ils constituent la nation
une et indivisible. La rationalisation des institutions par l'Assemblée constituante, le retour à la centralisation par le gouvernement révolutionnaire, l'effort administratif du Directoire, la reconstruction de l'état par Napoléon, achevèrent l'oeuvre de la
monarchie d'Ancien Regime par la destruction des autonomies et
des particularismes, par la mise en place de l'armature institutionnelle d'un état unifié. En même temps, par l'égalité civile,
par le mouvement des fédérations en 1790, par le développement
du réseau des sociétés affiliées aux Jacobins, par l'anti-fédéral-
isme et les congrès ou réunions centrales de sociétés populaires
en 1793, s'éveillait et se fortifiait la conscience d'une nation une

---

 [9]J. Roux, "Addresse présentée à la Convention nationale
au nom de la section des Gravilliers" (A. N. , W 20, d. 1073, imp.
in -- 8°, 12 p.).

 [10]Sur l'ensemble de ce problème, voir Albert Soboul, "De
l'Ancien Régime à l'Empire: problème national et réalités sociales, " L'Information historique (1960), pp. 59-64 et pp. 96-104.

et indivisible. Les progrès de la langue francaise allèrent dans le même sens. Des liens économiques nouveaux renforçaient la conscience nationale. Le morcellement féodal détruit les péages et les douanes intérieures, le "reculement des barrières" jusqu'à la frontière politique tendaient à l'unification du marché national, par ailleurs protégé de la concurrence étrangère par un tarif protectionniste. La Révolution française donnait à la souveraineté nationale une force et une efficacité qu'elle n'avait pas jusque là.

Un nouveau droit public international s'affirmait cependant. Cherchant à en degager les principes, à propos de l'affaire des princes allemands possessionés en Alsace, Merlin de Douai opposa en effet, le 28 octobre 1790, à l'état dynastique la nation conçue comme association volontaire. "Il n'y a entre vous et vos frères d'Alsace d'autre titre légitime d'union que le Pacte social formé l'année dernière entre tous les Français anciens et modernes dans cette Assemblée": allusion à la décision du Tiers Etat, le 17 juin 1789, de se proclamer Assemblée nationale, et à celle de l'Assemblée qui le 9 juillet suivant se déclarait constituante; allusion aussi au pacte fédératif du 14 juillet 1790. Une seule question "infiniment simple" se pose: celle de savoir "si c'est à des parchemins diplomatiques que le peuple alsacien doit l'avantage d'être français:. . . "Qu'importent au Peuple d'Alsace, qu'importent au Peuple François les conventions, qui, dans les tems du Despotisme, ont eu pour objet d'unir le premier au second? Le Peuple Alsacien s'est uni au Peuple François, parce qu'il l'a voulu; c'est donc sa volonté seule, et non pas le traité de Munster qui a légitimé l'union."[11] Cette volonté, l'Alsace l'avait manifesté en participant à la Fédération du 14 juillet 1790. Le droit public international était révolutionné comme le droit public intérieur: les nations avaient désormais le droit de se libérer et de disposer d'elles-mêmes.

Les traits que nous venons d'esquisser, rendent compte du retentissement de la Révolution française et de sa valeur d'exemple dans l'évolution du monde contemporain. Sans doute, dans les pays d'Europe qu'elles occupèrent, ce furent les armées de la République, puis celle de Napoléon, qui, plus que la force des idées, abattirent l'Ancien Régime. En abolissant le servage, en libérant les paysans des redevances seigneuriales et des dîmes ecclésiastiques, en remettant dans la circulation des biens de mainmorte, la conquête française fit place nette pour le développement du capitalisme. S'il ne resta rien de l'empire continental que Napoléon avait eu l'ambition de fonder, il anéantit pourtant l'Ancien Régime partout où il en eut le temps. En ce sens, son règne pro-

[11]Le Moniteur universel, 30 octobre 1790.

longe la Révolution, et il en fut bien le soldat, comme les souverains d'Ancien Régime ne cessèrent de le lui reprocher.[12]

Après Napoléon, le prestige de la Révolution ne s'évanouit pas. Avec le recul du temps, elle apparaît à la fois comme fille de la raison et fille de l'enthousiasme. Une puissante force d'émotion s'attacha à son souvenir, la prise de la Bastille demeurant le symbole de l'insurrection populaire, la Marseillaise le chant des guerres pour la liberté et l'indépendance. En ce sens, la Révolution française a bien valeur de mythe, au sens où Georges Sorel l'entendait: elle séduit l'imagination et les cœurs; annonciatrice de temps meilleurs, elle excite à l'action. Par delà ce romantisme révolutionnaire, son attrait idéologique n'est pas moins puissant, la Révolution française s'affirmant comme un immense effort pour asseoir la société sur des fondements rationnels.

Reprenons, une fois encore Tocqueville: "On l'a vue [la Révolution française] rapprocher ou diviser les hommes en dépit des lois, des traditions, des caractères, de la langue, rendant parfois ennemis des compatriotes et frères des étrangers; ou plutôt elle a formé au dessus de toutes les nationalités particulières, une patrie intellectuelle commune dont les hommes de toutes les nations ont pu devenir citoyens."[13] Etape nécessaire dans la transition du féodalisme au capitalisme, la Révolution française, par les solutions qu'elle a su successivement apporter au problème de l'égalité des droits, s'est encore imposée à l'histoire contemporaine. La transformation de l'économie par le capitalisme, en concentrant les entreprises, en multipliant et en agglomérant les salariés, en éveillant et précisant leur conscience de classe, a placé à nouveau au premier plan des préoccupations des hommes, le principe de l'égalité des droits. Si bien que ce principe essentiel que la bourgeoisie de 1789 avait posé avec éclat pour justifier l'abolition du privilège nobiliaire fondé sur la naissance, manifesta des conséquences que les Constituants n'avaient pas prévues, malgré les avertissements malveillants de certains adversaires clairvoyants. "Les nègres de nos colonies et les domestiques dans nos maisons," écrivit Rivarol dans le Journal politique national, "peuvent, la Déclaration des droits a la main, nous chasser de nos

---

[12]Voir Albert Soboul, "Le bilan du monde en 1815. Esquisse d'un bilan social," Comite international des sciences historiques. XIIᵉ Congrès, Vienne, 1965. Rapports, Tome I: Grands thèmes, p. 517.

[13]"Comment la Révolution française a été une révolution politique qui a procédé à la manière des révolutions religieuses, et pourquoi," L'Ancien Régime et la Révolution, p. 87.

héritages.   Comment une assemblée de législateurs a-t-elle feint d'ignorer que le droit de nature ne peut exister un instant à côté de la propriété?"14   C'était poser le problème du contenu des droits: égalité théorique ou égalité réelle?   A Vergniaud affirmant le 13 mars 1793: "L'égalité pour l'homme social n'est que celle des droits," répondent le 20 août suivant Félix Lepeletier: "Faire disparaître l'inégalité des jouissances," et en l'an IV Babeuf préconisant "la communauté des biens et des travaux," pour atteindre enfin à "l'égalité parfaite." La Révolution française ouvrait les trois voies dans lesquelles s'engagea successivement l'histoire du monde contemporain.

Pour le <u>libéralisme</u> <u>bourgeois</u>, celui des Constituants de Quatre-vingt-neuf comme celui des Anglo-Saxons, l'égalité n'est qu'une égalité des droits.   Tous les citoyens sont libres d'en user, mais tous n'en ont pas les moyens. Si dans la Déclaration l'égalité a été associée à la liberté, il s'agissait d'une affirmation de principe qui légitimait l'abaissement de l'aristocratie et l'abolition du privilège nobiliaire, plus qu'elle n'autorisait les espérances populaires. En plaçant au rang des droits naturels imprescriptibles celui de propriété, les Constituants introduisirent dans leur oeuvre une contradiction qu'ils ne purent surmonter: le maintien de l'esclavage et l'organisation censitaire du suffrage la portèrent au grand jour.   L'exercice du droit de vote fut dosé suivant le paiement d'une contribution déterminée, c'est-à-dire suivant le degré d'aisance et de richesse.   Ainsi les droits que la bourgeoisie constituante avait reconnus à l'homme et au citoyen, n'étaient que ceux de l'homme bourgeois; ils demeuraient abstraits et théoriques pour la masse des citoyens passifs.

La bourgeoisie révolutionnaire s'en tint toujours là, affirmant nettement ses principes, chaque fois que le mouvement populaire menaçait l'édifice nouveau. "Allons-nous terminer la Révolution, allons-nous la recommencer?" interroge Barnave, après la fuite à Varennes le 15 juillet 1791, dans un discours véhément, "vous avez rendu tous les hommes égaux devant la loi; vous avez consacré l'égalité civile et politique.... Un pas de plus serait

---

14<u>Journal</u> <u>politique</u> <u>national</u>, no. 19 (fin août 1789). Les Constituants "déclarent donc, à la face de l'univers, que tous les hommes naissaient et demeuraient libres, qu'un homme ne saurait être plus qu'un autre homme, et cent autres découvertes de cette nature, qu'ils se félicitaient d'avoir révélées les premiers du monde, se moquant bien philosophiquement de l'Angleterre qui n'avait pas su débuter comme eux, lorsqu'elle se donna une Constitution en 1688."

un acte funeste et coupable; un pas de plus dans la ligne de la
liberté serait la destruction de la royauté; dans la ligne de l'égalité,
la destruction de la propriété. Si l'on voulait encore détruire,
quand tout ce qu'il fallait détruire n'existe plus; si l'on croyait
n'avoir pas tout fait pour l'égalité, quand l'égalité de tous les
hommes est assurée, trouverait-on encore une aristocratie à anéantir, si ce n'est celle des propriétés? "[15] Dans cette même ligne,
Vergniaud dans son discours à la Convention, le 13 mars 1793, au
moment où s'affirme la poussée sectionnaire parisienne: "L'égalité, pour l'homme social, n'est que celle des droits. Elle n'est
pas plus celle des fortunes que celle des tailles, celles des forces,
de l'esprit, de l'activité, de l'industrie et du travail. "[16] Après
Thermidor, la bourgeoisie se raidit. Elle ne cache plus que les
droits de l'homme sont ceux du propriétaire. "Vous devez garantir
enfin la propriété du riche," déclare Boissy d'Anglas dans son
discours préliminaire au projet de Constitution, "L'égalité civile,
en effet, voilà tout ce que l'homme raisonnable peut exiger... Nous
devons être gouvernés par les meilleurs: les meilleurs sont les
plus instruits et les plus intéressés au maintien des lois; or, à
bien peu d'exception près, vous ne trouverez de pareils hommes
que parmi ceux qui, possédant une propriété, sont attachés au
pays qui la contient, aux lois qui la protègent, à la tranquillité qui
la conserve, et qui doivent à cette propriété et à l'aisance qu'elle
donne [leur] éducation. Un pays gouverné par les propriétaires
est dans l'ordre social, celui où les non-propriétaires gouvernent,
est dans l'état de nature. "[17] Propriétaire héréditaire, si bien que
subsiste en un certain sens le privilège de la naissance.

La voie du libéralisme bourgeois s'affirma avec éclat au
XIXe siècle. Par son compromis conservateur rassurant, elle
n'a rien perdu de sa valeur.

Pour les tenants de la démocratie sociale, telle qu'elle
s'est esquissée en l'an II, le droit à l'existence prime le droit de
propriété, l'égalité doit être celle "des jouissances." Dans son

---

[15]Moniteur, 17 juillet 1791.

[16]Ibid., 16 mars 1793.

[17]Ibid., 30 juin 1795. "L'égalité absolue est une chimère,"
poursuit Boissy d'Anglas; "pour qu'elle put exister, il faudrait
qu'il existât une égalité entière dans l'esprit, la vertu, la force phy-
sique, l'éducation, la fortune de tous les hommes." Singulière
continuité de vues des Girondins aux Thermidoriens.

discours du 2 décembre 1792 sur les troubles frumentaires d'Eure-et-Loir, Robespierre, subordonnant le droit de propriété au droit à l'existence, pose le fondement théorique d'une nation égalitaire. "Les auteurs de la théorie n'ont considéré les denrées les plus nécessaires à la vie que comme une marchandise ordinaire; ils n'ont mis aucune différence entre le commerce du blé et celui de l'indigo; ils ont plus disserté sur le commerce des grains que sur la subsistance du peuple... Ils ont compté pour beaucoup les profits des négociants ou des propriétaires, la vie des hommes à peu près pour rien.... Le premier des droits est celui d'exister: tous les autres sont subordonnés à celui-là."[18] Robespierre en vint, dans son discours du 24 avril 1793, à une nouvelle formulation du droit de propriété: "La propriété est le droit qu'a chaque citoyen de jouir et de disposer de la portion des biens qui lui est garantie par la loi." Ce n'était donc plus un droit naturel imprescriptible, antérieur à toute organisation sociale, comme l'avait affirmé la Déclaration de 1789; il s'inscrivait dorénavant dans des cadres sociaux et historiques, il se définissait par la loi.

C'est bien ainsi que l'entendaient aussi les masses populaires. Elles s'étaient toujours montrées hostiles à la liberté économique qui ouvrait la voie au capitalisme et à la concentration des entreprises, donc à leur prolétarisation: outre que pour elles les droits de l'homme et du citoyen demeuraient illusoires, la propriété privée de la terre et des ateliers les plaçait sous la dépendance de ceux qui en fait avaient seuls le privilège d'en jouir. Elles invoquèrent donc le droit à l'existence et mirent en avant, à l'encontre de la bourgeoisie propriétaire, le principe de "l'égalité des jouissances." Après le 10 août 1792, la bourgeoisie révolutionnaire se résolut, pour l'emporter, à l'alliance populaire: le suffrage universel fut institué, une république démocratique et sociale esquissée. La communauté nationale, investie du droit de contrôle sur la propriété privée, intervient pour maintenir une égalité relative par la reconstitution de la petite propriété, à mesure que l'évolution économique tend à la détruire, afin de prévenir la reconstitution du monopole de la richesse comme la formation d'un prolétariat dépendant. De là, les lois montagnardes pour multiplier les petits propriétaires, la direction de l'économie

---

[18]Moniteur, 4 décembre 1792. Voir Lefebvre, "Sur la pensée politique de Robespierre," Etudes sur la Révolution française, pp. 95-98, extrait du discours prononcé, le 15 octobre 1933, à l'occasion de l'inauguration du buste de Robespierre dans l'hôtel de ville d'Arras, publié dans Annales historiques de la Révolution française, X (1933), 492-510.

pour mettre en harmonie les prix et les salaires, un système d'enseignement ouvert à tous, "la bienfaisance nationale" enfin. Ainsi se réaliserait le but assigné à la société par la Déclaration des droits du 24 juin 1793: "le bonheur commun." Ainsi s'inscrirait dans les faits cet idéal d'une société égalitaire que Saint-Just précisait dans ses Institutions republicaines: "donner à tous les Français les moyens d'obtenir les premières nécessités de la vie, sans dépendre d'autre chose que des lois et sans dépendance mutuelle dans l'état civil." Ou encore: "Il faut que l'homme vive indépendant."

La tentative de démocratie sociale de l'an II, si elle remplit d'effroi le bourgeoisie, n'en prit pas moins valeur d'exemple après 1830, quand reparut le parti républicain et surtout après 1848, quand le suffrage universel rétabli conféra à ses principes une forme multipliée. La tentative de l'an II a nourri la pensée sociale de XIXe siècle, son souvenir a pesé fortement sur ses luttes politiques. Les esquisses montagnardes se sont lentement précisées sous la Troisième République; et d'abord cette instruction publique accessible à tous, vainement réclamée par les sans-culottes comme l'une des conditions nécessaires de la démocratie sociale.

Mais dans le même temps la liberté économique et la concentration capitaliste accroissant les écarts sociaux et renforçant les antagonisme, "l'égalité des jouissances" s'éloignait de plus en plus, hors de portée. Cramponnés à leur condition, artisans et boutiquiers, descendants des sans-culottes de Quatre-vingt-treize, toujours attachés à la petite propriété fondée sur le travail personnel, oscillaient de l'utopie à la révolte. La même contradiction entre les exigences de l'égalité des droits proclamée en principe et les conséquences du droit de propriété et de la liberté économique, et la même impuissance pesèrent sur les tentatives de démocratie sociale: la tragédie de juin 1848 en témoigna, pour ne pas parler des péripéties de la Troisième République. "Temps des anticipations," a dit E. Labrousse de l'an II. Ne serait-il pas le temps des utopies? Au quatrième fragment des Institutions républicaines, Saint-Just écrit: "Il ne faut ni riches ni pauvres." Mais il note en même temps sur son agenda: "Ne pas admettre le partage des propriétés." La république égalitaire de l'an II demeure bien du domaine des anticipations, Icarie jamais atteinte, mais toujours poursuivie.

Babeuf cependant, dès le temps de la Révolution, avait dénoué la contradiction, ouvrant à l'avenir une troisième voie, conférant au principe de l'égalité des droits une extension d'une

ampleur et un ressort d'une force extraordinaires. 19 Comme les
sans-culottes, comme les Jacobins, Babeuf proclame que le but de
la société est "le bonheur commun": la Révolution doit assurer à
tous les citoyens "l'égalité des jouissances." Mais la propriété
privée introduisant nécessairement l'inégalité et "la loi agraire,"
c'est-à-dire le partage égal des propriétés, ne pouvant "durer
qu'un jour" ("dès le lendemain de son établissement, l'inégalité
se remontrerait"), le seul moyen d'arriver à "l'égalité de fait" et
d' "assurer à chacun et à sa postérité, telle nombreuse qu'elle
soit, la suffisance, mais rien que la suffisance," est "d'établir
l'administration commune, de supprimer la propriété particulière,
d'attacher chaque homme au talent, à l'industrie qu'il connaît, de
l'obliger à en déposer le fruit en nature au magasin commun, et
d'établir une simple administration de distribution, une administration des subsistances, qui tenant registre de tous les individus
et de toutes les choses, fera repartir ces dernières dans la plus
scrupuleuse égalité."

Ce programme exposé dans le Manifeste des plébéiens
publié par Le Tribun du peuple du 9 frimaire an IV (30 novembre
1795), constituait par rapport aux idéologies sans-culotte et jacobine caractérisées l'une et l'autre par l'attachement à la propriété
privée fondée sur le travail personnel, un renouvellement profond
ou plus exactement une brusque mutation: "la communauté des
biens et des travaux" prônée par Babeuf fut la première forme de
l'idéologie révolutionnaire de la nouvelle société issue de la Révolution elle-même. Autrement dit, Babeuf présentait l'abolition de
la propriété privée des moyens de production et l'instauration d'une
démocratie communiste, comme seules capables de réaliser plei-
nement l'égalité des droits. Par le Babouvisme le communisme,
jusque là rêverie utopique, était érigé en un système idéologique
finalement cohérent; par la Conjuration des Egaux, il entrait dans
l'histoire des luttes sociales et politiques.

[19]Le point des études babouvistes est fait dans Babeuf
(1760-1797), Buonarroti (1761-1837), Pour le deuxième centenaire
de leur naissance, publication de la Société des études robespierristes (Nancy, 1961); Claude Mazauric, Babeuf et la Conspiration
pour l'égalité (Paris, 1962); Babeuf et les problèmes du babouvisme, recueil collectif sous la direction d'A. Soboul (Paris, 1963);
V. M. Daline, Gracchus Babeuf avant et pendant la Révolution
française (1785-1794) (Moscou, 1963) en russe; compte-rendu par
A. Soboul, Revue d'histoire moderne et contemporaine, XIII
(1966), 166-171; V. Daline, Armando Saitta, Albert Soboul, Inven-
taire des manuscrits et imprimés de Babeuf (Paris, 1966).

L'importance de la Conjuration et du Babouvisme ne peut se mesurer qu'à l'échelle du XIXe siècle: dans l'histoire de la Révolution et du Directoire, ils ne constituent qu'un simple épisode qui modifia sans doute l'équilibre politique du moment, mais qui n'eut pas de résonance profonde. Dans sa lettre du 26 messidor an IV (14 juillet 1796), véritable testament politique, Babeuf recommandait à Felix Lepeletier de rassembler tous ses "projets, notes et ébauches d'écrits démocratiques et révolutionnaires, tous consequents au vaste but," entendons l'égalité parfaite, le bonheur commun. "Lorsqu'on en sera venu à songer de nouveau au moyen de procurer au genre humain le bonheur que nous lui proposions, tu pourras rechercher dans ces chiffons et présenter à tous les disciples de l'Egalité...ce que les corrompus d'aujourdhui appellent mes rêves."

Répondant à ce voeu, Buonarrotti publia à Bruxelles en 1828, l'histoire de la Conspiration pour l'égalité, dite de Babeuf. [20] Cet ouvrage exerça une profonde influence sur la génération de 1830; grâce à lui, le Babouvisme s'inscrivit comme un chaînon de la pensée communiste. Ainsi étaient nées de la Révolution française, des idées qui menaient, selon l'expression de Marx, "au delà des idées de l'ancien état de chose," celles d'un ordre social nouveau qui ne serait pas l'ordre bourgeois.

La Révolution française se situe dès lors au coeur même de l'histoire du monde contemporain, au carrefour des divers courants sociaux et politiques qui ont partagé les nations et les partagent encore. Révolution bourgeoise classique, elle constitue par l'abolition sans compromis de la féodalité et du régime seigneurial, le point de départ de la société capitaliste et du système liberal representatif dans l'histoire de la France. Révolution paysanne et populaire, elle tendit par deux fois à dépasser ses limites bourgeoises: en l'an II, tentative qui, malgré l'échec nécessaire, conserva longtemps valeur prophétique d'exemple, et lors de la Conspiration pour l'égalité, épisode qui se situe à l'origine féconde de la pensée et de l'action révolutionnaires contemporaines. Ainsi s'expliquent sans doute ces vains efforts pour dénier à la Révolution française, précédent dangereux, sa réalité historique ou sa spécificité, sociale et nationale. Mais ainsi s'expliquent aussi le tressaillement qu'a ressenti le monde et le retentissement de la Révolution française dans la conscience des hommes de notre siècle. Ce souvenir à lui seul est révolutionnaire: il nous exalte encore.

---

[20]Dernière édition, Paris, 1957, avec une préface de Georges Lefebvre.

THE MEANING OF THE FRENCH REVOLUTION:
A PANEL DISCUSSION

Beatrice Hyslop, Hunter College
Gérard Laurent, Musée National de Haïti
Robert Holtman, LSU in Baton Rouge
Albert Soboul, Sorbonne

Moderated by William Eccles, University of Toronto

Professor Eccles.   The only reason I can imagine for my being asked to serve as moderator today is that Canadians have had a great deal of experience at peace keeping.

I will ask our panelists to speak for five minutes each, then to direct questions or challenges to each other. We will begin with Miss Hyslop.

Professor Hyslop.   I would like to suggest my own definition of revolution with a capital "R" as a phenomenon in history.   I do not believe I would tend to use the word "total" which Professor Soboul used. I say it is a many-sided set of changes, not just a political one, not just an economic one, but many-sided, including changes in thought which may precede the other changes.   Secondly that these changes take place in a relatively short period of time which, therefore, distinguishes the term from the use for the industrial revolution and certain other such movements. Thirdly, where it is in a short time and you have opposition to the changes, there is almost inevitably more or less bloodshed.   That's my definition of a revolution and certainly it seems to me to apply to the French Revolution.

Now, I would like to highlight two things that I think are important in the meaning of that period for subsequent times. M. Soboul just gave a hint of the suggestion that it was the beginning of national unity or sentiment of national unity. The French themselves don't like the term "nationalism," and perhaps we Americans don't like it when it's a fight to bus by other people. But the sentiment of nationalism is a factor in modern history and I consider that the French Revolution is the beginning of the nineteenth- and twentieth-century type of nationalism.

When I was studying the cahiers, I felt that a good many of the elements that go to make up national sentiment were there, replacing provincialism, replacing sentiment for the class, etc. But it took the revolutionary wars and both the opposition as well as the support of revolutionary ideas to fuse those diverse elements into a national idea. Now out of the national idea defended by the revolutionaries themselves also arose the counternationalism of the émigrés and you hear about two Frances in French history in the nineteenth and twentieth centuries. But it is a change from any kind of sentiment directed primarily toward the king and the ruling classes of the Old Regime so that it seems to me the French Revolution, as it spread through the Napoleonic period to other areas, is a key to modern nationalism. When I say modern, I mean since 1789.

The second thing I would like to underline is Soboul's claim of the universality of rights. I do not believe we would have a universal Declaration of Human Rights by the U. N. in 1948 without the French Declaration of 1789. Certainly the idea spread from France that these were rights for all people, not just for Frenchmen. And by the twentieth century, in reaction to the denial of those rights by the Nazis, a universal declaration is written.

Our state constitutions with their bills of rights were inspired by the Enlightenment, and I differ from Taylor who does not think the cahiers show an influence from the Enlightenment. I cannot go into that in detail in five minutes, but I'll mention just two things. If you compare cahiers drawn up in 1614 or for earlier meetings of the Estates General with those of 1789, the differences for the most part I could track down as originating in ideas of the Enlightenment. And then secondly, there was an influence from the states' bills of rights. Franklin saw a translation of them, and those Frenchmen who had come over to America in the Revolution were aware of them. It is not our own constitutional Bill of Rights that plays a role, but rather the Enlightenment plus the American experience. And, therefore, I think there is a tie between the ideas, the great expectations, that the revolutionaries gather from the popularization of the Enlightenment as they followed the background of the Revolution itself.

I think that the volume of Lefebvre, Quatre-vingt-neuf, is fairly well appreciated in this country, and that is as it should be. I think it is probably the best written of his works, but the way it has appeared in translation, most American students do not perhaps realize that it was written for the hundred and fiftieth anniversary of the 1789 Declaration. In his chapter on the Declaration of Rights of Man, Lefebvre makes two statements that are, I think, to some extent a prophecy of the future as well as a repetition of the criticism by the English contemporaries of this document, perhaps in part because it is not quite the English Bill of Rights.

Now Lefebvre said of the Declaration that these generalizations were not nearly as vague in the minds of the drafters as we might be in reading them today. Freedom of the press, that certainly meant you were against royal censorship. Freedom of the individual, in the minds of the persons who drafted the Declaration, meant these rights extended to other people.

The other statement of Lefebvre I want to mention was that the Declaration of 1789 was as important for what it left out as for what it contained. The Declaration of '93 talks about freedom of work and guarantee of welfare. The universal Declaration of Human Rights during the twentieth century contains an extension of the concept of liberty and equality.

I do not have time to comment on Professor Soboul's statements about equality, maybe that will come with other speakers and their discussion. I merely want to put one question to Professor Soboul because I don't know whether it would come in appropriately later. Certainly the majority of the inhabitants of France in 1789 were peasants, but is it not true that the greater part of the Revolution was carried out by urban population, and what is the significance of that for the ideas of liberty and equality? Thank you.

Professeur Laurent. Pour moi, la Révolution française sur le plan local bouleversa la structure de la société. On a eu comme une prise de position contre le régime féodal, mais la bourgeoisie qui apparaît et qui se déclare contestataire a voulu quand même maintenir par devant elle certains avantages. Au début de ce mouvement, certainement, on ne peut encore parler d'une révolution nette, car l'on va constater que, en même temps que cette bourgeoisie dans sa Déclaration des Droits de l'Homme--c'est-à-dire lors de l'Assemblée Nationale Constituante--va réclamer le renversement des barrières sociales, la liberté de parole, de pensée, d'action, en même temps que cette bourgeoisie proclame que tous les hommes sont libres et égaux en droit, on verra cette bourgeoisie accepter des compromis tel le pacte colonial qui, somme toute, n'était que l'exploitation des colonies à l'avantage de la métropole.   On a vu encore l'Assemblée Nationale Constituante reconnaître, accepter, permettre le régime esclavagiste. Alors, qu'en France on déclarait que l'homme était libre et que l'on recherchait la dignité pour tout le monde et plus tard l'égalité, à St. Domingue le trafic négrier était toléré et, d'autre part, on prenait toutes les dispositions pour perpétuer le régime esclava- giste.

En somme, à envisager ces deux aspects de la question, au début la bourgeoisie française n'entendait pas faire une révolu- tion. Elle a voulu plutôt servir des intérêts, établir un change- ment de régime, en ce qui a trait aux abus, en ce qui a trait à la politique féodale et à la politique monarchique, c'est-à-dire prendre position contre la noblesse, contre les aristocrates, contre le clergé et parvenir ainsi à partager le pouvoir politique avec le gouvernement. Cela s'explique, car le pacte colonial en somme ne visait qu'à cela. Ce pacte colonial ne visait qu'à enrichir la bourgeoisie puisque avant tout c'était une association entre l'état et des particuliers qui étaient, eux, des membres de la bourgeoi- sie. Il faut attendre la Convention populaire pour voir la Révolu- tion s'entendre et prendre un autre aspect, l'aspect égalitaire. C'est à ce stade qu'il y eut révolution intégrale. On verra par ex- emple la Convention Montagnarde par son décret du 4 février 1794 déclarer libres les noirs des colonies et mettre définitivement fin au trafic négrier au nom de l'humanité. Merci.

__Professor Holtman.__ Professor Eccles said that maybe he was moderating because Canadians are experienced at peacekeeping. We do know, however, that they have threatened to walk out of this role, not a happy one. I am not sure just how happy our role is here this afternoon either, but at least we will see what we can do.

I agree completely with Miss Hyslop that nationalism as we know it is an offspring of the French Revolution. Fairly closely connected with this, I think, are a couple of other aspects we might consider. One is that individuals are now being treated as citizens rather than subjects. This, of course, has a good many ramifications. Also rather closely allied to this nationalism is a new concept of war. Even though we may think of war as being sort of abnormal, if we look at history we find it's only too normal. Certainly with the coming of the French Revolution--despite what some, like Civil War historians, would say--we have a new concept of war which is carried over right into the twentieth century.

I also agree with Miss Hyslop that we have to include the Napoleonic period along with the Revolution. We can't very well say that we can stop in 1799 and at the same time say that Napoleon was the consolidator of the French Revolution at home and extended many of the revolutionary gains abroad.

This morning Professor Soboul said he did not care very much whether we called it an Atlantic Revolution or referred to Democratic Revolution. I wouldn't go quite that far; I do care. I think the terms Atlantic Revolution or Democratic Revolution as Professor Palmer uses them are inaccurate in that historically we have to think of the French Revolution as being something unique. To be sure other revolutions did have certain similarities to it; but I think that Professor Caponigri would agree with me that whenever we speak of analogies, we are not being completely accurate, and they are not completely identical.

There is another thing we can say about the French Revolution, it was not monolithic. Not only was it multifaceted, as Miss Hyslop has mentioned, but it went through a good many different phases, and if we try to be too simplistic in our treatment, we may be led off on the wrong tack.

I think that the French Revolution was a revolution of rising expectations. In order to have a revolution, we need, of course, grievances which are actual. You also need a strength of feeling about these grievances in order that the people themselves may be willing to take some kind of action. One reason that they felt strongly was of course the writings of individuals. Another reason was the parasitism which they saw in too many people in their own neighborhood or in the country as a whole, and this might have some meaning for us. (I might also parenthetically add that Professor Soboul this morning said it would be very helpful if we defined the term revolution. Maybe we should define the meaning of the word "meaning" for this afternoon.)

Another thing about the French Revolution was that it did bring the people together, whether we speak in national or other terms. It did not atomize the French, but it did away with a lot of provincial boundaries, with internal tolls, with legal differences and that would include the Napoleonic period as well as the revolutionary decade itself.

And lastly, for now at least, I think we cannot overstress the meaning of the French Revolution to us in terms of individualism. People are now treated as individuals in a political sense where they have rights, in an economic sense where they have property, instead of being considered merely a part of a corporation or a social class or a State.

<u>Professeur Soboul</u>. Tout événement de l'importance de la Révolu-
tion française a une double signification, d'une part quant au pays
où se déroule l'événement en question, d'autre part une signification générale se rapportant à l'histoire universelle. Donc, un
double message.

Tout d'abord la signification générale: comment la Révolution française s'inscrit-elle dans l'histoire, (je ne dirais pas
celle du monde occidental, je ne suis pas d'accord avec la théorie
d'une "révolution occidentale"), mais dans l'histoire du monde
moderne? J'estime que toutes les nations et tous les pays ont
suivi, dans leur histoire, une ligne générale identique. L'histoire
a un sens. Mais c'est avec des modalités différentes que chaque
nation suit cette ligne générale. En ce sens, les XVIIIe et XIXe
siècles présentent une signification générale que nous comprenons
mieux à la lumière de la Révolution française.

La Révolution française constitue une étape dans la transition de l'ancienne société à survivances féodales à la société
moderne, celle dans laquelle nous vivons encore, société bourgeoise, société capitaliste du point de vue économique. Quelle est
plus précisément la signification de la Révolution française du
point de vue de l'histoire générale, de ce qu'on pourrait appeler
la "loi de transition du féodalisme au capitalisme"? (J'emploie le
mot "loi" en tant qu'historien, c'est-à-dire pour signifier une
"évolution tendantielle"; il ne s'agit evidemment pas de loi au sens
des sciences exactes.) En ce qui concerne le passage de la société
à survivances féodales à la société moderne définie théoriquement
par le capitalisme, l'histoire montre qu'il y a deux voies.

La voie française constitue la "voie révolutionnaire" par
excellence, celle qui détruit totalement les vestiges de l'époque
féodale. En 1789, ces vestiges étaient encore très vivants: si on
le nie, on ne comprend plus les révoltes paysannes. Les masses
ne se révoltent pas pour le plaisir de la violence et par goût du
sang: ce fut là l'explication de Taine, mais ce n'est pas une explication historique.

L'autre voie, du point de vue de l'histoire comparative
(j'estime nécessaire que les historiens aient recours à la méthode
comparative) est la "voie de compromis," ce que l'on a appelé la
"voie prussienne." Ce fut aussi la voie italienne, celle du <u>Risorgi-
mento</u>. Ce fut la voie de l'unification allemande, la voie du Meiji
japonais. C'est celle qui, dans le passage de l'ancienne société à
la nouvelle, intègre dans la nouvelle société des éléments de
l'ancienne. Ainsi la grande propriété foncière de Prusse orientale,
ou la grande propriété de l'Italie du sud dont les structures persis-
tantes posent encore tant de problèmes. Ainsi encore, le cas du
Japon: la question agraire n'y fut pas résolue par le Meiji, mais

seulement en 1945 par un acte de MacArthur. Cette évolution par la voie du compromis, avec ses conséquences lointaines, a pesé lourdement sur l'évolution de ces pays au vingtième siècle. La Prusse a emprunté la voie du compromis dans le passage de l'ancienne société à la nouvelle; vous en connaissez les conséquences: Hitler et le nazisme. Quant à l'Italie issue du Risorgimento, son évolution a abouti à Mussolini et au fascisme.

Il est un second aspect non moins important. Je rejoindrai là mon ami Cobb pour qui seule la spécificité compte en histoire. Je soulignerai donc la signification spécifique et l'originalité de la Révolution française, évidemment découlant des structures de la société d'Ancien Régime. Cette révolution fut la révolution du Tiers-Etat. L'aristocracie fut suffisamment puissante pour s'y opposer, elle refusa le compromis offert par l'Assemblée Constituante an cours de l'été 1789. La Révolution française fut, pour ainsi dire, poussée dans la voie qui fut spécifiquement la sienne: anti-féodale et anti-aristocratique.

Cette révolution du Tiers-Etat se définit mieux sur le plan négatif que sur un plan positif. Anti-féodale, elle a détruit complètement le système féodal, sans compromis, sans rachat des droits seigneuriaux comme en Italie. Elle a aboli le servage, elle a libéré le paysan, elle lui a donné la terre, alors que dans d'autre pays le servage a été aboli, mais le paysan n'a pas reçu la terre: ainsi en Italie du sud, en Pologne en 1807, plus tard en Russie. Là est la spécificité française: révolution anti-féodale et anti-aristocratique.

Si nous voulons maintenant définir plus précisément la Révolution française du point de vue social, dans ses aspects positifs et non pas négatifs, nous dirons qu'elle fut révolution bourgeoise: il n'y a aucun doute, ce sont des gens de la bourgeoisie qui ont dirigé la révolution. Sans doute nous ne devons pas entendre ici bourgeoisie au sens étroit de capitaliste. Il n'en reste pas moins que les hommes de 1789, les Girondins, les Montagnards, étaient des hommes qui, par bien des aspects, se définissaient comme bourgeois. On ne peut non plus nier les liaisons de ces hommes, même s'ils appartenaient aux professions libérales, avec la bourgeoisie d'affaires. Barnave était lié aux grands planteurs de Saint-Domingue, les Girondins à la grande bourgeoisie des ports. N'oublions pas que l'esclavage n'a pas été aboli aux colonies, que les droits politiques ont été refusés aux hommes de couleur libres. Il y avait à Paris, un lobby colonial, formé en particulier par les représentants des grands planteurs et par ceux des Chambres de commerce des ports: les intérêts capitalistes ont été bien défendus. Remarquons encore qu'il n'est pas besoin d'être capitaliste soi-même pour défendre les intérêts du capitalisme. A part du Directoire et plus encore du Consulat, ce sont

les notables, c'est-à-dire ceux qui se différencient du peuple par
la fortune et par la propriété, qui sont à la tête de la société,
même si ce n'est qu'à partir du milieu du XIXe siècle que la France
entre vraiment dans l'ère du développement industriel capitaliste.
En ce sens, la Révolution française fut bien bourgeoise et, à
échéance, capitaliste.

Il importe cependant d'apporter ici des nuances. Révolution du Tiers-Etat, révolution conduite par la bourgeoisie; mais
aussi, et pour répondre à la question de Miss Hyslop, révolution à
soutien populaire: c'est la force du peuple qui a détruit l'ancien
système, parce que le people ne pourait plus en supporter le
poids. Donc une révolution bourgeoise à soutien populaire. Mais
encore s'agit-il ici de préciser: je dirai volontiers que la Révolution française fut aussi une révolution paysanne. Nous avons peut-
être, depuis vingt ans et plus, porté trop d'attention aux masses
populaires urbaines, dites "sans-culottes," du 14 juillet et des
journées d'octobre 1789, au renversement du trône, le 10 août 1792,
et à l'élimination de la Gironde, le 31 mai 1793. La révolution
a-t-elle été faite par cette minorité urbaine seule? Non sans
doute. On ne saurait oublier les insurrections paysannes, la
Jacquerie toujours présente de 1789 à 1792, et qui n'a pas été suf-
fisament étudiée par les historiens français. En 1789, ce sont à
la fois les paysans et les gens des villes qui poussent la Révolution
en avant: nous ne pouvons pas oublier la Grande Peur. Mais en
1791 et jusqu'au printemps 1792, le peuple des villes n'intervient
pas ou peu. Ce sont alors les masses des campagnes, les paysans,
qui poussent la révolution en avant.

L'histoire générale des soulèvements paysans et de la
Jacquerie de 1789 à 1792, c'est-à-dire jusqu'au moment où le peuple
des villes prend le relai, cette histoire n'a jamais été faite en
France. Il existe des monographies, la plus célèbre est celle de
Georges Lefebvre sur les paysans du Nord; mais aucune synthèse,
aucun ouvrage général. Dernièrement, un historien soviétique, le
professeur Ado, après avoir travaillé plusieurs années dans les
archives de France, a publié une thèse sur ces problèmes. Je
peux donc maintenant répondre à Miss Hyslop: en 1789, la Révolution française a été faite à la fois par le peuple des campagnes et
par une minorité urbaine, mais de 1789 à 1792, ce qui pousse la
Révolution en avant, c'est la Jacquerie paysanne.

Ce qui me permettrait de définir cette révolution comme
bourgeoise et paysanne, et donc d'enrichir ainsi la signification de
la Révolution française.

Professor Eccles. I will ask you to limit your answer to three minutes, and I'll ask if any member of the panel has any challenge or question for the others. If not, I'll ask for questions from the floor.

Professor Hyslop. I'd like to add one challenge about the Rights of Man of 1789. Two years later in 1791, Olympe de Gouges proposed a Declaration of the Rights of Women. She did object to certain phrases of the Declaration of the Rights of 1789 and that may come to be known in this country maybe before it is known in France because of the Woman's Lib Movement and the history of women which seem to have aroused a great deal of interest of late. If the Declaration of Rights was not applied to blacks properly, it wasn't applied to Frenchwomen either.

Professeur Soboul. La Révolution Française fut anti-féministe. Les Jacobins, en particulier, se montrèrent très hostiles à la participation des femmes à la vie politique. Les sans-culottes, non.

Professor Eccles. Are there any questions from the floor? We have time for a few.

Professor Newman. This is directed primarily at Professor Soboul, but to anyone else, also. It is certainly incontrovertible from his work on the sans-culottes that the people wanted freedom, and democracy, and equality, yet it is also incontrovertible that the people, the former sans-culottes, were for Bonaparte. They cheered Bonaparte as the true representative of their desire. Yet he created a new aristocracy and crushed democracy. How can one explain that the French wanted democracy and equality, then threw it all away under Napoleon?

Professeur Soboul. A ceci je répondrai d'abord que ce n'est pas Napoléon, ou plutôt Bonaparte, qui a écrasé la liberté et l'égalité telles que l'entendaient les sans-culottes: ce sont les Thermidoriens, ce sont les Directoriaux. Le Directoire n'était plus le régime du peuple. Les Brumairiens ont porté Bonaparte au pouvoir, mais cet événement s'inscrit très logiquement dans la suite de Thermidor. Thermidoriens, Directoriaux, Brumairiens: ce sont les mêmes hommes. Lorsque Bonaparte s'empare du pouvoir par le coup d'Etat de brumaire, l'essentiel de la tâche était accompli: depuis 1795, le peuple n'était plus concerné par la politique, la liberté n'existait plus, l'égalité encore moins. La Constitution de l'an III (1795) a instauré un système censitaire. Bonaparte a eu l'astuce de rétablir, par la Constitution de l'an VIII (1799), le suffrage universel, en l'accomodant, il est vrai, au bénéfice des notables.

Mais cependant, Napoléon s'est maintenu fermement sur certains principes de la Révolution. Il a rétabli une noblesse, c'est vrai, mais ces nouveaux titres de noblesse n'entraînaient aucun privilège, l'égalité devant la loi et devant l'impôt fut maintenue. Napoléon n'a jamais rétabli le privilège aristocratique, n'est jamais revenu sur les deux conquêtes essentielles de 1789: l'égalité civile et la laïcité de l'Etat. Ce sont là les deux fondements de la société moderne en France, Napoléon n'y a pas touché. Les puissances d'Ancien Régime ne s'y sont pas trompées, qui ont combattu dans Napoléon jusqu'au bout, le soldat de la Révolution. Le régime napoléonien, à mon avis, se soude étroitement à la Révolution celle de 1789 naturellement, et non celle de 1793.

Pour en revenir en peuple, que pouvait lui importer une liberté dont il y n'avait pas les moyens de jouir. Depuis 1795, il était rejeté du système politique. Ajoutons que les masses populaires ont connu une réelle prosperité sous l'Empire. Je ne suis pas d'accord avec les historiens économistes qui le nient, ajoutant que le Révolution française a rompu la croissance économique. Encore s'agirait-il de savoir à qui profite la croissance...Or, la Révolution en supprimant le prélèvement féodal, en abolissant les droits seigneuriaux et la dîme, en permettant à des paysans déjà propriétaires d'acquérir plus de terre, a permis une réelle prospérité paysanne. Il n'est que de lire les rapports des préfets pour le constater. Dans les villes, à partir de la fin du Directoire, en 1798, il y a une reprise économique. Les salaires ont monté jusqu'à la grande crise de 1811-1812, si bien que les ouvriers des villes ont été reconnaissants à Napoléon, même si la tendance s'est renversée après 1812.

Napoléon a été surnommé "l'empereur des faubourgs": s'il l'a été, c'est justement parce que, du point de vue **populaire**, il n'est jamais revenu sur les conquêtes essentielles de la Révolution, et qu'il a, dans une certaine mesure, apporté la prospérité aux masses populaires.

Professor Eccles.   Thank you, ladies and gentlemen.

DES RAPPORTS ENTRE LA REVOLUTION
FRANÇAISE ET CELLE DE SAINT-DOMINGUE

Gérard M. Laurent

En même temps qu'une révolution éclatait en France, démantelant l'arsenal monarchique, abolissant les privilèges féodaux, ouvrant les artères politiques et administratives aux ambitions d'une bourgeoisie contestataire, allégeant le fardeau d'un peuple fatigué de ses entraves, à Saint-Domingue, à 1800 lieues de la France, trois mouvements à tendance subversive faisaient sauter des cadres vermoulus, libérant en définitive un peuple de noirs qui s'asphyxiait.

On attribue généralement à la Révolution française les bouleversements qui agitèrent la prospère colonie de Saint-Domingue. Des écrivains hasardèrent même l'opinion que la révolution dans cette colonie était fille de la révolution métropolitaine. C'était soutenir à l'encontre des principes de la théorie de l'histoire moderne la possibilité d'exporter une révolution. Or, celle-ci naît de causes locales; souvent elle se présente comme le résultat des contradictions du milieu. Etrangère à toute spontanéité, une révolution évolue graduellement vers l'éclatement final. L'analyse des sociétés conduit à la déduction qu'une révolution est la conséquence logique de conflagrations sociales, de mauvaise distribution des richesses, d'une situation volcanique créée par un esprit d'exploitation et d'iniquité. Je suis enclin à penser que la Révolution française laisserait indemne l'ossature économique et sociale de Saint-Domingue, si des facteurs primordiaux ne bouleversaient à la même époque la société coloniale menacée de dislocation.

Avant de nous interroger sur une possible influence de la Révolution française sur celle de Saint-Domingue, ou d'expliquer la nature des rapports entre elles, il nous semble urgent de montrer l'état d'esprit des différentes catégories sociales: les noirs, les affranchis, les blancs, tous ces artisans des troubles de la colonie.

***

L'installation sur cette terre d'apport qu'était Saint-Domingue de travailleurs tirés de l'Afrique et condamnés à se plier à la cupidité coloniale et métropolitaine annonçait une révolution. Cette transplantation répondait à une exigence de la monoculture. La canne à sucre réclamait une main-d'oeuvre abondante et de grandes habitations d'au moins 300 carreaux de terre. Les travailleurs européens n'étaient plus intéressés à venir dans les Antilles. Ils s'étaient offerts comme travailleurs, mais on les avait engagés comme esclaves. Quoique blancs, ils connurent la flétrissure de la fleur de lys, la fustigation, la mutilation. Les planteurs de Saint-Domingue devaient tourner ailleurs leurs regards. L'Afrique, grâce aux guerres tribales, était une pourvoyeuse idéale. Les prisonniers de guerre étaient vendus. L'Edit de 1685 ou Code Noir, dans son article 44, légalisait l'exploitation des noirs, considérés comme des "choses" et déclarés tels. Les colons alors se virent à la tête d'un matériel humain de production sur lequel ils avaient des droits illimités. Pressés de s'enrichir, ils recoururent au régime du fouet pour tirer de l'esclave le maximum de rendement. Et, comme la bourgeoisie métropolitaine s'associait aux colons, ces esclaves déracinés devinrent l'objet d'une double exploitation. Le travail exigé d'eux sera intensif et incessant, aussi épuisant qu'abrutissant. Mais il fallait perpétuer le régime. Aux châtiments corporels, au travail forcé, on adjoignit la contrainte morale qui impliquait la dépersonnalisation des noirs, leur isolement dans un milieu décadent, leur ignorance par le retrait de tout moyen d'alphabétisation. Ce système esclavagiste se suffisait à provoquer l'étincelle de haine et de colère propre à détruire la colonie. Le mécontentement des esclaves, sous-hommes plongés dans une abjecte condition de vie, et leurs rancoeurs accumulées devaient, à l'occasion d'une prise de conscience, les conduire à la démolition du régime et la conquête de leurs droits humains.

Ces esclaves n'étaient pas les seuls mécontents.

En dépit de leur morgue et de leurs préjugés, les planteurs de Saint-Domingue ne purent rester insensibles aux charmes physiques des négresses, leurs esclaves. Et de leurs rapports intimes naquirent des citoyens se rapprochant des blancs par leur nuance epidermique. Jouissant de leur prérogative de fils de colons, ces bâtards furent émancipés à leur naissance. Certains affranchis, habiles à jouir de la succession d'un père complaisant, se trouvèrent à leur majorité à la tête d'une belle fortune. D'autres, également favorisés par leur ascendance blanche, eurent le privilège de partir pour la France afin de poursuivre leurs études et parachever leur éducation. De retour a Saint-Domingue, après le cycle de leurs études, et poussés par un esprit de solidarité, ils fondèrent des écoles que fréquentèrent leurs frères de même condition, mais moins fortunés. Généralement, ils étaient de rudes travailleurs. Ils avaient essaimé dans les montagnes isolées du Sud. Ils avaient transformé ces régions, bonifié les terres qu'ils cultivèrent avec courage. Bref, à la veille de la Révolution Française, ces affranchis étaient au nombre de 28.000; ils possédaient le tiers des terres de la colonie et le quart des 500.000 esclaves. Leurs richesses, leur formation culturelle, leur poussée démographique suscitèrent chez les petits blancs une féroce jalousie et chez les colons et négociants une profonde inquiétude. On redoutait cette évolution tentaculaire qui menaçait de domination l'empire des blancs. Alors pour se satisfaire et se tranquilliser, par prudence comme par vengeance, les blancs dressèrent des barrières à l'évolution des sang-mêlés. Une situation sociale humiliante leur fut imposée. Une dégradante avanie leur fut réservée dans leurs activités sociales et professionnelles, dans l'administration, dans l'armée, dans la politique. Déclarés citoyens passifs, ils furent contraints d'essuyer la bave impertinente des petits blancs et la jactance vexatoire des colons. Mécontents, ils rêvaient de se soulever contre cet état de choses qui les ravalait; ils réclamaient, au nom de la justice, leurs droits civils et politiques; ils étaient prêts à lutter pour une égalité avec les blancs.

Constituaient la lie de la classe blanche des gens de métier, des artisans tumultueux, bouillants, pleins de rancoeurs. Victimes de la révolution de la canne, ils se voyaient refoulés par une société fortement hiérarchisée. Ils étaient opprimés sur le plan économique et méprisés des colons et grands planteurs. Ces hommes ruminaient leur vengeance, tout en convoitant la situation économique des colons.

Ces derniers, à leur tour, écumaient de rage contre la métropole qui les assujettissait aux rigueurs excessives du Pacte Colonial. Ce pacte fut la formule inventée par Colbert pour tirer la France du marasme économique provoqué tant par les fautes de Mazarin comme homme d'Etat que par la politique de gloire de Louis XIV. A la vérité ce système dit Colbertisme aida puissamment la France à améliorer sa situation économique, à réduire son taux de chômage (grâce à l'établissement de nouvelles industries et au développement des villes côtières) à accumuler des capitaux, tout en enrichissant la bourgeoisie. Mais, par contre, ce pacte était conçu dans un esprit de subordination des intérêts coloniaux à ceux de la métropole. C'était le mercantilisme. Les habitants des îles, de Saint-Domingue en particulier, étaient astreints à des obligations qui n'étaient que des formes déguisées de servitude. Y furent proscrites toutes relations commerciales avec une nation autre que la France. Seule la bourgeoisie commerçante ou négrière approvisionnait Saint-Domingue en marchandises ou en bois d'ébène. Et la métropole fixait elle-même le prix des denrées tropicales. Toute forme d'industrie y était prohibée. La censure était exercée même sur la diversité des cultures tropicales. Certains produits étaient autorisés, d'autres pas, selon les intérêts métropolitains. L'étranglement, systématique, s'étendait sur le plan politique. Ainsi les colons se voyaient condamnés à ne vivre que pour assurer l'aisance de la bourgeoisie et de la noblesse de France. Eux aussi aspiraient à un mouvement qui adoucirait le régime de l'exclusif.

Ainsi tous ceux qui composaient la société de Saint-Domingue: noirs, citoyens de couleur, petits blancs, colons, étaient des mécontents, des aigris qui, tapis dans l'ombre, guettaient une occasion propice pour renverser à leur avantage l'ordre colonial. Sans doute les planteurs, sans entendre changer les conditions des autres catégories sociales, aspiraient à abolir le régime du pacte colonial, à administrer la colonie, à légiférer au nom de la Métropole. Les petits blancs travaillaient au chambardement de la colonie; ils rêvaient de ruiner les colons et nourrissaient l'espoir de les remplacer à la tête de la colonie. Les affranchis revendiquaient en faveur d'une réforme sociale: mais, comme les blancs, ils étaient partisans du régime esclavagiste. Aucun de ces mouvements, organisés sans la participation de la classe majoritaire, ne répondait à la définition d'une révolution qui implique avant tout un changement dans la structure d'une société et sous-entend la recherche du bien-être pour les masses refoulées et dégradées, exploitées et ravalées. Ces observations autorisent à noter que seul le mouvement des ateliers avait un caractère vraiment révolutionnaire. Il était appelé à balayer tout un système, à changer des mentalités viciées, à faire éclater des digues qui fossilisaient toute une catégorie d'hommes, enfin à élever des esclaves au niveau de la dignité humaine.

Au rappel des contradictions qui gangrenaient le corps social, on s'explique les mobiles qui ont poussé des observateurs sagaces à comparer Saint-Domingue à un baril de poudre exposé à la moindre etincelle. Mais cette explosion pourrait se faire

attendre, se ferait même attendre sans les flammèches sorties
du brasier qui consumait le régime féodal en France. A ce point
de vue, il est difficile de ne pas reconnaître d'étroits rapports
entre les événements à Saint-Domingue et le mouvement qui déchi-
rait la société française.

Incontestablement la Révolution française a créé à Saint-
Domingue un climat d'effervescence. Elle y a inauguré l'ère de la
violence et des revendications. La Convocation des Etats-Généraux a favorisé le mouvement réactionnaire des colons. Ceux-ci,
encouragés par ce premier coup de bélier porté au régime monarchique, ont osé s'attaquer à la puissance gouvernementale en
affrontant le gouverneur. En dépit de l'interdiction de ce dernier,
ils ont organisé des élections clandestines et, au su des autorités,
envoyé en France une délégation chargée de présenter leurs
doléances. De son côté la Déclaration des Droits de l'Homme,
charte de la libération sociale, par son cri de justice, par ses
principes de liberté et d'égalité au niveau des hommes, a ranimé
les espoirs des citoyens de couleur dans leurs luttes éperdues pour
leur réhabilitation sociale. Leur action fut d'ailleurs stimulée par
la campagne humaniste des membres de la Société des Amis des
Noirs, avocats de leur cause. Face à leur action s'alignaient les
membres du club Massiac, amis et protecteurs des colons, partisans de leur politique de discrimination. Donc dès le début, la
Révolution française, par la Convocation des Etats-Généraux, par
la Déclaration des Droits de l'Homme, et par l'action des clubs
antagonistes, a poussé à un affrontement les colons et les membres de l'appareil d'Etat, les affranchis et les blancs. Ces
derniers, tout comme les administrateurs royaux, tentèrent vainement d'endiguer le torrent par leur irascible réaction. Mais le
comportement social de ces groupes contestataires, plaidoyer en
faveur de la violence, tout comme les rumeurs qui circulaient
parmi les libres à l'entendement des nègres domestiques et des
nègres de métier, provoquèrent chez les esclaves les plus éveillés
une prise de conscience. Ils avaient enfin compris que la liberté
ne se donne pas à 500.000 esclaves; elle s'acquiert; on l'arrache
aux forces obscurantistes. Et un tel enjeu mérite bien qu'on expose sa vie. Lorsqu'on est fatigué des siècles de servitude, d'op-
probre, de misères, on doit y mettre fin par une révolte sanglante.
Tel fut l'enseignement de la Révolution française à travers le
rayonnement du mouvement des colons et de celui des affranchis.

***

La Révolution française n'a pas seulement créé pour les
differentes categories sociales l'occasion si fiévreusement attendue

de se manifester.   Elle a fait mieux.   Elle a précipité les événements par sa politique coloniale.   Cet autre aspect souligne avec éclat l'influence qu'elle a exercé sur les groupements sociaux de Saint-Domingue.

L'étude de cette politique nous conduit à l'analyse des décrets du 8 mars 1790, du 15 mai 1791, du 24 septembre 1791, du 4 avril 1792 et du 4 février 1794 et à l'examen des actes posés par les agents de la Métropole soit dans le plein exercice de leur mission soit sous la dictée des circonstances.

L'Assemblée Nationale Constituante a sérieusement perturbé le climat de Saint-Domingue par ses indécisions, ses contradictions, ses tâtonnements.   D'essence bourgeoise, cette assemblée qui a rayonné dans la Déclaration des Droits de l'Homme, orientait sa politique coloniale, par intérêt, vers la perpétuation du régime esclavagiste.   Ce résultat exigeait une coalition des propriétaires.   Colons   et affranchis,   intéressés à ce régime d'exploitation, devaient s'entendre.   L'assemblée manifesta une vélléité de regroupement en offrant aux affranchis par son décret du 8 mars 1790, les droits civils et politiques.   Cette politique métropolitaine se heurta à l'intransigeance des colons bourrés de préjugés et fracassa dans un choc sanglant entre colons et affranchis. (Affaire d'Ogé) Craignant une révolte des ateliers, menace contre le régime esclavagiste, l'Assemblée vota le décret du 15 mai 1791, qui déclarait citoyens actifs les affranchis propriétaires, nés de père et mère libres.   Cette loi également fut la cause d'un affrontement armé entre colons et affranchis.   (Affaire des Confédérés de l'Ouest).   Appréhendant ce climat de violence susceptible de mettre en cause le sort des esclaves, la Constituante fit une volte-face par sa loi du 24 septembre 1791.   Les blancs furent déclarés les arbitres du sort des citoyens de couleur.   Ces derniers, quoique pleins de haine contre les colons et les petits blancs, se plièrent à la décision métropolitaine.   Ils croyaient à l'instar de leur chef, Julien Raimond, gagner par cette soumission les bonnes grâces de la Métropole.

En France la révolution poursuivait sa marche ascensionnelle.   L'Assemblée Nationale fut remplacée par la Législative (1791-1792).   Au sein de cette dernière se trouvaient les Brissot, les Pétion, les Condorcet, les Abbé Grégoire, les Mirabeau etc. Son action se signala en faveur des affranchis.   Elle reposa sur eux sa politique coloniale et sortit son décret du 4 avril 1792 qui les réhabilitait.   Il fallait constituer un bloc puissant contre les esclaves, partant réconcilier colons et affranchis afin de sauvegarder le régime.

Mais cette loi du 4 avril 92 créa à Saint-Domingue un climat d'effervescence.   Les colons, les blancs en général, ne

reculèrent pas devant la rigueur des moyens pour paralyser les
Commissaires Civils chargés de la faire appliquer. Ils prirent
l'initiative de quatre grands mouvements qui éclatèrent sous le
gouvernement de la Convention Girondine (1792-1793). Or cette
assemblée symbolise la bourgeoisie moyenne libérale; en France,
elle combat l'aristocratie féodale qui organise la contre-révolu-
tions. Dans les colonies, elle s'attaque également aux colons
royalistes, déjà engagés dans des tractations avec le cabinet de
Londres. La Convention Girondine veut sauvegarder ses intérêts
matériels, les principes du Pacte Colonial en particulier. L'in-
quiète la politique séparatiste des colons de Saint-Domingue. Elle
veut maintenir et la traite négrière et l'esclavage. "C'était la
sueur et le sang des esclaves de Saint-Domingue qui payaient le
luxe des négociants bordelais." Avec la Convention Girondine, la
bourgeoisie des ports défendait ses droits. Et dans la lutte qui
opposa à Saint-Domingue ses représentants, en l'occurence les
Commissaires Civils Sonthonax, Polverel, Ailhaud, aux colons,
deux forces esclavagistes, les vrais bénéficiaires seront les esclaves. Car après chaque manoeuvre des colons, les commissaires réagissaient avec une violence accrue. Ils confiaient leur
défense aux affranchis ou citoyens du 4 avril. Mais ceux-ci faiblis-
saient, parvenant difficilement à tenir en respect les blancs coa-
lisés. Alors en désespoir de cause et pour sauver la colonie,
Sonthonax fit appel aux noirs, qui surent faire apprécier leur
valeur comme force de frappe. La guerre entre la France et le
bloc monarchique davantage souligna aux yeux des dirigeants de
Saint-Domingue l'importance des noirs.

En vue de mieux résister à l'agression anglo-espagnole
et désireux de réorganiser le travail sur les habitations, Sonthonax
dut, nonobstant sa mission, libérer tous les noirs qui furent incor-
porés dans les armées républicaines. Il n'y avait pas d'autre
formule, car les esclaves s'échappaient en masse des habitations,
se faisaient marrons et allaient s'engager, comme soldats libres,
dans les armées espagnoles. C'est cette mesure de Sonthonax que
ratifia la Convention montagnarde le 4 février 1794.

Tout s'enchaînait tant en France qu'à Saint-Domingue.

Alors que la Métropole, à la défense de ses intérêts, re-
courait tour à tour aux blancs de Saint-Domingue (24 septembre
1791), aux affranchis (4 avril 1792) et enfin aux noirs (4 février
1794), on vit d'autre part les esclaves preter leurs services aux
affranchis contre les blancs (affaire des suisses), aux royalistes
contre les colons (août 1791), aux colons contre les Commissaires
Civils (affaire Borel), aux Commissaires Civils contre les colons
(affaire Galbaud), et, lorsqu'ils devinrent une force de frappe
appréciée, à la République contre les anglo-espagnols (revire-
ment de T. Louverture). En France, la révolution a évolué vers

une dictature populaire fondée sur la terreur; elle était partie des griefs d'une bourgeoisie à sentiments pro-monarchiques. Elle influença de la même façon, selon la même courbe, la colonie de Saint-Domingue. Celle-ci fut bouleversée par des colons propriétaires, qui cédèrent leur place à des affranchis esclavagistes, avant d'être saccagée par des esclaves insurgés. Conduits par un chef extraordinaire, qui exploitait les contradictions au niveau local et international, ces anciens esclaves marchèrent, de conquêtes en conquêtes, vers une consécration de leur liberté garantie par une Constitution en 1801.

Mais le Directoire Exécutif (1795-1799) freina la révolution en France. Une république bourgeoise s'y installa. Sa politique coloniale sera également rétrograde. On prôna la nécessité de l'ancien régime qui prévalait à Saint-Domingue avant 89. Et contre ce retour à l'esclavage campa Toussaint Louverture. Afin d'avoir la haute main, ce chef se débarrassa des agents métropolitains dont la politique le gênait. Sonthonax, qui y était revenu nanti d'une seconde mission, fut rembarqué en 1797. Le général Hédouville, un an plus tard, l'agent Roume, en 1801, connurent le même sort.

Puis, ce fut en France le coup d'état du 18 brumaire qui acheva de démolir les conquêtes révolutionnaires. A la révolution des noirs également le Premier Consul entendit mettre fin. Il décida de se débarrasser de tous les indigènes qui, embrigadés sous le commandement de Toussaint Louverture, entendaient lutter pour une liberté fondée sur l'indépendance. En vue de les anéantir tous et pour proclamer le retour du régime esclavagiste, une armada commandée par le propre beau-frère de Bonaparte fit voile vers Saint-Domingue. Alors grâce à une prise de conscience nette due à l'endoctrinement de leur chef, grâce encore à leur fanatisme, à leur conviction, à leur courage, les nègres de Saint-Domingue eurent raison de tous obstacles. Sur les vestiges de cette puissante et prestigieuse armée européenne, la Nation Haïtienne fut édifiée. La révolution des masses, débutée le 22 août 1791, avait triomphé le 1er janvier 1804.

En conclusion nous pouvons soutenir qu'indépendamment des contradictions du milieu qui annonçait des troubles graves à Saint-Domingue, la Révolution française, par ses principes et sa politique coloniale, y a influencé les événements. De l'assemblée Nationale Constituante à la Convention Montagnarde, du Directoire Exécutif au Consulat, elle a perturbé le climat de Saint-Domingue tant par ses décrets que par l'action de ses agents ou Commissaires Civils. Et cette influence a été telle que les nègres, brisant leurs chaines, ont occupé le théâtre des événements de 1793 à 1804. Certes ces résultats ont dépassé les voeux des révolutionnaires de

France. Ceux-ci, en libérant les esclaves, pensaient avoir bouclé la révolution dans cette colonie, si précieuse. Par ce geste libérateur, ils pensaient avoir définitivement rivé Saint-Domingue à la Métropole. Ils ont même tenté d'assimiler les noirs en les coupant de leurs racines. Ils y parviendraient, n'étaient les circonstances. La contre-révolution en s'installant au pouvoir en France a engendré la méfiance à Saint-Domingue. Des propos pleins de menaces contre les noirs ont tiré ces derniers de leur torpeur. La peur d'un retour du régime esclavagiste les a exaltés. Ils voulaient tous mourir ou vivre dans la dignité.

Reconnaissants, les anciens esclaves n'ont jamais renié la France de la Déclaration des Droits de l'Homme, qui leur dessilla les yeux; ni la France de la Convention Montagnarde qui officiellement fit d'eux des hommes libres. Ils sont restés attachés à un Laveaux, à un Sonthonax qui leur révélèrent la valeur de l'éducation et de l'instruction comme facteurs de civilisation. Grâce à ces heureuses influences, ils prirent conscience de leurs droits; leur personnalité s'affirma. Certains pensaient même à une indépendance qui n'entrainerait pas pour autant une rupture avec la France. Mais la politique des réactionnaires tapis dans le Directoire et surtout le Consulat coupa les ponts avec des nègres irréductibles. Fiers de leur dignité, ces anciens esclaves, prosélytes de la Déclaration des Droits de l'Homme, ne pouvaient abdiquer cette belle conquête sociale. Et c'est sous sa bannière qu'ils marchèrent contre les armées de Leclerc, ultime espérance des anciens colons.

REVOLUTIONS IN TASTE AND SENSIBILITY

Albert J. Griffith

"The great variety of Taste...which prevails in the world," the philosopher David Hume wrote in 1757, "is too obvious not to have fallen under every one's observation."[1] And what was true about taste two hundred years ago was also true two hundred and even two thousand years before that, and is still true today. There once would have been every reason to suppose that this truth about the variety of tastes was an eternal one which would hold its validity throughout all the eons yet to come, as it has held its validity throughout all the past. Now, however, for perhaps the first time in human history, at least some influential thinkers have raised the question as to whether a homogenization of taste may not be on the horizon: they forecast a point in the not too distant future when--under the combined influences of the political power of the corporate state and the technological efficiency of the mass media--that variety in taste which so fascinated Hume may disappear and be replaced by a monolithic cultural standard imposed on all from without.

This vision of a future in which human differences, including these long-standing and inexplicable differences in taste, will be erased in favor of a production-line uniformity of opinion is not altogether a new one. Utopian philosophers have often presented

[1]"Of the Standard of Taste," in Of the Standard of Taste and Other Essays, ed. John W. Lenz (New York, 1965), p. 3.

95

glimmerings of it, but it was Aldous Huxley who in 1931 gave us the full-dress scenario in his Brave New World. In the society presented in Brave New World, such science fiction marvels as bokanovskification, hypnopaedia, and soma vaporization were used by the totalitarian state to eliminate all individuality since individuality was seen as a threat to social stability. Questions of truth and beauty were replaced by questions of comfort and happiness. There was indeed in this imagined society no disputing of taste--for neither disputation nor taste was allowed. Those who resisted the cultural conditioning process, or who, like the "savages" on the New Mexico reservation, clung to the individual freedom of choice of the pre-Fordian past, were isolated and ostracized from the brainwashed populace of the programmed society.

Huxley, of course, projected his dystopian nightmare some six hundred years into the future. "In 1931, when Brave New World was being written," he has said, "I was convinced that there was still plenty of time." But only twenty-seven years later, Huxley noted with alarm in Brave New World Revisited that the prophecies of 1931 were coming true "much sooner" than he had thought they would; by that time, 1958, he could sense the horror of "total organization" as "just around the next corner."[2] Increasingly today, there is a swelling chorus of voices to tell us that we are ready to round that corner at any moment.

It is this possibility, whether proximate or remote, that the historical diversification of taste and sensibility, which we have always known, may not be forever with us, that makes an exploration of the question of how tastes and sensibilities change far from irrelevant in a symposium devoted to "The Revolutionary Experience." How are tastes and sensibilities formed? How do they change? Why do they change? Do they evolve gradually or do they burst forth in revolutionary turmoil? What is the impact of revolutionary change in other areas on the esthetic preferences of an individual or a society?

I do not find that these questions have been given very systematic or satisfactory answers up to now, and I certainly do not have the competence to try to provide final answers here. I do think, however, that there are certain reflections we can make about the nature of taste and sensibility, about historical patterns of change affecting these, and about some of the present dilemmas in contemporary esthetics, all of which will, perhaps, have some value as we contemplate the future possibilities. If I tend to talk

---

[2]Brave New World Revisited (New York, 1960), pp. 1-2.

about the subject primarily in reference to American culture, and if I tend to give my examples principally from literature, this should not be taken as a disparagement either of other cultures or of other art forms, but merely as limitations imposed by my own narrow area of expertise and by my own timidity in stepping very far afield from the home ground of my own specialization when exploring so complex a subject.

For purposes of our discussion here, let us assume that taste and sensibility are two aspects of the same phenomenon, since both terms are commonly used to refer to the individual perception of and preference for or against the various objects and events in external reality. As applied to art, taste is perhaps more often used to describe the awareness and feeling of the artistic audience, and sensibility to describe the awareness and feeling of the artist himself. Obviously, however, one feeds upon the other. The artist very largely sees and re-creates that which others before him have thought worthy of notice and expression; art imitates other art at least as much as it directly imitates life. The individual's artistic sensibility is often circumscribed by the tastes of those around him. There is a moving piteousness in the lament of the frustrated artist who, like Melville, resents the limitations of his audience: "What I feel most moved to write, that is banned,--it will not pay. Yet, altogether write the other way I cannot. So the product is a final hash, and all my books are botches."[3]

But just as the tastes of the society influence the artist in what he is capable of doing and in what he is permitted to do, so the artist can have a counterinfluence on the tastes of that same society. If we may extend what Wordsworth says about poets to artists in general, we can say that the artist is "a man speaking to other men: a man, it is true, endowed with more lively sensibility, more enthusiasm and tenderness, who has a greater knowledge of human nature, and a more comprehensive soul, than are supposed to be common among mankind," but still only a man, "nothing differing in kind from other men, but only in degree."[4] And it is

---

[3]Herman Melville, Letter to Nathaniel Hawthorne, June 1 (?), 1851, in The Portable Melville, ed. Jay Leyda (New York, 1952), p. 430.

[4]William Wordsworth, "Preface to Lyrical Ballads," in The Norton Anthology of English Literature, ed. M. H. Abrams et al, Major Authors Edition, rev. (New York, 1968), pp. 1275-1277.

this man of more acute feelings and perceptions who must himself, Wordsworth elsewhere reminds us, create the taste of the audience who will appreciate him.

Susan Sontag, in one of her provocative essays on modern culture, has argued that "Art today is a new kind of instrument, an instrument for modifying consciousness and organizing new modes of sensibility."[5] I would not dispute this claim; I would rather extend this definition to include not just contemporary art, which certainly does modify our consciousness in dramatic ways, but art of the past as well, which has also performed to greater or lesser degree this same function. Art is, in the words of Sir Herbert Read, "eternally disturbing, permanently revolutionary." "It is so," Read says, "because the artist, to the degree of his greatness, always confronts the unknown, and what he brings back from that confrontation is a novelty, a new symbol, a new vision of life, the outer image of inward things. His importance to society is not that he voices received opinions, or gives clear expression to the confused feelings of the masses"; he is rather "an upsetter of the established order." Because of this, Read says, "the greatest enemy of art is the collective mind" against which the artist must struggle to "seek a higher level of individual sensibility and perception."[6] Only so-called "popular art," which is defined by Abraham Kaplan as that art which is "never a discovery, only a reaffirmation" of what is already standardized into a stereotype,[7] lacks this capacity for modifying consciousness.

The revolutionary potential of the artist has been recognized at least as long ago as Plato's time, when Plato's Socrates argued for the exclusion of the poet from the ideal republic on the grounds that poetry "feeds and waters the passions instead of drying them up" and letting them be controlled by the reason.[8] If art seemed

---

[5]"One Culture and the New Sensibility," in Against Interpretation and Other Essays (New York, 1967), p. 296.

[6]"Art and Society," in The Arts and Man (1969), rpt. in The Pop Culture Tradition, ed. Edward M. White (New York, 1972), pp. 135-36.

[7]"The Aesthetics of the Popular Arts," in Modern Culture and the Arts, ed. James B. Hall and Barry Ulanov (New York, 1967), pp. 66-67.

[8]The Republic, trans. Benjamin Jowett, in The Dialogues of Plato, 3rd ed. (London, 1892), Book X, pp. 595a-608b.

dangerous enough to warrant suppression even at the dawn of western civilization, how much more dangerous might it seem today when the pace of change is so accelerated that new conscious- nesses can spring Venus-like from fertile brains almost overnight? If we accept Charles A. Reich's analysis in The Greening of America of the development of the three major consciousnesses which have dominated our culture, we can readily see the increas- ing rapidity with which alterations of sensibilities take place. Consciousness I, the world-view based on the Puritan work ethic and the American dream, Reich says, began with the new American nation and developed over a period of two centuries. Conscious- ness II, which celebrates the institutions and organization of the Corporate State, began to replace Consciousness I only after World War II. But already Consciousness II is beginning to be replaced by Consciousness III, the youth movement's attempt to gain a "recov- ery of self" from the technocratic society.[9] The trend is obvious: each succeeding consciousness has a shorter lifespan than the previous one. Despite Reich's own hopes for a permanence to Consciousness III, we would be justified in suspecting that Consciousness IV may not be too far ahead of us.

As change accelerates in everything else around us, then, we can also suspect that there will be an acceleration of change in the interactions of taste and sensibility. Mass tastes--shifting back and forth as fashions emerge, prosper, and die--will more and more tend to limit the expressive possibilities open to the artist ("What I feel most moved to write, that is banned,--it will not pay!"). But artistic sensibilities, ever probing the unknown but having the unknown made familiar overnight through the mass media, will redirect the fickle tastes of the same public to each year's newest discoveries. Obsolescence in art forms will become as predictable as obsolescence in automobiles or women's clothing.

Changes in taste and sensibility, we can see from this, are at least partially inner-determined: that is, the artist's sensibili- ties tend to transform his culture at the same time that the tastes of his culture shape his sensibilities and hence his art. But to what extent are nonartistic actions and responses also determina- tive of alterations and adjustments in taste and sensibility? How do ideas and events outside the spectrum of esthetics affect what happens within that spectrum? In short, what historical factors influence our perceptions and preferences in the arts?

---

[9]The Greening of America (New York, 1970).

Obviously, esthetic response is not a constant forever fixed by the inherent value of the art object. "The various feelings of enjoyment or of displeasure," Kant observed, "rest not so much upon the nature of the external things that arouse them as upon each person's own disposition to be moved by these to pleasure or pain."[10] "The sentiments of men," Hume noted in a similar vein, "often differ with regard to beauty and deformity of all kinds, even while their general discourse is the same."[11] And both Kant and Hume commented at length about the variety of taste found from place to place and from time to time.

It is reasonable to presume, I dare say, that if the taste of Germany is not like that of France, or if the taste of the eighteenth century is not quite that of the nineteenth, then these differences in taste may possibly have correlations with other variables discoverable between the two nations or the two epochs. What happened in France that did not happen in Germany and what happened in the nineteenth century that had not yet happened in the eighteenth--these historical facts influence esthetic receptiveness. As T. S. Eliot put it:

> No poet, no artist of any art, has his complete meaning alone. His significance, his appreciation is the appreciation of his relation to the dead poets and artists. You cannot value him alone; you must set him, for contrast and comparison, among the dead.... The existing monuments form an ideal order among themselves, which is modified by the introduction of the new (the really new) work of art among them. The existing order is complete before the new work arrives; for order to persist after the supervention of novelty, the whole existing order must be, if ever so slightly, altered; and so the relations, proportions, values of each work of art toward the whole are readjusted; and this is conformity between the old and the new.[12]

---

[10]Observations on the Feeling of the Beautiful and the Sublime, trans. John T. Goldthwait (Berkeley, 1965), p. 45.

[11]Hume, "Of the Standard of Taste," p. 3.

[12]"Tradition and the Individual Talent," in Selected Essays, new ed. (New York, 1950), pp. 4-5.

I would like to expand Eliot's argument to include a logical corollary; if the past history of art is involved in the judgment of artistic value, so too is the past history of all that is outside art. If the existing relationships in art history shift a little with each new addition, so too do the existing relationships in history as a whole.

Just as there was a two-way interplay between the internal relationships of artist's sensibilities and audience's tastes, so there is a two-way interplay between past history and present art; the history influences what will be done in the art and how the art will be appreciated, but the art, by expanding (even if ever so slightly) man's total insights into life, creates a necessary reinterpretation of history--in short, art alters history by organizing a new mode of sensibility towards it.

I would like to use the American Revolution as an example of an historical event involved in this two-way interplay with art. The American Revolution, like any other historical event, is theoretically capable of description through a listing of a set of finite details. Certain actions occurred on certain dates and certain effects followed. Certain persons thought and said and did certain things, and these things became stimuli which aroused certain other persons to think and say and do other things in response. Empirical methodology will authenticate or disprove facts or supposed facts such as these. The raw factual data, however, does not yield meaning; the meaning emerges as the facts are sifted through the consciousness of the historian. Alongside the historian, however, is the artist, who is also sifting historical facts through his consciousness and releasing meaning from them. What happened determines what he can see; but what he can see determines if not what happened at least what we understand of what happened.

The American Revolution is not, in one sense, an objectifiable reality; it is an abstraction, a way of comprehending as a unity a wide array of discrete facts that often have rather tenuous interrelationships. What was the American Revolution? The inevitable result of the application of the rational principles of the Enlightenment to the sphere of practical politics? An emotional bloodletting by unprincipled romantic radicalism? A courageous American victory? An absurd British blunder? The birth of a new civilization? The death throes of an old one? The liberation of the common man? Or his enslavement by the corporate state? The facts create the meaning, but the meaning seen determines which facts will be noticed and remembered and be called our history.

In 1787, one of the first belletristic works inspired by the Revolution and its results found the meaning of the Revolution to lie in the vindication and exoneration of an authentic American culture, based on standards of behavior and judgment far removed from the effete norms of the decadent British culture. This work, of course, was Royall Tyler's The Contrast, a blatantly nationalistic play, whose theme is not unfairly represented by a rhetorical question in the doggerel-filled prologue: "Why should our thoughts to distant countries roam, / When each refinement may be found at home?" We have the whole conflict of the play before us when the comic villain (Dimple) declares to the hero (Manly), "When you shall have seen the brilliant exhibitions of Europe, you will learn to despise the amusements of this country as much as I do," and the hero avers, "Therefore I do not wish to see them; for I can never esteem that knowledge valuable which tends to give me a distaste for my native country."[13]

Shortly after The Contrast, Hugh Henry Breckenridge's picaresque novel Modern Chivalry appeared in installments with a celebration of the freedom which the Revolution had brought to the common man to enable him to escape from class distinctions and to pursue his own ambitions and self-interests. Philip Freneau and William Cullen Bryant began to celebrate the rugged American landscape and the noble savage who was closest to it, the American Indian. Frontier journalists, such as A. B. Longstreet and George Washington Harris, applauded the individualism and nonconformity of the frontiersman in their comic tales and anecdotes; genteel poets, such as Lowell, Holmes, and Longfellow, found patriotic inspiration in the achievements of the new nation. James Fenimore Cooper discerned a mythic new American hero in Natty Bumppo, who was Daniel Boone reconceived to embody the post-Revolutionary American dream of manifest destiny.

In all of these writers (as in all of the artists of other media who were contemporaneous with them), certain historical facts were stimulating their creative imaginations. America had had its revolution. It had broken its ties with the motherland. It had set off on its own to determine its own future. It had created a new kind of republic for a new kind of free man. It had sent the common man into the primitive wilderness, like Adam into the New Eden, like Israel into the New Canaan, like Christian into the New City of Light. And these events that had transpired redirected the eyes of the artist to new kinds of experience and his creative talents to new kinds of expression.

---

[13]"The Contrast," in The Literature of the United States, ed. Walter Blair et al., rev. ed. (Chicago, 1953), I, 424, 445.

The apotheosis of this new American experience and this new American form of expression is found preeminently in the "barbaric yawp" of the solitary singer, Walt Whitman. Ralph Waldo Emerson had prophesied Whitman's coming: "The poet is...the man without impediment, who sees and handles that which others dream of, traverses the whole scale of experience, and is representative of man, in virtue of being the largest power to receive and to impart....The poet has a new thought: he has a whole new experience to unfold; he will tell us how it was with him, and all men will be the richer in his fortune."[14] At first, Emerson looked in vain for the messianic poet he hoped America would produce, but when in 1855 he received a copy of Leaves of Grass he stoutly declared it "the most extraordinary piece of wit and wisdom that America has yet contributed."[15] "Books are the best type of the influence of the past," Emerson said, adding: "Each age, it is found, must write its own books; or rather, each generation for the next succeeding."[16]

Emerson was right, Whitman himself declared in his preface to Leaves of Grass:

> America does not repel the past or what it has
> produced under its forms or amid other politics
> or the idea of castes or the old religion....accepts
> the lesson with calmness...is not so impatient as
> has been supposed that the slough still sticks to
> opinions and manners and literature while the life
> which served its requirements has passed into the
> new life of the new forms...perceives that the
> corpse is slowly borne from the eating and sleep-
> ing rooms of the house...perceives that it waits
> a little while in the door...that it was fittest for

---

[14]"The Poet," in The Literature of the United States,   I, 826-827.

[15]Letter to Walt Whitman, July 21, 1855, in A Century of Walt Whitman Criticism, ed. Edwin Haviland Miller (Bloomington, 1969), p. 1.

[16]"The American Scholar," in The Literature of the United States, I, 796.

its days...that its action has descended to the
stalwart and wellshaped heir who approached...
and that he shall be fittest for his days.[17]

With this life of the past now reincarnated in himself, Whitman
sees himself as "commensurate with a people," enclosing the old
and the new, becoming the "arbiter of the diverse" and the "equal-
izer of his age and land." As such, he will respond to the United
States as "essentially the greatest poem"--because in this new
nation are what he calls "ampler largeness and stir," "action un-
tied from strings," "hospitality which forever indicates heroes,"
"roughs and beards and space and ruggedness and nonchalance that
the soul loves," the "crampless and flowing breadth" of its perspective, and the "self-esteem and wonderful sympathy" of the
common people.

　　　　And identifying so with the country itself, what does Whitman
sing about? "I celebrate myself, and sing myself," he says, and
proceeds to weave the "Song of Myself" out of the multifarious
experience he has subsumed through his democratic sensibility.
"I am an acme of things accomplish'd, and I an encloser of things
to be," he declares. "I know I have the best of time and space,
and was never measured and never will be measured." And out of
this celebrating and singing and enclosing and having the best of
time and space comes the unique form of Whitman's verse. "The
poetic quality," he told us in his preface, "is not marshalled in
rhyme or uniformity or abstract addresses to things nor in melancholy complaints or good precepts, but is the life of these and
much else and is in the soul.... The rhyme and uniformity of perfect poems show the free growth of metrical laws and bud from
them as unerringly and loosely as lilacs or roses on a bush, and
take shapes as compact as the shapes of chestnuts and oranges and
melons and pears, and shed the perfume impalpable to form." All
the technical features of Whitman's poems, in fact, are organically
related to the sensiblity which produced them--they are manifestations in form of the content they express, they are medium but
message as well. "One's Self I sing, a simple separate person,/
Yet utter the word Democratic, the word En-Masse," and the
technical elements--the all-inclusive lists and catalogs, the contradictions and paradoxes, the refusal to discriminate and judge,

---

[17]"Preface 1855--Leaves of Grass, First Edition," in Leaves
of Grass, ed. Harold W. Blodgett and Sculley Bradley, Comprehensive Reader's Edition, The Collected Writings of Walt Whitman
(New York, 1965), p. 709. All subsequent references to Whitman
are to this same edition.

the colloquial language, the rambling structures, the carnal imagery, the progress without completion--all these reinforce the overt democratic, all-American message of the words.

That which the American Revolution was, then, has in Whitman been fully absorbed into the sensibility of an artist so that he sees and expresses instinctively that which the Revolution has prepared him to see and express: the grandeur of the new nation, the glory of the common man, the supremacy of the democratic principle. Furthermore, his mythic vision of the post-Revolutionary world suggests an artistic form which is a mirror of the world perceived and re-created in the poetry. Whitman's poems are only comprehensible in terms of the political foment from which they were generated; but after Whitman, part of our interpretation of the American democratic revolutionary experience will always be Whitman's. The first interplay is between history and the sensibility of the artist; the second is between the sensibility of the artist and the tastes of the mass audience. "The proof of a poet is that his country absorbs him as affectionately as he has absorbed it," Whitman prophesied, and his proof was not long in coming. Today, Whitman's vision of the American experience is to some degree the vision of all us--those of us who read Whitman and those who don't, those of us who think about our past and those who are unaware that the past impinges on our present. We have absorbed Whitman into our mass tastes, not always directly from the original, but often from his artistic descendants, Frost and Lindsay and Sandburg and William Carlos Williams and Ginsberg and Kerouac, and also sometimes from a collateral line in the other arts, John Philip Sousa and Agnes deMille and John Houston and Andy Warhol and Robert Indiana and Woodie Guthrie and Will Rogers and George Gershwin and Dennis Hopper.

A political upheaval, like the American Revolution, is only one of many types of historical changes which can have stunning impacts on taste and sensibility. Tastes and sensibilities changed significantly, for instance, during the epochs when great religious conversions or reversals took place. Thus, the switching of the classical pagan world to Christianity, the Muslim subjugation of much of the Mediterranean world, the breakup of the Roman Catholic Church by the Protestant Reformation were all occasions for major changes in taste and sensibility. One has only to compare the Parthenon with a Gothic cathedral, a Dante with a Milton, an El Greco with a Picasso to see what changes in the religious sphere do to artistic sensibility.

Economic, educational, social, scientific, and technological upheavals, reversals, or breakthroughs can have equally compelling effects. The Renaissance, perhaps more than any age other than our own, was witness to revolutions in one area after another--the replacement of a universal language, Latin, by distinct vernaculars, the subversion of the Holy Roman Empire by nationalistic states, the breaking of the boundaries of a finite world by the great voyages of discovery and exploration, the shattering of the concept of an anthropocentric universe with the Copernican theory, the collapse of feudalism and its rigid class structure with the rise of a mercantilistic middle class, the decline of the agrarian economy with incipient industrialism, etc. And what age, including our own, ever made more breakthroughs in art? What age ever altered more drastically the sensibility and taste of a preceding era?

There is a change aplenty in our current age as well, and there are consequent rapid shiftings in taste and sensibility today. Cultures and countercultures seem to rise and meld in a dialectic process so speeded up we can hardly keep track of it. The one factor that is significantly different in this age, however, is the unique presence of a virtually all-pervasive system of mass media. Unquestionably, the media are responsible to a large degree for the acceleration of change--both social and esthetic. But the question with which we began this discussion, the question of the ability of individuals or societies to maintain individual freedom of perception and choice, in the face of the tremendous homogenizing pressures of the media, is still not an easy one to find an answer to. "The effects of technology," Marshall McLuhan says, "do not occur at the level of opinions or concepts, but alter sense ratios or patterns of perception steadily and without any resistance."[18] If this is so, then we are all having our tastes and sensibilities altered, and the probability is that we are all having them altered in pretty much the same way. Will we soon be Aldous Huxley's dreaded army of Epsilons--robot-like creatures with only those opinions that have been programmed into us?

Though McLuhan can be frightening, he also offers one of the few words of consolation for our future prospects. "The serious artist," McLuhan says, "is the only person able to encounter technology with impunity, just because he is an expert aware of the changes in sense perception."[19] Futurologist John McHale states further: "Common charges of 'standardized taste'

---

[18]Understanding Media: The Extensions of Man (New York, 1964), p. 18.

[19]Ibid.

and 'uniformity' confuse the mass provision of items with their individual and selective consumption. The latter remains more than ever, and more widely, within the province of personal choice--less dictated than ever formerly by tradition, authority and scarcity."[20] And if Susan Sontag is right, the serious artist will be responding to the electronic media technological revolution just the way Whitman responded to the political-social Revolution of 1776--by absorbing it, making it a part of himself (in this case an extension of his central nervous system), and organizing in his art the new modes of sensibility it permits.

　　　Is the end of our differences in taste and sensibility at hand? The answer seems to be: "Not here, not quite, not yet."

　　　[20]"The Plastic Parthenon," in The Futurists, ed. Alvin Toffler (New York, 1972), p. 53.

NEOCLASSICAL ART:
THE MIRROR OF REVOLUTION AND ENLIGHTENMENT

Keith Marshall

An opera would seem an unlikely place to begin a study of French neoclassical painting, if only because one associates opera with flamboyant emotion--so great that one must sing not speak--and late eighteenth-century painting with the coolness of strict academic training. But painting, just before the French Revolution, existed in a state of tense equilibrium that charged its themes and figures with potential emotion; and, as the first political blows were struck, the art seemed to sing forth a message that inspired, as well as condoned, revolutionary activity. Strictly speaking, one should turn immediately to Gluck's operas for the musical counterpart of neoclassical painting; for, just as painters sought a return to the noble simplicity of ancient art, a respite from baroque or rococo fantasies, so Gluck in _Orfeo_ returned directly to Greek legend in an attempt to purify his master.

It is to Mozart, however, that I should like to turn, to _The Marriage of Figaro_. It is difficult to believe that in 1785 this work could have met with such distrust from public officials: but at that time all plays were suspect, and Beaumarchais's story of a servant outwitting his master was viewed with great suspicion. It is not, however, the proto-revolutionary sentiments of the Figaro-Almaviva relationship on which I wish to dwell, but rather the atmosphere--particularly in the final scenes.

Throughout the opera, jest has triumphed; frivolity, in the old style, still holds sway. Cherubino is banished to the war, but

Figaro dismisses all thoughts of hardship or danger in the jaunty
non più andrai. And of course a lawsuit turns into a double wedding.
Yet the undercurrent of tension remains, much as it must have
been felt in France itself. Near the end of the opera, Figaro
muses, "Tutto è tranquillo e placido" but in a moment the whole
scene explodes into the madness of confused identities and ambiva-
lent emotions.

That same year, Jacques-Louis David, who would become
the premier painter of the Revolution, showed his Oath of the
Horatii (Fig. 19), a scene of stoic calm and heroic resolution in
which the men of the family swear vengeance. What David does
not represent is the madness which follows, the brothers' return
from combat, their sister's death, their lives endangered. All
remains poised, through David's brush, on the brink.

Such tension is not surprising in a society that was overtly
analytical in all it did. The Enlightenment was certainly the major
impetus to the mind's forging its way into the modern world; but in
its wake it swept away much necessary compromise and attempted
to affirm and distinguish all areas of thought. Of particular importance to art was the distinction, first heralded in the eighteenth
century, between romantic and classic art. Previous centuries
had been able to accept the two characteristics united in a single
person; and indeed even the sternest French painters of the time
were sometimes unable to quell all "romantic" impulses. But
Winckelmann's On the Study and Imitation of Greek Art, published
in 1755, was followed only a year later by Burke's On the Sublime;
and suddenly the lines were firmly drawn between sublime and
beautiful, romantic and classic. The minds that had divided French
art into the warring factions of Poussinistes and Rubenistes in the
early years of the century could rest assured that, even with their
own particular controversy forgotten in the new artistic climate,
aesthetic unrest would continue unabated for at least another
century.

Artistic turmoil was not evident only at the end of the century; indeed, the very art against which the neoclassical painters
reacted had begun the century as the new art. The grandeur of
baroque forms was too heavy a load for the infant eighteenth century to bear: gradually painting moved from the sphere of ennobling the monarch to the expression of his, and his followers',
delight in the elegant pleasures of life. A LeBrun drawing for an
almanac (Fig. 1) expresses the baroque formality of the previous
century. The new taste, however, was more in harmony with the
style and subject matter of a painting like Claude's Ascanius
Shooting the Stag of Sylvia (Fig. 2) which represented the culmination of European landscape painting at the time. And even Claude's

mythological pastiche was too serious for the new age. If it sought a god or goddess in this landscape, she was Love.

The art of Watteau, Boucher, Fragonard, and their schools was a rêverie; and it is ideally approached as a dream. Two brothers, just a century later, were well suited to do just that. Jules and Edmond de Goncourt sought a Golden Age, and they discovered it in the works of these painters. More important, they discerned that the magic of the age and its art had never completely faltered. In their Art of the Eighteenth Century, the Goncourts begin at the end of the century, penetrating the aura of high seriousness to reach the delicious frivolity that beckoned from the fêtes champêtres:

> Let us return to the beginnings of the present century: French taste declares its attitudes in the form of a public disavowal of all the eighteenth century masters, great and small. Their works are thrown into the junk stands on the quays, moulder in the street air or leave the country, banished from this France that is now too poor to buy them back. No one troubles about them, no one wants them, no one looks at them. ... There is hardly more than a handful of collectors sufficiently audacious to be tempted by their cheapness into acquiring works of art of the Louis XV period; and they have to buy clandestinely, almost with shame, hiding their purchases as an extravagance, a caprice, an act of wanton curiosity, a collector's debauch.

Surely they discharge too much buckshot at the specter of neoclassical taste. The Revolution and the Jacobin tradition had left the school of Boucher and Watteau in disgrace and had turned to ancient Greece and Rome for prototypes. Only Greuze survived their scorn, for he had represented a trend of sentimental morality that was more akin to their desire for a lofty morality that would inform the new art.

Nevertheless, the Academies and new aesthetic doctrines, however severely applied, were incapable of banishing an artistic taste. Official Paris might bow to new demands (which of course reflected new social and aesthetic aspirations); but in the provinces, the old taste held sway. And in Paris itself, collectors nourished the older tradition, both by collecting the works of its artists and by inspiring contemporary artists to paint in that manner to ensure sales. Even within official circles, Prud'hon survived; and, in a casual manner, David was sometimes called the Boucher of his time!

But the Goncourts' prose, although somewhat misleading, is as delightful as the art which it evokes; and the two brothers are perhaps our most congenial guides to the art that immediately preceded the Revolution. With the first words of their essay on Watteau, we enter the dream world of the past. Watteau was, for the Goncourts, the great poet of the eighteenth century, a man who created in his imagination a visual world that in effect became the most easily recognized type of the real world. His particular gift was that of assimilating the beauties of the world, reshaping them through his imagination, and returning them to the world to enliven the image of the age. Watteau, they claimed, renewed

> [the] quality of grace. It is no longer the grace of antiquity [certainly not as Claude viewed it] that we meet with in his art: a precise and tangible charm, the marble perfection of Galatea, the seductiveness--exclusively plastic--the material glory of a Venus. The grace of Watteau is grace itself. It is that touch that bestows upon women a charm, a coquetry, a beauty that is beyond mere physical beauty.

The painter's Rendez-vous de Chasse (Fig. 3) presents this exquisite natural idyll in all its charm--the beauties of its "deities" not superhuman, but elegantly refined. The harshness of nature is dismissed, and the whole is suitable for the decoration of a bauble, as precious as the figures themselves. Gravelot recognized this; and his design for the lid of a snuffbox (Fig. 4), focusing on a reversed image of the woman being helped from her horse, captures the essential quality of Watteau's work: its delicacy, frivolity--its non-heroic nature. Although this particular painting is quite large, the figures are appropriate to the decoration of a box, which might then be found among them. If they drank the cup of life to the fullest, it was, no doubt, from a delicate Sèvres piece that they partook.

The fanciful nature of the age is obvious from the opposite end of the telescope as well. Watteau might populate a vast landscape with diminutive figures. Other artists might snatch heroic plums from the past and re-create them in the miniature scale of the new age. The lid of another snuffbox, attributed to Louis Ouizille, portrays an emasculated version of Poussin's Et in Arcadia Ego,

entitled merely Lovers Beside a Statue of Cupid (Fig. 5). Such
was the taste of the age, the heritage of Watteau, who through delicate fancy gave shape and form to the emotions of the time.

    But if Watteau created the atmosphere of the age, Boucher--
the Goncourts claim--fully embodied it. He took Watteau's achievement for his own and created a type of beauty which suited the particular society that he served. But it was, at the same time, an
artistic vision of less scope than Watteau's: a vision that seemed
to rotate around the blatant sensuality that was absent from
Watteau's world:

> [Boucher] was able neither to envelop the human
> form with its beauty nor to veil it with modesty;
> the flesh he paints has a kind of inviting effrontery;
> his divinities, nymphs, nereids, all his female
> nudities are women who have undressed; but who
> knew better how to undress them? The Venus of
> whom Boucher dreamt and whom he painted was
> only the physical Venus; but he knew her by heart.

This all took place in the realm of the gods where anything might
be allowed: The Judgment of Paris   (Fig. 7) certainly provided
such an opportunity, and its style and motives found their way onto
the lids of more suggestive snuffboxes (Fig. 6).

    When Boucher treated earthly subjects--gently erotic pas-
torals--he generally banished from his idylls "that particular
crudity that is always somewhat distasteful." But in the service of
Madame de Pompadour, whom he painted frequently (Fig. 8) in the
more innocently suggestive style, a bit of sensuality was often
demanded:

> Whenever she deemed it necessary to reawaken
> the king's sensuality with the stimulus of indecent
> suggestion, she turned to Boucher, who would
> throw off a series of panels illustrating a story
> that began in the idyllic and ended in the porno-
> graphic vein.

The most noted of the models, Nellie Murphy, often appears in
what might be called "bottom-scapes" (Fig. 9); and, although the
works involving her show a certain warmth of personal involvement, one feels that the depths of poor Nellie's character might
more discreetly have been plumbed through more "proprietous"
portraiture.

　　　　For in the end it is not a matter merely of taste, but of style: the painter's taste must ultimately surface in his manner of painting. Diderot, firm in his belief that art must both avow and convey moral purpose, condemned many of Boucher's works, claiming that in his paintings, degradation of style had accompanied corruption step by step. The Goncourts, less stimulated by idealism, expressed a more purely artistic evaluation of his oeuvre:

> He was simply an original, highly gifted painter
> who lacked one superior quality, the birthmark of
> all great painters, namely distinction. He had his
> own particular manner, but lacked style in the best
> sense of the term. Elegant vulgarity, that is the
> hallmark of Boucher--

a hallmark that would be disgraced by the new undercurrents of morality and enlightenment.

　　　　It is in Fragonard, however, that style, subject, and technique all seem to merge to produce the characteristic image of the age. For he seizes the delicacy, the fancy of the time, and portrays it in the most perfectly delicious and invitingly amorous of worlds. And the chief glory of this world is Fragonard's color, which exceeds the power of his rivals. His work quite simply possesses that elusive attribute, style: the felicitous marriage of manner and matter.

　　　　Fragonard's Swing (Fig. 10) is not yet another fête champêtre, nor a prolonged inspection of a nude body. It is a fleeting glimpse, captured in the full blush of radiant, jewel-like color, of an exquisite moment of amorous joy. Idea and expression are one. But, like the swing itself, the age was reined; and a sudden jolt might spill the lady--or topple a king!

　　　　For morality was on the prowl; and, although its first manifestations were sentimental and artistic, philosophers of the age envisioned a more potent role for the arts, one which would eventually lead it into the service of politics. Initially, the change in outlook seemed comparable merely to the succession of Watteau's frivolous rococo motives to LeBrun's heavier baroque monumentality. But when one examines works that treat similar themes, a greater change in orientation is obvious. Watteau's L'Accordée de Village (Fig. 11) is a fête champêtre that just happens to have a bride and groom in its midst instead of some anonymous amorous pair. And the couple are by no means the focal point of the work; indeed, activity is rampant everywhere except where the couple are seated. In stark contrast to this is Greuze's treatment of the same subject (Fig. 12), in which the theme is the emotion of the

couple and families, intimately expressed in their humble sur-
roundings--not the festivities that might ordinarily surround such
an event.

Today Greuze suffers in our estimation, for his overt
morality seems a bit offensive and his sentimentality too sugary for
our hardened hearts. Even the Goncourts, rapturous over the
glories of eighteenth-century painting, find Greuze a descent from
the heights:

> When centuries grow old, they become sentimental;
> their corruption melts. It was a strange moment
> for the aging eighteenth century, as if the heart of
> a rake had declined into its second childhood!
> Humanity, charity, these words seemed suddenly
> to have the quality of a revelation....On all sides,
> the prevailing aridity sought dew, the mind re-
> quired freshness, tears prepared to flow.

The important phrase in their evaluation is not, however, "they
become sentimental," but "their corruption melts"; for if sentimentality replaced "delicacy," morality definitely prevailed over
licentiousness.

The initial triumph of morality came through the virtues of
the fairer sex, women such as Greuze's Inconsolable Widow (Fig.
13), gazing enraptured at the bust of her late husband, his remembered love leaping forth from the letter and rending her heart.
Here, interestingly enough, we see the introduction of antique
motives, forms which make her bare breasts seem noble instead of
erotic, images that later artists would use to set the mood for acts
of heroic virtue.

Closer to the common heart--even in France--were such
exempla as Richardson's Pamela, the story of a virtuous servant
girl who wins her master's respect and hand in marriage by steadfastly refusing his advances. Her diaries and letters, when viewed
by the skeptical, suggest that she knew quite well what she was
doing; but for those to whom virtue was supreme, Gravelot's drawing of Pamela (Fig. 14) portrayed the simple rewards that await the
righteous.

Such works satisfied the new moralist appetites of the
masses; but on a higher level the philosophes promulgated new
ideals that art could--and should--serve a moral function in society.
Their program divided theoretically into two parts: a message,
morality--and a medium, neoclassicism...which in practice often
formed a unique and convincing whole.

Frenchmen were no strangers to either classical philosophy or ancient art. Theorists of the day knew that Plato had argued in the Republic the moral influence of art--and that therefore artists should portray only the good. Likewise, Aristotle, in the Politics, hypothesized that figures, colors, lines, etc., are not only imitations--but that they in themselves express emotions that denote moral habits. Thus today, on a much lower intellectual plane, we talk of a sensuous curve, or an incident that makes us "see red."

These thinkers, influenced by Locke's epistemology, the idea of a tabula rasa, felt that art could be a major influence in the reformation of morality; and they were clever enough to realize that cold logic alone could never content men. Although reason was to replace revelation, it was reason that cracked its whip through the gauze of essays, poems, drama, and paintings.

Diderot was a noted enthusiast of the moral role; reading his Salons, one is conscious of a growing revulsion against works like Boucher's and a rich enthusiasm for works that idealize innocence and decency. And in his Essai sur la peinture, his call to artists to reform the salons into mirrors of virtue rang clear through his evaluations of art.

Rousseau, in his Discours sur les sciences et les arts, was even harsher on the times. He attempted to determine whether or not the revival of the arts and sciences--The Enlightenment--had contributed to the moral improvement of mankind. He concluded that the arts, themselves depraved by voluptuous taste, only added to the evil consequences which luxury brought in its train.

The message determined, the medium reared its head. It was only logical that the age which provided the philosophy should also furnish the imagery. Greece and Rome, to the men of the Enlightenment, were the only true homes of an ideal secular society, noble by nature--severe perhaps, but in moral and intellectual agreement with the ideals of late eighteenth-century philosophes. Conveniently, the earth disgorged the secrets of the past at Pompeii and Herculaneum--and painters such as Joseph-Marie Vien, whose Cupid Vendor and innumerable sketches employing antique imagery (Fig. 15) set the stage for the proliferation of late Roman imagery, were present to convey the severe forms to the Academicians. Thus while Diderot, Rousseau, and others pursued their ideal of art as a positive influence on public and personal life, the growth and development of neoclassical art forms provided a suitable vehicle for their plans.

In the seventeenth century, Poussin had established the classical tradition in France, guiding it from Rome. He held that a work of art could be created while pursuing a rational plan; and, for him, classical meant "a coherent union of every detail in a

transformation of disorderly nature into a disciplined harmony."
He realized these ideals, he felt, in works such as his Death of
Germanicus (Fig. 16) which served as a background to much of the
classical art of the late eighteenth century. Works such as Vien's
Vendor can hardly bear comparison with Poussin's masterpieces.
But, exhibited in 1763, it summed up the qualities that Vien had
derived from his "rigorous study and imitation of the antique":
a grand simplicity of the figures, static and without movement;
simplicity of clothing and ornament; sobriety in all accessories and
their arrangement. In 1788, Marie Antoinette, in an extraordinary
betrayal of her role as a pastoral milkmaid, had a Sèvres set produced in which Greek motives order a starkly beautiful finish, with
the images of the cows corresponding to every dictum of Vien's
antique vision. A stunning contrast it must have been to the earlier
Sèvres "Rose"--thus called after Madame de Pompadour's Christian
name--and an indication that the neoclassical mode had invaded
society not only at the level of reform, but also at the very seat of
luxury.

This universality of the mode--its initial association with
both the pastoral fantasies of the royalty (infinitely preferable to
the licentiousness of its predecessors) and the sentimental moral
strains of the populace--perhaps explains why it was, even in its
most violent poses, not associated with revolutionary fervor until
after the revolution. Its goal seemed to be the reform of morality,
not of politics.

Greuze's The Emperor Septimus Severus Reprimanding His
Son Caracalla for Having Plotted Against His Life (Fig. 17), which
relies so heavily on Poussin's Germanicus, is a moment of re-
proach: the father reprimands the son, and the viewer, impressed
by the severe nobility of the scene (its action portrayed in frieze-
like dignity against a shallow pictorial plane) is to be impressed
and instructed by this single majestic act. All excess detail is
eliminated: the message is severe; likewise the means of representation. It is almost an A-B-C or multiplication table of stern
morality.

This painting was Greuze's morceau de réception at the
Académie; and it was a great disappointment to him that he was
accepted not as a history painter--the highest category--but as a
genre painter. Yet, with hindsight, we realize that this is precisely what he, and even men like David, were doing: producing
highly specific genre scenes, elevated versions of Hogarth's Rake's
Progress clothed in garb robbed from the wardrobe of antique
painting.

This cool but obsessively moralistic orientation is obvious
in another of Greuze's works. A Father's Curse: the Son Punished

(Fig. 18) employs the motives of Germanicus in a typical genre situation, adding a higher nobility to a poor interior by stripping it of rustic ornament. The simplicity of the scene immediately links it in the viewer's mind to the noble chastity and piety of ancient life; and the moral of the scene, given full emotional expression, is obvious. In the Salon of that year (1765), Diderot responded to the work with the greatest admiration: "What a lesson for parents, and for children!" he exclaimed.

All this seems like prehistory, however, when one approaches David's Oath of the Horatii (Fig. 19), painted appropriately in Rome in 1784 and exhibited at the Paris Salon of the following year. All of a sudden, in the presence of this work, men seemed to become aware of moral responsibility. The public might have responded emotionally to Greuze's morality--but David's painting filled them with the determination to make noble actions triumph.

David's success was instantaneous; he became famous throughout Europe as both the embodiment of the new morality and the painter of the manifesto of the neoclassical school. No one would have thought, however, to suggest that he was a social or political radical.

As the philosophes had envisioned, means and message had merged in a unified, steelhard vision that would ennoble life. And perhaps this precision, the lack of emotion or sentimentality in the male figures, is the key to the painting's success. The figure of the leading brother is often assumed to be derived from the similar figure in Poussin's Sabines (Fig. 26). But compare the two: the classical grace of Poussin's figure, presiding over a licentious rout, belongs with Greuze's limp morality; David's figure is stern, painted in rigid outline that rivals bas-relief.

Yet while he insisted on purity of line and emotion, David understood the psychological heritage of his viewers: a tug at the heartstrings was necessary, and the group of women, so boldly isolated from the figures of the men, provided this. One can sense and appreciate the drastic morality of the men's oath more fully when it is contrasted to feminine sentimentality, a prominent motif from Greuze with which most viewers would have sympathized. Nevertheless, these are "Roman women," a step above "Inconsolable Widows"--and through their classical demeanor the old sentimentality is recast in a more noble form: still soft, though, still feminine, still a foil to heroic male virtue.

One should not forget the lesson that Frenchwomen took from their Roman predecessors: presenting their jewels to the National Assembly to aid in payment of the national debt. Appropriately, many of the women who gave their jewels were wives of artists, and Madame David was prominent in the ceremony. Paintings that recorded The Spirit of Roman Women in French Ladies might not be the moral thunderbolt that the Horatii was, but they did reveal the difference between the noble sentiments of the French women of the Revolution and the sentimentality of their predecessors.

An interesting and important aspect of David's method is his handling of the classical vocabulary. For, just as the spirit of Roman women appeared in the French, so David's neoclassicism was a new and timely creation. Germinal, Thermidor, and Brumaire are new words with Latin roots. In the same manner, David has taken bits of Roman history and imagery and essentially recast them into a very elevated--and inverted--form of genre painting: genre in that it is the expression of a particular time and atmosphere, late-eighteenth-century France, even though it attempts to be timeless. It is hardly historical painting--which attempts to take a contemporary event and clothe (or, in most cases, unclothe) it in ancient forms. David takes a hypothetical moment from the past, isolates and selects details that will convey his message, and confronts the public with it. Of course, they are more elevated subjects than Pamela or Mariage à la Mode, but still a tract for the times.

After his Death of Socrates, an experiment in the Greek key that did not suit David either stylistically or moralistically, the artist returned to the more convenial Roman mode for the theme and imagery of his Lictors Returning to Brutus the Bodies of His Sons (Fig. 20) of 1789. Once again he chose a moment away from crowds, a scene in which he conveys intense emotion through various painterly techniques (among others, the shadow that envelops the dejected Brutus and the stunning contrast of blue and red, around which the painting is organized) and the juxtaposition of the stoic--and in this case dreadful--morality of Brutus and the intensely--but highly justifiable--emotion of the women. For Brutus has just ordered the death of his sons for their part in a revolutionary plot; he now sits isolated, noble but broken in spirit. The women faint and cry out in anguish, the servant covering her head as she weeps. In this work, one senses the full measure of the tension that threatened to break forth and destroy both social and pictorial harmony.

Amazingly, Brutus--even more overtly political in its implications than the Horatii--was not viewed as a revolutionary document when it first appeared. Although the General Director of the Salon had suggested that caution be exercised in choosing the works exhibited, the high moral sentiment, which informs the painters, seems to have banished from thought any recognition of

a baser motive. (What a tribute to David's power as an artist!)
David himself mentions that Brutus is the work of his that to date
has caused the greatest "fuss"--but only over its undisputed
genius, the noble conception of Brutus, the effectiveness of his
placement in shadow.

But the days were growing steadily darker. An artist
like Mozart must have sensed the imminent holocaust; for whereas
Count Almaviva in Figaro is chastized but forgiven, Don Giovanni,
in the opera of that name, is carried to destruction. A marvellous
comment on the action, the subtle change in the times, is the recall
of Figaro's non più andrai in the last act of Don Giovanni. Figaro
had sung to the departing Cherubino:

> You'll not flutter or twirl any more, sir,
> Or make eyes day and night at the ladies,
> Or disturb their repose as before, sir,
> You Adonis, you young knave of hearts.

The young page faced at most a diversionary stint in a sophisticated
regiment. But as Giovanni devours his meal, Leporello sings the
same verse--now more sinister in its implications--under his
breath--and within minutes the Commendatore has appeared and
concluded in tragic fashion the rake's amorous adventures. In
Figaro, small transgressions are forgiven, and harmony prevails;
but in the later work, high morality triumphs, even if vindication
involves death.

By 1790, morality had become particularized: no longer a
general message to the age, it was to become the backbone of the
revolutionary stance. Brutus, seen before as the tragic conflict
between two types of virtue (paternal love and patriotic duty), became a symbol of devotion to a cause. And this, I feel, is the
tragedy of David's career. For at this point, the fusion of medium
and message is fractured, and a new message is forced into the
framework. Once this happens, the painting loses much of its
dynamic force, and, more importantly, the painting ceases to exist
as a whole. Its figures become actors; and, when the emotional
fervor is lost, the intensity of the painting as a work of art departs.
Petty questions arise--What do the women represent in the new
French Republic? ... to postulate just one--and we have before us a
forged document instead of a work of art.

To rend the fabric further and wrench message and expression apart, the painting was "translated" into action. In 1790,
at a performance of Voltaire's Brutus which David attended, the
scene was recreated on stage exactly as it appeared in the painting.
As a work of art it became superfluous. It had passed into the

public mythology, and the virtue which had <u>inspired</u> the work, when narrowly defined, destroyed it.

In the liberalized <u>Salon</u> of 1791, David exhibited his noted <u>Oath of the Tennis Court</u> (Fig. 22) which in effect moved him into the realm of contemporary history painting--the act of consciously ennobling an event. Significantly, it was in the same <u>Salon</u> that <u>Brutus</u> and the <u>Horatii</u> were "recognized" as proof of David's politically revolutionary sentiments--thus depriving them of their status as perhaps the greatest genre works ever painted.

For a while, even in his role as official painter of the Jacobins, David's movement to history painting did not seem to restrict his creativity or depth of perception. One need only compare Gainsborough's <u>Mrs</u>. <u>Siddons</u> (Fig. 23) to David's <u>Madame Trudaine</u> (Fig. 24) to distinguish the deep and forceful neoclassicism (in the latter) from a Grand Style that relied perhaps too heavily on association, trappings, and pose.

And certainly <u>The Death of Marat</u> (Fig. 25), triumphantly serene and <u>classical</u>, not neoclassical, reveals his power as a painter--the strong geometry, acid colors, and radiantly brushed background forcing forward the funerary image of Marat. It became, immediately, the secular pietà of the Revolution.

Look at the illustration for a moment; feel what the pure, unadorned image itself--isolated--conveys to you of perfect peace realized through the tempering fires of intense emotion. Here is the essence of classical art, in both theme and stark realization. Then read Thomas Carlyle, in <u>The French Revolution</u> (1837), not on Marat's death, but on Charlotte Corday's:

> On Wednesday morning, the thronged Palais de Justice and Revolutionary Tribunal can see her face; beautiful and calm: she dates it "fourth day of the Preparation of Peace." A strange murmur ran through the Hall at the sight of her; you could not say of what character. Tinville has his indictments and tape-papers; the cutler of the Palais Royal will testify that he sold her the sheath-knife; "All these details are needless," interrupted Charlotte; "it is I that killed Marat." By whose instigation?--"By no one's." What tempted you, then? "His crimes." "I killed one man," added she, raising her voice extremely (extrêmement), as they went on with their questions, "I killed one man to save a hundred thousand; a villain to save innocents; a savage wild beast to give repose to my country. I was a Republican before the Revolution: I never wanted energy."

> There is nothing to be said. The public gazes astonished: the hasty limners sketch her features, Charlotte not disapproving: the men of law proceed with their formalities. The doom is Death as a murderess. To her Advocate she gives thanks; in gentle phrase, in high-flown classical spirit. To the priest they send her she gives thanks; but needs not any shriving, any ghostly or other aid from him.

In words, we have the Revolution before us; in paint, still, the highest morality.

David's concern with becoming an official history painter almost destroyed him as an artist. Poussin's Rape of the Sabines (Fig. 26) was his inspiration; but in The Intervention of the Sabine Women (Fig. 27), David insisted on returning to heroic nudity--just when Benjamin West was insisting on the propriety of portraying the figures in his Death of Wolfe (Fig. 28)--greatly idealized--in the garb which actually would have been worn. Yet he was still able to create one of the most perfect images of the Empire period, timeless in its simplicity and beauty, the portrait of Madame Récamier (Fig. 29).

Unfortunately, such classical appearance suited only a particular sort of person, and, as the fashion became more popular, its excesses were obviously open to satire. La Manie de la Danse (Fig. 30) is a light interlude in the serious business of the Empire. And What Fashion is Likely to Become (Fig. 31) presents an Englishman's jaded view of what next to expect from the besieged Continent.

David's Coronation (Fig. 32), a grandiose yet uninspiring view of a state occasion, is worth mentioning only as it reminds us of David's official role as premier peintre of the Republic. Among his other duties was the organization of public spectacles, a task at which he revealed a surprising incapacity for invention. His genius, it seems, lay in classical refinement, not in baroque elaboration.

Let us turn again to Carlyle for a vision of one such spectacle:

> Painter David has not been idle. Thanks to David and the French genius, there steps forth into the sunlight, this day, a Scenic Phantasmagory unexampled:--whereof History, so occupied with Real Phantasmagories, will say but little.

For one thing, History can notice with satisfaction, on the ruins of the Bastille, a Statue of
Nature: gigantic, spurting water from her two
mamelles. Not a dream this; but a fact, palpable
visible. There she spouts, great Nature; dim
before daybreak.

. . . .

And now mark, in the Place de la Revolution,
what other august statue may this be, veiled in
canvas,--which swiftly we shear off, by pulley and
cord? The Statue of Liberty! She too is of plas-
ter, hoping to become of metal; stands where a
Tyrant Louis Quinze once stood. "Three thousand
birds" are let loose, into the whole world, with
labels round their necks, We are free; imitate us.
Holocaust of Royalist and ci-devant trumpery,
such as one could still gather, is burnt; pontifical
eloquence must be uttered by handsome Herault,
and Pagan orisons offered up....

The whole, no doubt, was as formalized as Prud'hon's technically
exquisite sketch for The Triumph of Bonaparte (Fig. 33), a work
which, for all its delights, is still just a sketch that cannot rival
the singular grandeur of David's Napoleon Crossing the Alps (Fig.
34) or the haunting presence of his painting of the emperor burning
the candle at 4 a.m. for the glory of his people (Fig. 35). In all
these paintings, however, the trappings of neoclassicism are used
simply as props to an image; and the works are properly classified
as either history or occasional painting of the Empire.

With the decline of the vitality of neoclassical painting,
the first seeds of a more romantic vision began to spring forth in
the official image. Most notable of this type are two works executed
by Baron Antoine-Jean Gros: Napoleon at the Pesthouse at Jaffa--
(Fig. 36) in which the emperor is seen as a present-day Edward
the Confessor--and Napoleon at Eylau (Fig. 37)--where he appears
almost a messianic figure. Strangely enough, a movement that began by turning to Greece and Rome to ennoble its leaders finally
discovered its most powerful imagery in a highly romantic tradition.

Classical allegory, however, was by no means a casualty
of the change in taste. Pure allegory, that seemed to return to the
halcyon days before the turmoil of the late eighteenth century,
evoked a Golden Age (in itself a "romantic" concept--a return to a
past time that just happened to be classical in its imagery!) to provide an ideological escape from the disappointments of the Napoleonic era. Virtue triumphs (Shades of Greuze) in Prud'hon's

Innocence Chooses Love Over Riches (Fig. 38), and his Venus and
Adonis (Fig. 39) share a more noble affection than Boucher's pair.

But greater changes were yet to come; for with the Bourbon's restoration and David's exile, the neoclassical style that
had reflected the Revolution found itself in disgrace. The great
experiment had failed; virtue had been extinguished, it seemed, in
the crucible of public and Imperial fervor. The grand subject, the
noble morality, was gone; and artists began to indulge in fancies
and exotic yearnings--both within the residual clear forms of neoclassical art, and in many forms that would usher in yet another
artistic revolution, one that would be more capable of expressing
the plight of the average man.

Ingres's Odalisque (Fig. 40) is neoclassical only in the
artist's adherence to clarity of form: the mood is exotic, oriental.
Indeed, the self-portraits of the two men--David's painted while he
was in prison in 1794 (Fig. 41), Ingres's when he was a confident
youth of twenty-four (1804) (Fig. 42)--reveal their different orien-
tations. Anything that I might say about the character expressed
would be merely a personal opinion, so that I leave each person to
contemplate the portraits himself.

But would you not select Ingres as the man who painted the
extraordinary portrait of Madame d'Haussonville (Fig. 43), the
face clear and diagrammatic, the hand poised underneath the chin
almost like an invader from another civilization--a bit of exotic
ornament to complement the severely classical form of the face?
Or the mysterious image of Jupiter and Thetis (Fig. 44), her body
supple and as improbable as a dream, the hand, caressing his
chin, like a strange wild orchid...? There is certainly little
moral severity in this premier student of David's atelier: all is
exotic, the world not of the Greeks, but of Ossian (Fig. 45), the
tales of the Scottish bard (published by Macpherson in the late
eighteenth century) that read like an exotic northern dream when
compared with the sun-drenched imagery of Greece and Rome.

Part of this enthusiasm for the exotic must, of course, be
attributed to the influence of tales from North America, the center
of romantic aspiration for the Frenchman--whether it be the noble
imagery of Girodet's portrait of Jean-Baptiste Belley (Fig. 46) of
Santo Domingo or the same artist's moonlit evocation of the arche-
typically romantic scene of Atala's Entombment (Fig. 47) from
Chateaubriand's novel of the Indian maid's love for the noble
warrior Chactas.

The story goes on and on, ever more distant from David
and his Horatii. Men now die on a raft, floating on the ocean (Fig.
48), their grim fate as ordinary mortals expressed in Géricault's
monochromatic palette; or spirits break loose in Hell, thrashing

in a river of Delacroix's explosive color (Fig. 49). If a musical theme were to be chosen for these works, it would have to be Beethoven's <u>Fidelio</u>--Géricault himself had chosen as a subject the opening of the gates of a prison of the Inquisition.

Finally, toward mid century, the new romantic ideals fired the imagination of the people once again. But this time they had no Brutus or Horatii to emulate. That had failed. They were ordinary men, and force now seemed the answer.

Over the Barrier! Can't you see her, Liberty! Press on! (Fig. 50) The strains of the Marseillaise guide them, not Mozart or Beethoven, Rome or the East. In the new day, art must be itself--perhaps a recorder of events or sentiments--and leave revolution to the people.

Figure 1. Le Brun. Plate from an Almanac. Ashmolean Museum, Oxford.

Figure 2. Lorrain. *Ascanius Shooting the Stag of Sylvia*. Ashmolean Museum, Oxford.

Figure 4. Gravelot. Design after Watteau, for the lid of a snuffbox. Ashmolean Museum, Oxford.

Figure 5. Ouizille. Snuffbox: *Lovers Beside a Statue of Cupid.* Ashmolean Museum, Oxford.

Figure 6. Cherrier. Snuffbox: *An Allegory of Love.* Ashmolean Museum, Oxford.

Figure 7. Boucher. *Judgment of Paris*. Reproduced by permission of the Trustees of the Wallace Collection, London.

Figure 8. Boucher. *Madame de Pompadour*. Reproduced by permission of the Trustees of the Wallace Collection, London.

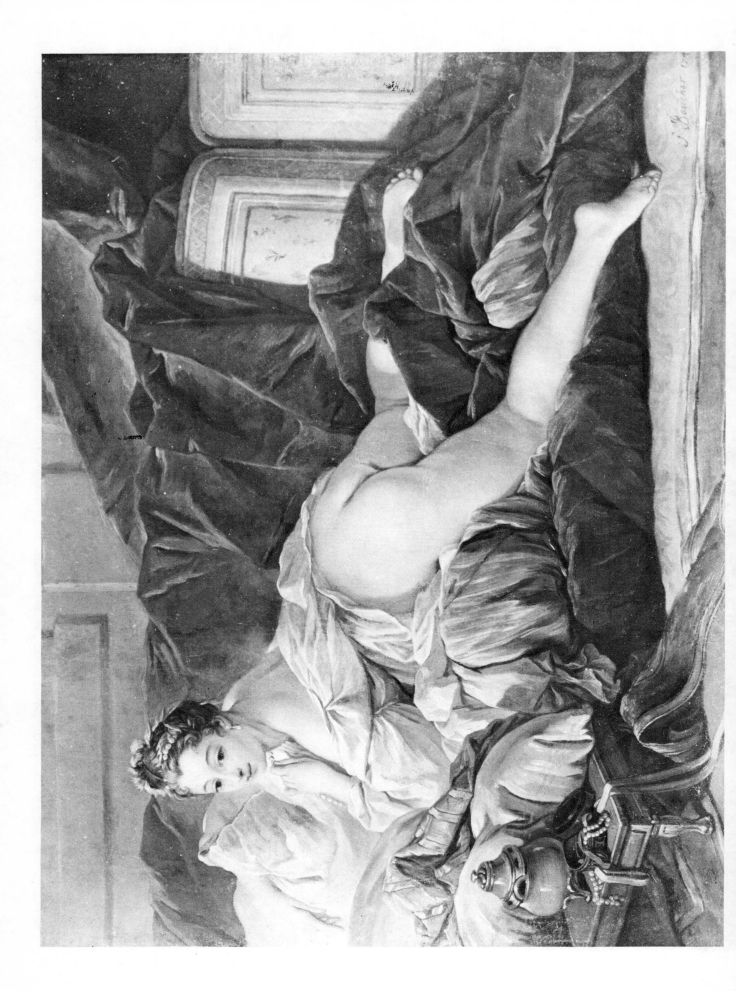

Figure 10. Fragonard. *The Swing*. Reproduced by permission of the Trustees of the Wallace Collection.

Figure 11. Larmesan. Engraving after Watteau's *L'Accordée de Village*. Ashmolean Museum, Oxford.

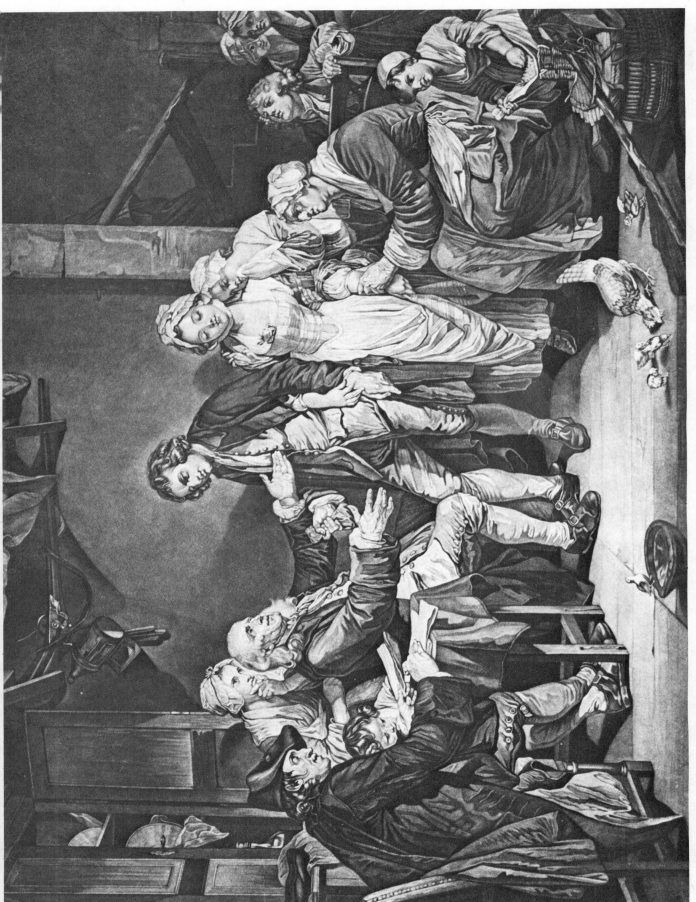

Figure 12. Colored lithograph after Greuze's *L'Accordée de Village*. Victoria and Albert Museum, London.

Figure 13. Greuze. *The Inconsolable Widow*. Reproduced by permission of the Trustees of the Wallace Collection, London.

Figure 14. Gravelot. Design for *Pamela*. Ashmolean Museum, Oxford.

Figure 15. Vien. *Prisoners of War Led to Execution*. Ashmolean Museum, Oxford.

Figure 16. Poussin. *The Death of Germanicus.* Minneapolis Institute of the Arts. Photo courtesy Giraudon, Paris.

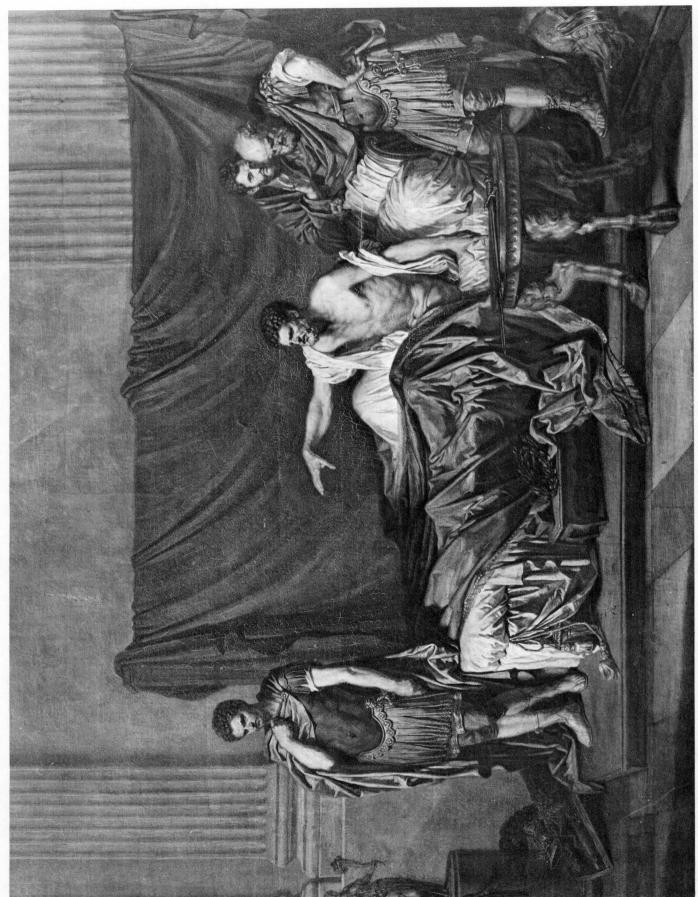

Figure 17. Greuze. *The Emperor Septimus Severus Reprimanding His Son Caracalla For Having Plotted Against His*

Figure 18. Greuze. *The Father's Curse: The Son Punished*. Musée du Louvre, Paris. Photo courtesy Giraudon, Paris.

Figure 20. David. *Lictors Returning to Brutus the Bodies of His Sons.* Musée du Louvre, Paris. Photo courtesy Giraudon, Paris.

Figure 21. Boucher. Standing Figures. Ashmolean Museum, Oxford.

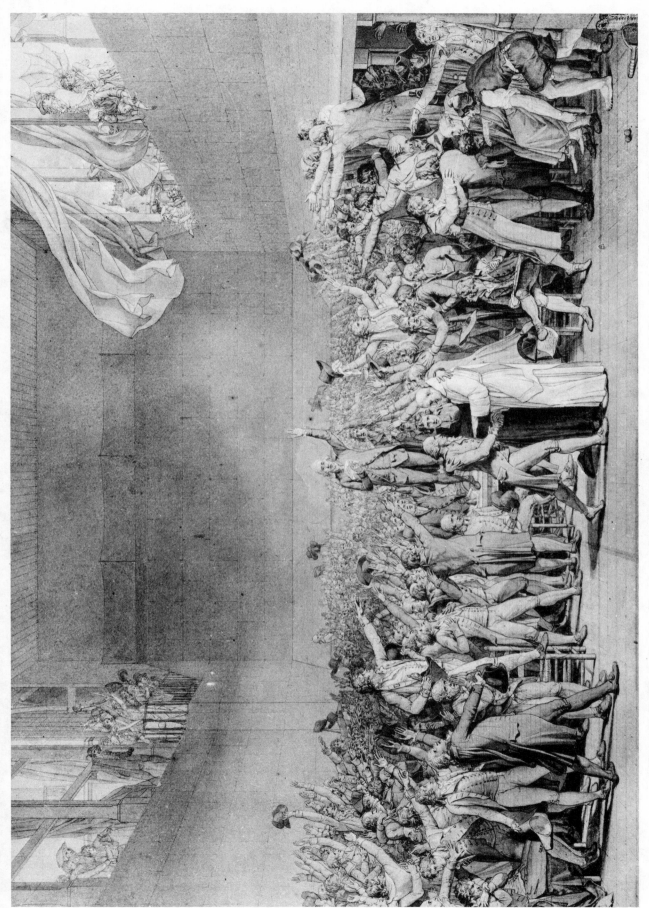

Figure 22. David. *Oath of the Tennis Court*. Cabinet des Dessins du Louvre, en dépôt au château de Versailles. Photo courtesy Giraudon, Paris.

Figure 23. Gainsborough. *Mrs. Siddons.* Reproduced by courtesy of Trustees of the National Gallery of Art, London.

Figure 24. David. *Portrait of Madame Trudaine*. Musée du Louvre, Paris. Photo courtesy Giraudon, Paris.

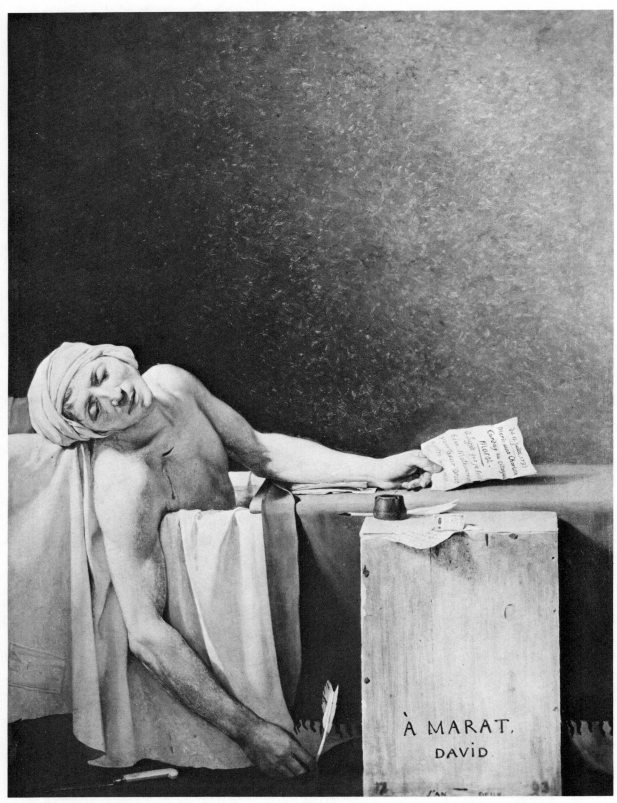

Figure 25. David. *The Death of Marat*. Musée Royal des Beaux-Arts, Brussels. Photo courtesy Giraudon, Paris.

Figure 26. Poussin. *The Rape of the Sabines.* Musée du Louvre, Paris. Photo courtesy Lauros-Giraudon, Paris.

Figure 27. David. *The Intervention of the Sabine Women.* Musée du Louvre, Paris. Photo courtesy Lauros-Giraudon, Paris.

Figure 28. West. *The Death of Wolfe.* The National Gallery, Ottawa.

Figure 30. Debucourt. *La Manie de la Danse.* Bibliothèque Nationale, Paris. Photo courtesy Giraudon.

Figure 31. Anonymous caricature. *What Fashion Is Likely to Become.*

Figure 32. David. *The Coronation* (detail). Musée du Louvre, Paris. Photo courtesy Giraudon, Paris.

Figure 33. Prud'hon. *Triumph of Bonaparte*. Musée Condé, Chantilly. Photo courtesy Giraudon, Paris.

Figure 34. Engraving after David's *Napoleon Crossing the Alps*.

Figure 35. David. *Napoleon*. Samuel H. Kress Collection. National Gallery of Art, Washington, D. C. Photo courtesy Giraudon, Paris.

Figure 36. Gros. *Napoleon at the Pesthouse of Jaffa*. Musée du Louvre, Paris. Photo courtesy Giraudon, Paris.

Figure 37. Gros. *Napoleon at Eylau* (detail). Musée du Louvre, Paris. Photo courtesy Giraudon.

Figure 38. Prud'hon. *Innocence Chooses Love Over Riches*. Ashmolean Museum, London.

Figure 39. Prud'hon. *Venus and Adonis*. Reproduced by permission of the Trustees of the Wallace Collection, London.

Figure 40. Ingres. *La Grande Odalisque*. Musée du Louvre, Paris. Photo courtesy Giraudon, Paris.

Figure 41. David. *Self-Portrait*. Musée du Louvre, Paris. Photo courtesy Giraudon.

Figure 42. Ingres. *Self-Portrait*. Musée Condé, Chantilly. Photo courtesy Giraudon, Paris.

Figure 43. Ingres. *Madame d'Haussonville*. Frick Collection, New York. Photo courtesy Giraudon, Paris.

Figure 44. Ingres. *Jupiter and Thetis*. Musée Granet, Aix-en-Provence. Photo courtesy Giraudon, Paris.

Figure 45. Ingres. *The Dream of Ossian*. Musée Ingres, Montauban. Photo courtesy Giraudon, Paris.

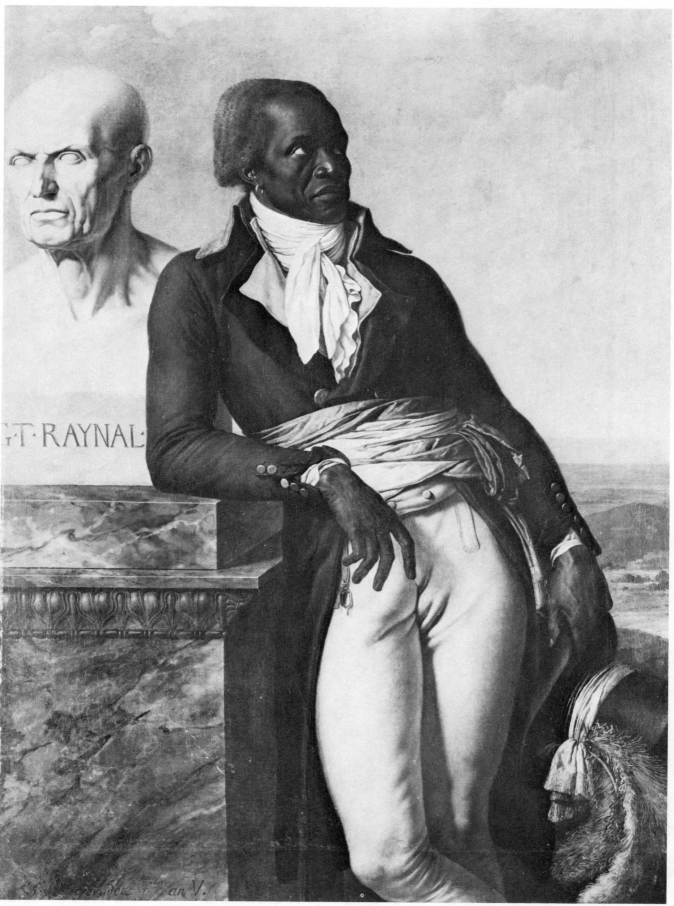

Figure 46. Girodet-Trioson. *Portrait of Jean-Baptiste Belley, Deputy of Santo Domingo*. Musée de la Révolution, Versailles. Photo courtesy Giraudon, Paris.

Figure 47. Girodet-Trioson. *Atala's Entombment*. Musée du Louvre, Paris. Photo courtesy Lauros-Giraudon, Paris.

Figure 48. Géricault. *The Raft of Medusa.* Musée du Louvre, Paris. Photo courtesy Giraudon, Paris.

Figure 50. Delacroix. *Liberty Leading the People*. Musée du Louvre, Paris. Photo courtesy Giraudon, Paris.

REVOLUTIONARY ARCHITECTURE:
THE IMPACT OF FRENCH EMIGRE ARCHITECTS IN AMERICA

Roy Graham

The French Revolution affected a considerable portion of the globe and reached into all areas of human activity, including architecture. It scattered to distant shores large numbers of itinerants, and so it was that French émigrés carried the architectural ideas of the Enlightenment to the rest of the Western World. Almost all of them revolutionaries in their artistic theories, they were forced to leave France because in one way or another they had become unacceptable to the leaders of the political revolution. Their stay in North America was brief, but their influence was profound because of the paucity of trained architects in the New World.

The United States, a new country, wanted to build and build quickly so that architects found ready employment throughout the Republic. Moreover, ideological considerations also made the French designers especially welcome in America. Although the political break with England had been sharper than the cultural division, there was a new sense of intellectual liberation in the United States. France's active part in the American Revolution had increased the exchange between the two countries. Furthermore, American and French leaders had strong political ties, possessing a common passion for reason, intellectual clarity, and justice. In Thomas Jefferson's America, the French émigré architects found receptive clients.

It was a time of aesthetic turmoil, with no directions yet established. Prerevolutionary American architecture had been dominated by the ideas of Englishmen, particularly Wren and Gibbs. After the war, a newly affluent mercantile class in New England began to turn to a more delicately attenuated, decorative kind of neoclassicism patterned after the work of Robert and James Adam. These conservative merchants, still linked to their counterparts in England by strong economic and cultural ties, embraced the innovative refinements in proportion, scale and interior decoration which were characteristic of the Adams.

At the other intellectual pole of the new country, in Virginia, the aspirations of the young nation found more heroic visual exemplification. Jefferson's fondness for classical, and specifically for French attitudes, is well known. His own architectural designs injected into American building the attitudes of French neoclassicism, a discipline of rigueur intellectuelle and ordre visuel which soon came to dominate governmental building of that period.

These evolving styles rested solidly on a base which had been worked out by French architects in the years between 1750 and 1790, a réactionnaire architecture that art historians have called "Romantic Classicism." The style eventually emerged as part of a general revulsion from the excesses of the Baroque style and its more lavish extension, the Rococo. Adherents of the emerging cult of Reason ridiculed wasteful extravagance in all things, including architecture. Classical architecture offered an alternative which came to be regarded as the guide to rational perfection. The pure Greek and Roman forms, already simpler than the Baroque, were further refined to the point of geometric severity, and the resulting forms were placed against a natural background. The Classical Greeks had sought harmony in nature; the Romantic Classicists tried to integrate their geometric forms into nature.

For critics already repelled by the exaggerations of Italian baroque and the frivolity of continental Rococo, the pure, sun-bleached forms of the newly rediscovered Doric temples at Paestum and the perfectly preserved buildings unearthed at Pompeii and Herculaneum were a revelation. Beginning in the middle of the eighteenth century, archaeology took shape as an entity, not yet a science but already more than mere antiquarianism. Its early discoveries reinforced the evidence of history, literature, and art; connoisseurs, collectors, and artists traveled to Italy and Greece to see the new wonders and returned with new ideas of taste and new ideals for society. The German archaeologist Johann Winckelmann expressed something of the spirit of the age when he argued for the perfectibility of man and the general progress of the human race. These two notions, perfectibility and progress, were deeply imbedded in the ideology of the French Enlightenment. Its philosophers argued that systematic study and physical imitation of antiquity would again lift man to the niveau de perfection et d'harmonie known only at the peak of Greek civilization.

This passion for the classical model soon went beyond mere theory and permeated many practical fields from the design of furniture to architecture and town planning. Nor was it confined to France. The Venetian etcher Piranesi fueled the movement with impressive, romantically exaggerated engravings of ruined Rome. Robert Adam himself, the premier British architect of his day, led expeditions which made exact architectural drawings of the ruined temples on the Acropolis and at Spalato in Yugoslavia. The rediscovery of Etruscan art, the first systematic explorations of ancient Egyptian sites added to the growing appreciation of the past. The Abbé Laugier's Essai sur l'architecture disparaged the fading Baroque style and supported the neoclassical, fonctionaliste arguments.

These varied activities had an impact, gradual but profound, on the architecture of prerevolutionary France and, eventually, on American architecture. The more thoughtful architects were well aware of the tendency to idealize the classical past, but they had also inherited from their Renaissance predecessors a strong national tradition, a French style which remained a part of most designs. They designed with a new sobriety and restraint, but many buildings remained modifications of older forms, with stylistic innovations that were subtle, almost inconspicuous. Nevertheless, new trends could be discerned.

The distance traveled by French architecture in the eighteenth century can be best illustrated by buildings not too different from that crowning achievement of the Baroque, Louis XIV's great palace at Versailles. The Petit Trianon, begun in 1762 by Gabriel, and even more the lesser-known pavillon of Louveciennes designed by the young Claude-Nicolas Ledoux in 1771, displayed an increasingly classical architectural vocabulary, but applied it to the traditional French style. The resultant forms resembled temples, however, rather than French country houses; they were virtually square blocks, with a minimum of architectural embellishment, the few decorative features being concentrated at the points of entry and fenestration. In the Petit Trianon, the classical elements are three-dimensional additions to the principal facade. In Louveciennes, Ledoux used the ancient motifs with more certainty, employing a favorite Roman entrance device consisting of a hemicycle preceded by a screen of columns. In both these small pavillons, however, the plans of the walls were emphasized by minimizing projections, by framing fenestration, and by allowing the rustication to extend over all wall surfaces. Wall openings were graduated and proportionally related to each other, similar shapes delicately varied. The total impression is of sublime understatement. In the new buildings, the different architectural elements were not expressed in a single movement as they were during the Baroque period, but the various parts of the composition were proportioned so as to appear self-sufficient. There was no need to carry an echo from one part to another. Independence and individuality of parts now called for calm, smooth transitions--surfaces unies-- between them. The division of ingredients into unités géométriques élémentaires was clearly defined (Fig. 1).

Though devotees of reason, the French revolutionary architects were contemporaries of Jean-Baptiste Greuze and Jean-Jacques Rousseau. In an emotionally charged time, they loved to give their feelings free rein. The architects wished to touch the soul of the beholder through an architecture appropriée which would make each building express its nature and function. (At the time, "function" nearly meant "rôle.") The theory of appropriateness, or rôle, soon became translated into a literal symbolism which was called by Étienne-Louis Boullée, one of its main exponents, une architecture parlante, an architecture in which the function was revealed as interpreted allegorically. The movement began with a return to truthfulness in architecture advocated by the philosophes. Components such as columns were to hold up entablatures, that is they must be appropriately structural and not decorative. An architecture of feeling, it called for character, grandeur and emotion.

Romantic Classicism, as this style came to be called, also has another side: a fondness for "nature" which is obviously romantic, thus justifying the somewhat awkward name. Whatever its origins--the cult of nature taught by Rousseau, the popularity in France of English theories in gardening, the whimsical interest in ruins, the Orient, or the Middle Ages--the pittoresque was established in France by the time the future émigré architects received their training. Nothing revealed its popularity more than Marie-Antoinette's hameau at Trianon. Built between 1783 and 1786, during the years which saw much development of neoclassical architecture, the hameau consisted of an English garden in the natural style with rustic dwellings and service buildings resembling those of a quaint Norman farm. The fashion set by the queen became popular, and numerous guidebooks were published.

The pittoresque did not always merge with the neoclassical in eighteenth-century France. Because the purity of white classical forms was set off by the contrast with a rich palette of nature, pittoresque and neoclassical existed as separate but parallel tendencies. The pittoresque appeared primarily in the garden--mysterious, irrational, and organic--where Gothic architecture was particularly appropriate. The juxtaposition of the pittoresque with the classical aesthetic of Greek and Roman architecture achieved something of the same austere and stoical beauty to be found in the heroic paintings of David.

The designs of the architect who imigrated to America may seem tame compared to the megalomaniac later visions of Boullée and Ledoux, but they were necessarily tempered and diluted according to the realities of construction techniques and financial hardship during the unsettled years at the end of the century.

The first French émigré architect in America was Major Pierre-Charles L'Enfant, born in Paris in 1754, the son of a peintre ordinaire to the king at the Gobelins factory.[1] He came to America in 1777, a month before Lafayette, and "spent freely of his modest means for American independence."[2] It is assumed he had received instructions in engineering and architecture in Paris. He is not listed among architectes experts-jurés du Roi, but he had been a student of the Académie Royale de Peinture et de Sculpture.[3] In America he was commissioned a captain of engineers, attached to Inspector General Steuben.[4] In 1782, while still in the revolutionary army, he saw his first design realized in Philadelphia: a fête to celebrate the birth of the Dauphin.[5] The celebration, which brought recognition to L'Enfant, showed the immense popularity of France, but also of the monarchy which had helped to liberate America. L'Enfant became a personal friend of George Washington and was admired by Jefferson and Hamilton as well.[6] In 1783 he went back to France, either because of lack of work or because

---

[1]H. Paul Caemmerer, Life of Pierre Charles L'Enfant (Washington, D. C., 1950), p. 1

[2]Francis W. Kervick, Architects in America of Catholic Tradition (Rutland, Vt., 1962), p. 84.

[3]Information of the Ordre des Architectes Conseil Superieur; Caemmerer, p. 9.

[4]Caemmerer, p. 53.

[5]Ibid., pp. 87-88.

[6]July 15, 1782, Dr. Benjamin Rush, "The French Fete in Philadelphia in Honor of the Dauphin's Birthday, 1782," Pennsylvania Magazine of History, XXI (May-August, 1897), 257.

of his distaste for unsettled political conditions. [7] He did return permanently to the United States in 1786.

He lived first in New York where he practiced architecture. In 1786-1788 he worked "to adorn the building" of prerevolutionary St. Paul's Church on Broadway, his major work being a design for the reredos and the communion rail.(This design exemplifies the late French Baroque rather than the new revolutionary architecture.). In 1787 he designed the Erasmus Academy at Flatbush, New York. Over fourteen more houses in the same style were done by L'Enfant in New York. [8] He redesigned the old New York City Hall in 1788 and worked on many Philadelphia private homes, including a house for Robert Morris. This house, similar to the Hotel Biron designed by Jacques Gabriel, resembles the earlier eighteenth-century French houses with high mansard roofs.

When the decision was made to lay out the new federal capital on the Potomac, L'Enfant wrote to Washington to offer his services. It was according to plans he published in 1791 that the city of Washington was built. Radiating streets and squares centering on the Capitol and the White House were used to symbolize union, much in the way of the architecture parlante of the revolutionary architects. The plan, however, shows the influences of Versailles and of the layout of earlier French cities. Conceived on a grand scale "to symbolize the future greatness of the nation, "[9] the project was to make him the most famous of all the French architects in America.

L'Enfant had returned to America intending to create an official style and a capital for the country. Other émigrés arrived with more modest ambitions. Some, like Hallet, came to teach. Very little is known of Étienne-Sulpice Hallet's early years in France, although he appears to have been the best educated of the émigrés with the possible exception of Ramée. In 1785, he was listed as one of three admitted as architectes experts-jurés du Roi and he was still so listed in 1790. [10] He had come to America a year before, in 1789, presumably to teach in the New York branch

---

[7]J. J. Jusserand, With Americans of Past and Present Days (New York, 1916), p. 145.

[8]Caemmerer, pp. 103-106.

[9]Ibid. , pp. 87-88.

[10]William Partridge, "L'Enfant's Vision," Federal Architect, VII (April, 1937), 103.

of the Richmond Académie des Sciences et Beaux-Arts, established by the French educator, Quesnay de Beaurepaire, since his name is found on a list of New York patrons in Quesnay's 1788 Mémoire. Hallet neglected to bring any recommendations to America because he felt he was known sufficiently to several persons interested in "l'établissement pour lequel je m'étais destiné." He remained in America in 1793 when the outbreak of the Reign of Terror placed supporters of the royal family in danger of their life. By 1791 Hallet was actively working in Philadelphia, and in the same year he sent Jefferson a design for the capitol in Washington which included a dome like the one finally used.[11] Hallet also advised Jefferson in his design of the Virginia capitol.

Although Washington preferred Hallet's designs and Jefferson praised them highly, the plans approved were those of Dr. William Thornton.[12] Hallet was given an identical prize, however, and was appointed superintendent of the capitol. Later he was employed to make alterations to Thornton's plans. His own designs, very much in keeping with eighteenth-century French thought, include a large classical pediment with a Corinthian peristyle as the featured design elements of the front while the rear had a projecting domed semicircle. It suggests a gigantic version of the Hôtel de Salm in Paris. Hallet also submitted a plan for the White House competition which was won by another immigrant, James Hoban of Ireland. Because of a general misunderstanding or because of "insubordination," Hallet was dismissed from government services in 1794.[13] The rest of his life was marked by the same misfortunes as many of his compatiorts. He received his last payment in 1795,[14] and, after some minor works in Georgetown in 1796, dropped from sight. He died, almost forgotten, in New Rochelle, New York.

Another émigré architect was Maximilien Godefroy who, when the Revolution erupted in France, rallied to the side of the king and, as "Comte la Marde," raised and outfitted a regiment at

---

[11]Louis Réau, Histoire de l'expansion de l'art français (Paris, 1931), p. 227.

[12]Wells Bennett, "Stephen Hallet and His Designs for the National Capitol," Journal of the American Institute of Architects, IV (July-October, 1916), 379.

[13]Ibid.

[14]National Archives Microfilm Copy # M37.

his own expense. [15] He became a captain in the Royal Engineers of
Louis XVI and before escaping France, was imprisoned first in the
infamous Château d'If and later in a prison in the Pyrenees. In
1805 he came to Baltimore to teach architecture, military engineering, and drawing at St. Mary's Seminary--he had a degree in
engineering from the Academy in Paris. In 1807 he designed for
the college the Seminary Chapel, one of the earliest Gothic Revival
buildings in the country. He was also the architect of the Commerce and Farmer's Bank in Baltimore, built in 1810, a severely
geometric building with a corner opening and appliqué decoration.
In 1813 he designed the Ledoux-like Masonic Hall (Fig. 2).   His
Battle Monument in Baltimore was built in 1815 (Fig. 3). He also
designed the First Presbyterian Church and the Unitarian Church
(Fig. 4), a domed, temple-like building with an arched loggia under
a classical pediment. In 1816 he designed the courthouse in
Richmond, Virginia. [16]

Godefroy unsuccessfully entered the competition for the
Washington Monument in Baltimore (Fig. 5), losing to Robert Mills.
He and Latrobe made studies for the Baltimore Exchange contest
which they subsequently won. [17] Arguments over the design, however, led to the dissolution of the partnership, and Godefroy
tried unsuccessfully to practice on his own in Baltimore. He designed the fortifications of the city, and in 1819 left for England
where he exhibited paintings in London, trying desperately to establish a practice, but doing only small amounts of architectural work.
Acute poverty made him return to France in 1827 to take a small
official position as architect of the Department of Maine-et-Loire.
After 1842 he cannot be traced in France. Godefroy's most important contribution to American architecture may have been his brief
collaboration with Benjamin Henry Latrobe, soon to emerge as the
first important American neoclassicist.

New York City's dominance had not yet been established,
but it was already a city of importance, and therefore drew a share
of the émigré architects. Joseph-François Mangin, who descended
from a long line of famous architects, had been born and educated

---

[15] National Archives Microfilm Copy # M37.

[16] Robert Alexander, "The Art and Architecture of Maximilien
Godefroy," unpublished Ph. D. dissertation, New York University,
1961, passim.

[17] Kervick, 58.

in France.[18]   He first appeared in New York in 1794 as an advisor especially recommended by General Washington for the fortifications of "New Buildings" and first served as assistant to Vincent, engineer-in-chief of the city's fortifications whom he later succeeded.[19]   After becoming city surveyor, he established an architectural and engineering practice in partnership with his brother Charles. In 1797 he drew the plans for the New York State Prison,[20] and, five years later, after he and John McComb, Jr., had formed a partnership, drew the plans for the New York City Hall (Fig. 6).[21] The same year he designed one of the first Gothic Revival buildings erected in this country, St. Patrick's Cathedral on Prince and Mott streets, a structure which antedates Godefroy's designs for St. Mary's Seminary in Baltimore by four years. After those architectural works, Mangin appears to have worked mainly with fortress design, his original interest.[22]   The Mangin brothers disappeared from the American scene in 1817, perhaps to return to France.

Marc Isambard Brunel trained as an engineer in France. On the very day the Convention pronounced sentence on Louis XVI, Brunel, who was on leave from the navy, could not control his emotions and denounced the government in a tavern only a few doors away from Jacobin headquarters. Having managed to forge a passport hastily, he left France and boarded an American vessel. He landed in New York in 1793 where he first occupied himself with the plans for canals in the state and then with improvements to make New York rivers navigable.[23]

---

[18]Louis Hautecoeur, Histoire de L'architecture classique en France (Paris, 1952), IV, 327.

[19]Kervick, 94.

[20]Plans and elevations in Schuyler Papers, New York Public Library.

[21]Original drawings 1, 2, 3, McComb Papers, New York Historical Society. Damie Stillman, "New York City Hall: Competition and Execution," Journal of the Society of Architectural Historians, XXIII (October, 1964), 136.

[22]Ebeneezer Stephens to Joseph F. Mangin, July 3, 1798. Ebeneezer Stephens Letters, New York Historical Society.

[23]Richard Beamish, Life of Sir Marc Isambard Brunel (London, 1862), 32.

Soon after Brunel entered the competition for a new structure to replace the "building which served as the great council
chamber of the nation at Washington." Along with him in this competition was a friend, M. Pharoux, a French "architect by profession" who had come over with Brunel from Belgium. Brunel's
biographer tells us that his designs were so "superior in arrangement, elegance and grandeur of design" that the judges were re-
lieved from all difficulty of selection. "Principles of economy,"
however, interfered with the execution of the work.[24] No information indicates that this was the competition for the Capitol or any
other Washington-area building.

From 1795 to 1798, Brunel collaborated with the Mangin
brothers, Joseph-François and Charles, on the design of the Park
Theatre in New York, a competition also entered by Pharoux and
other French émigrés. The plan (Fig.7),[25] which resembles
greatly that of contemporary French theatres, is probably more
the work of the Mangins than that of Brunel. Brunel is also supposed to have "worked with his countryman, Major Pierre-Charles
L'Enfant, upon other buildings"[26] in New York. However well
planned and unusual the designs for the Park Theatre, their execution did not bring Brunel a more general architectural practice of
any direct benefit. Unfortunately this building burned in 1821, and,
except for an undated and unidentified floor plan, there remains no
authenticated drawing to show the architectural concept. The cupola
which surmounted it is said to have resembled the one over the
Corn Market in Paris.[27]

Brunel resolutely declined urgent and repeated invitations
to return to France, "still apprehensive that the leaders of the
revolution were scarcely prepared to understand the true principles
for which they were contending."[28] But on June 20, 1799, he did
sail for England where he achieved his greatest success as a bridge
builder and was awarded a knighthood for his inventions.

---

[24]Beamish, 32.

[25]Unidentified, unsigned, undated floor plan in John McComb
Papers, New York Historical Society.

[26]Kervick, 24.

[27]Beamish, 34.

[28]Ibid., 37.

The Eastern Seaboard cities, where most of the culture and the economic power of the fledgling country were concentrated, naturally attracted most émigrés. But they had competition from an outpost of French culture at the mouth of the Mississippi. Even while it was still under Spanish rule, French-speaking New Orleans had become a natural refuge for émigrés of all kinds, including architects.

Among them was Barthélemy Lafon who left his native province of Languedoc and went to Spanish-held Louisiana at the outbreak of the political turmoil in 1789. He quickly gained stature as an architect as well as "un instituteur," builder, real estate appraiser, cartographer, publisher, theatrical impressario, and "the best surveyor in Louisiana."[29] In 1795 he planned public baths which were never built because funds had to be diverted to re-building New Orleans after the devastating fire of that year.[30] The plans for the public baths are very much in the eighteenth-century French style, resembling many contemporary Parisian buildings. It would have been one of the finest examples of eighteenth-century French architecture in America had it been built.

After a colorful career, including service with the pirate Jean Lafitte for whom he laid out a "capital" near Galveston,[31] Lafon became a major during the Battle of New Orleans.[32] He laid out the plans for the faubourg St. John, giving the streets and squares classical names which reflected French neoclassical tastes: Tivoli Place, rue du Prytanée, and Cours du Colisée in what used to be Lafayette and Orphée in the faubourg Ste. Marie.[33]

In 1795 Lafon also designed the Lemonnier House and in 1800 the Bank of the United States and the Bosque House. During the American domination Major Lafon was appointed Chief Engineer of

---

[29]Stanley Faye, "Privateersmen of the Gulf and Their Prizes," Louisiana Historical Quarterly, XXII (1939), 1069.

[30]Louisiana Purchase: An Exhibition Prepared by the Louisiana State Museum in Co-operation with the Louisiana Landmarks Society (New Orleans, 1953), 29

[31]Testimony of Perera and Lopez, Aury Papers, University of Texas at Austin.

[32]Faye, "Privateersmen of the Gulf," 1069.

[33]Information of the Vieux Carré Survey, New Orleans, Louisiana.

the District of the Mississippi, [34] and drew up a list of points of defense for the Territory of Louisiana. Included in the defense works was a series of wooden phares at the mouth of the Mississippi. This Ledoux-like structure illustrated was replaced later by the limestone lighthouse built by Latrobe.

In 1816 newspaper legal notices made it clear that Lafon was all but bankrupt. [35] On September 9, 1820, the Louisiana Courier reported: "Died this morning . . . Barthélemy Lafon, Engineer, Geographer, and Architect, an old inhabitant of this place . . . His death is much lamented by a number of respectable citizens who had known how to appreciate his talent and his heart."[36]

Other émigrés sought refuge first in Santo Domingo, and then because of the slave uprising fled again to New Orleans and Charleston. Arsène Lacarrière Latour and Hyacinth Laclotte, both natives of Bordeaux, had been attending the Paris Academy of Fine Arts when they were forced to flee by way of Santo Domingo to Louisiana. They are supposed to have reached New Orleans in 1802, though there is no proof of their presence in the colony until 1810, after the Louisiana Purchase. [37]

On October 17, 1811, Latour and Laclotte advertised their services as architects and engineers in the Louisiana Courier.

> On the 26th of this month Messrs. Latour and Laclotte will open a school, in which they will teach drawing in its various branches, portrait, landscape, the designing and coloring of plans, leveling, perspective, ornament, architecture in all its branches, as the composition of plans, the details of carpenter's work, joinery, masonry, smith's work . . . the distribution, ornamenting, and furnishing of apartments in the newest taste, and according to the principles adopted in the Paris Academy of Fine Arts, of which they are both pupils. [38]

---

[34]Charles-Étienne-Arthur Gayarré, History of Louisiana, 4 vols. (New York, 1854-1866), IV, 385.

[35]L'Ami des Lois, April 27, 1816.

[36]Louisiana Courier, September 9, 1820.

[37]Information of the Vieux Carré Survey, New Orleans, Louisiana.

[38]Louisiana Courier, October 17, 1811.

In the same year they designed the Orleans Street Theatre (Fig. 7) which was finished in 1813. The façade, which resembled that of many theatres built in France at the time, was broken by two rows of arcades, one forming a loggia and the other a pilastrade which framed a series of rectangular windows.

The architectural team, both of whom had served as majors in the United States Army during the War of 1812, remodeled the Lemonnier residence and built several town houses, among them one for Pierre Roger and Sieur George. In 1813 they designed the Girod House (Fig. 8), a standard eighteenth-century town house with vague Louis XVI detail, which seems to be a provincial adaptation of the great Paris houses. In 1814 the team split; Latour went into partnership with Henry S. Boneval Latrobe to design the Thierry House in New Orleans, and Laclotte continued the atelier on his own. [39] After 1820 neither is heard of again in this country.

Joseph-Jacques Ramée is typical of the émigré architects, but that he was better educated than the others and that he was successful, at least in Europe, while the others, with the exception of Brunel, were not. Ramée, moreover, was more deeply involved in the revolution and had absorbed the revolutionary spirit. Born in the Ardennes and trained as a military builder, he was in 1780 inspecteur dans les bureaux des bâtiments for the comte d'Artois, the future Charles X. He was apprenticed to the famous architect François-Joseph Bélanger until 1790 when he entered the service of William Beckford, the wealthy and eccentric English writer for whom he designed extravagant fêtes. Ramée's noble clientele and royal patronage did not prevent him from joining the society of the Jacobins for whom he designed the settings for the Fête de la Fédération of 1790. The same apparatus was carried to Nancy for a revolutionary funeral. A captain in the Montmartre grenadiers in 1792, he was a major in Dumouriez's army when the general decided to march on Paris and free the imprisoned king. After this unsuccessful attempt, they fled to Central Europe and Ramée passed from city to city according to the fortunes of war, eventually reaching Hamburg in December 1794. There he successfully worked for the German nobility and Danish royalty doing interior design, architecture, and landscape architecture until David Parish, who dreamed of building a great feudal territory in the northern New York wilderness, discovered him and brought him to America.

Ramée designed a house for Parish in Ogdensburg as well as some notable residences nearby and two handsome estates for

[39]L'Ami des Lois, July 27, 1813.

Parish's friends, the Duane Mansion in Duanesburg and Calverton in Baltimore. With Parish as a patron, he entered a magnificent triumphal arch in the Baltimore Washington Monument competition (Fig. 9) and competed unsuccessfully for the design of the Baltimore Exchange.

Ramée's most ambitious commission in this country was for the Union College in Schenectady in 1813 (Fig. 10). Here he was to design the first example of an entirely new principle in campus layout. With a focal pantheonic library and a cour d'honneur with pavillons and enclosed arcades, Union College astoundingly resembles Jefferson's University of Virginia built in 1828. The picturesque setting of Union provides a fitting backdrop for the classic grouping. The uniformity of style for all buildings and their common orientation toward a central library is believed by some to have been intended to symbolize education according to the laws of reason. Some historians see this architecture parlante as symbolizing the fact that the privilège royal of education was now available to all. Ramée's plan emphatically rejected the monastic self-containment of the English Oxford and Cambridge traditions. This proclamation of "la carrière ouverte aux talents" embodied the ideals of both the French and American revolutions.

The émigrés' designs present no tendency not already found in European architecture. In general, their designs were facile examples of the eighteenth-century tradition. The émigré architects had received their training in the last decades of the eighteenth century and therefore were only fledglings when the revolution swept them to the New World. They generally followed the style of the older revolutionary architects from whom they inherited a predilection for elementary geometry. They reformed planning and were willing to experiment with surface treatment as well as spatial patterns. The changed attitude toward material which characterized late eighteenth-century French architecture foreshadowed twentieth-century attitudes. Practically all of them, Ramée in his landscapes, Mangin and Godefroy in their Gothic designs, exemplified the trend toward the pittoresque.

The pittoresque of French revolutionary thought found its way into the imagination of the American architects who followed. The émigrés also introduced a variety of architectural styles which are found side by side in their designs: Greek, Roman, Tuscan, Egyptian, Italian Renaissance, and modern. Consequently, the revolutionary era is thus related to the development of romanticism and the rise of eclecticism in Ameria.

The contrast between the émigrés' drawings and the others submitted in American competitions yield a most valuable historical commentary of early architectural knowledge. The émigrés established a wholly new standard of design, partly because they were highly trained. Acceptance of both professionalism and contemporary European styles was slow. Yet, despite continual compromises, the emphasis on training, on theory and principles, on the art of design and the science of construction, and on professional duties and conduct became accepted. An equally important contribution of the émigrés was the establishment of a standard of architectural draftsmanship: émigrés ranked as much above the native architects in this respect as in facility of design. The circulation of their drawings and their exhibition in public cannot fail to have been markedly educational for the American builders.

The French architects had the advantage of riding on the great revolutionary wave of pro-French enthusiasm, but the disadvantages of living in a country conscious for the first time of its own nationality. The émigrés thus were active for a few years only and either left or faded into obscurity, leaving a variety of monuments to every shade of French eighteenth-century taste. Although certain monuments of Romantic Classicism and the pittoresque met with much success during the Federal period, their French-born designers were not so fortunate. L'Enfant, Latour, Laclotte, Lafon, and Hallet died in poverty. Godefroy, Mangin, Brunel, and Ramée gave up their struggle and returned to Europe. The fruits of their labors were enjoyed by their American successors.

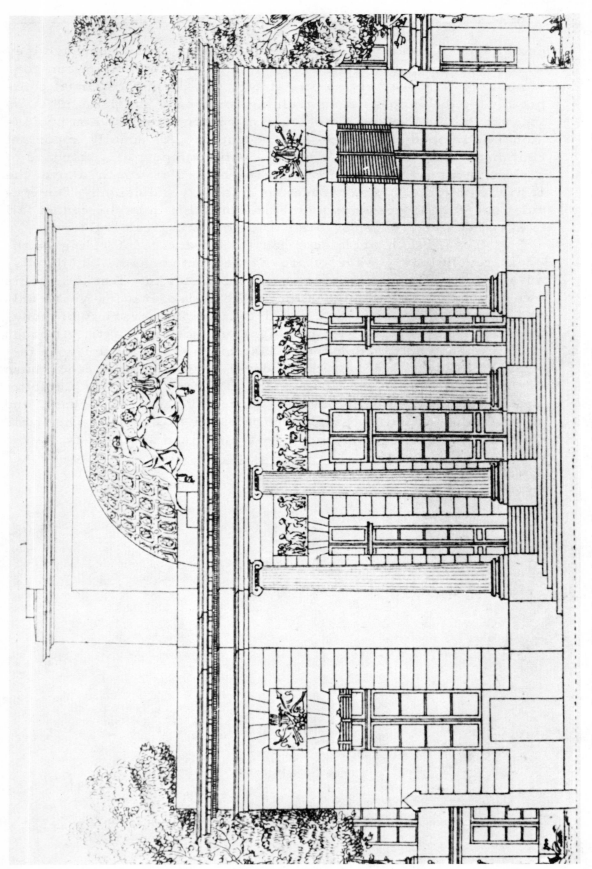

Figure 1. Ledoux. Hôtel Guimard, Paris. From Kraft and Ransonette, *Plans, coupes, élévations de la plus belle maison à Paris*. Photo courtesy of Colonial Williamsburg, Williamsburg, Virginia.

Figure 2. Godefroy. Masonic Hall, Baltimore, Maryland. From map in Peale Museum, Baltimore, Maryland. Photo courtesy of Colonial Williamsburg, Williamsburg, Virginia.

Max. Godefroy Esqr P.A. &: invenit & delin.^t 1815.

Engraved by B. Tanner.

Figure 3. Godefroy. Battle Monument, Baltimore, Maryland. Original in Peale Museum, Baltimore, Maryland. Photo courtesy of Colonial Williamsburg, Williamsburg, Virginia.

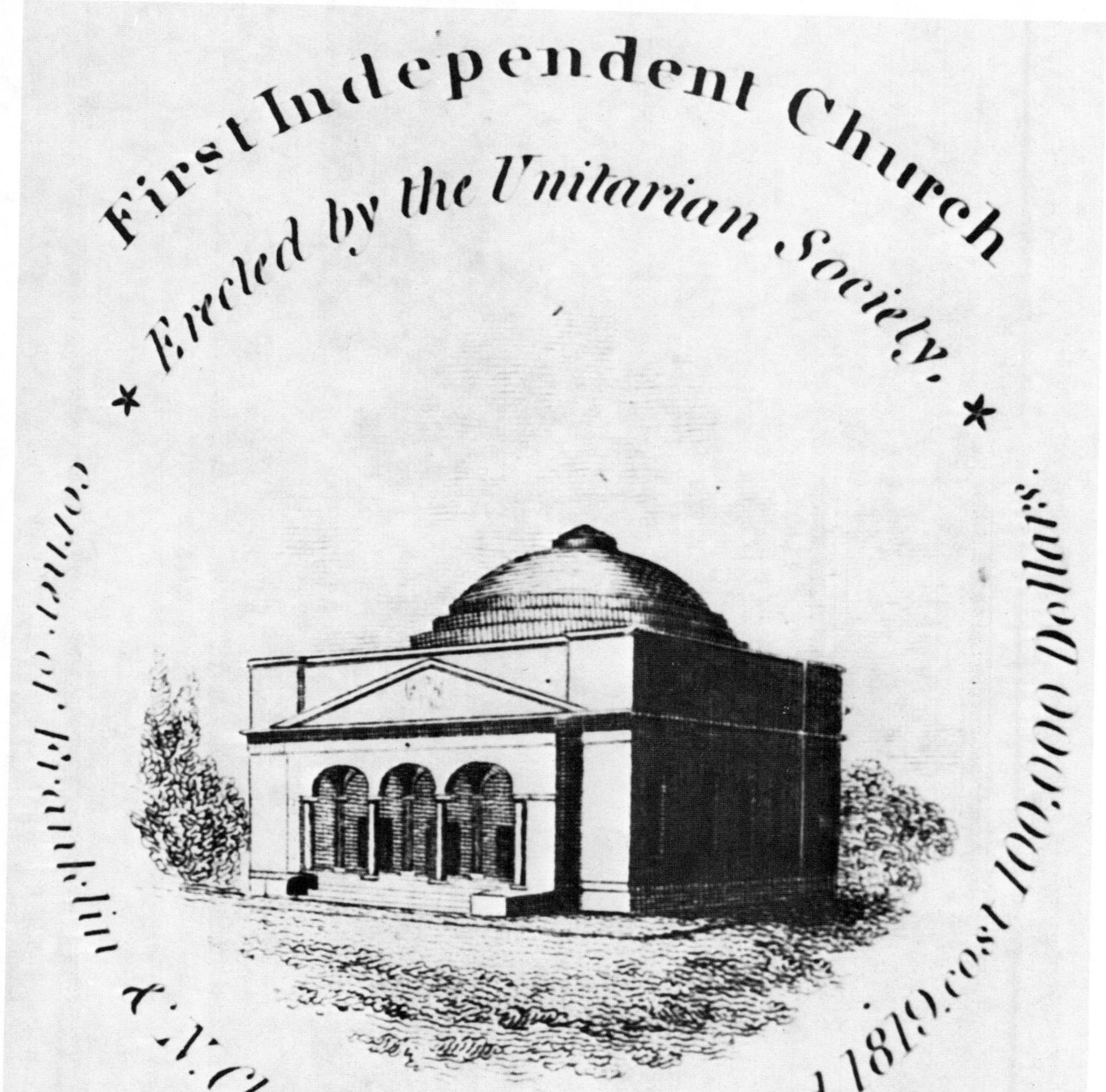
First Independent Church
Erected by the Unitarian Society.
corner of Franklin & N. Charles Streets, dedicated 1819. cost 100,000 Dollars.
M. Godefroy Arch!

Figure 4. Godefroy. First Unitarian Church, Baltimore, Maryland. From map in Peale Museum, Baltimore, Maryland. Photo courtesy of Colonial Williamsburg, Williamsburg, Virginia.

Figure 5. Godefroy. Washington Monument (unsuccessful entry). Original in Peale Museum, Baltimore, Maryland. Photo courtesy of Colonial Williamsburg, Williamsburg, Virginia.

Figure 6. Mangin. New York City Hall. Original in possession of The New York Historical Society. Photo courtesy of Colonial Williamsburg, Williamsburg, Virginia.

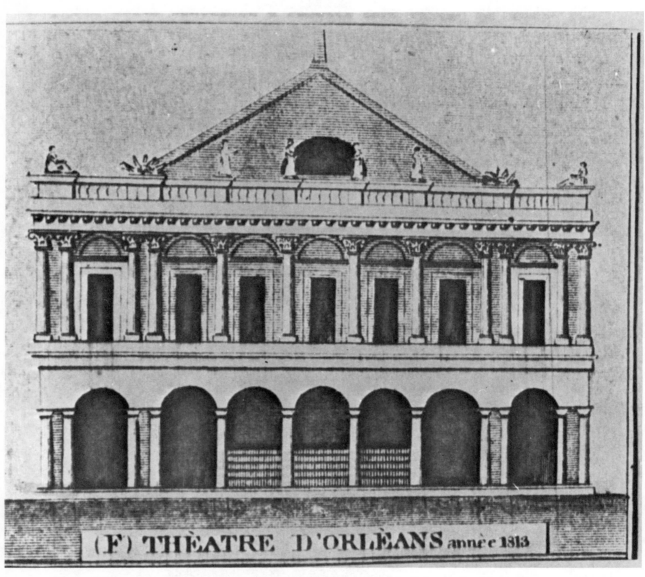

Figure 7. Lacarrière Latour and Laclotte. Orleans Theater, New Orleans, Louisiana. From map in Historic New Orleans Collection. Photo courtesy of Colonial Williamsburg, Williamsburg, Virginia.

Figure 8. Lacarrière Latour and Laclotte. Girod House, New Orleans, Louisiana. HABS photo from the library of Congress. Photo courtesy of Colonial Williamsburg, Williamsburg, Virginia.

Figure 9. Ramée. Project for the Washington Monument. Original in Peale Museum, Baltimore, Maryland. Photo courtesy of Colonial Williamsburg, Williamsburg, Virginia.

Figure 10. Ramée. Plan of Union College. Schenectady, New York. Original in the library of Union College. Photo courtesy of Colonial Williamsburg, Williamsburg, Virginia.

REVOLUTION AND POPULAR IDEOLOGY

George Rudé

My topic is revolution and popular ideology and, more generally, the revolution within the revolution. Every revolution has its popular components. However bourgeois one may say that the English or the American or the French revolutions of the seventeenth and eighteenth centuries were, they had other contenders and were seedbeds for something else besides.

In England in the 1640s there were the leaders of Parliament, the Presbyterians and Independents; but there were also the Levellers and Diggers and lower-class sectaries. In America there were Southern planters, the large merchants and the Sons of Liberty of Boston; but there were also the mechanics, the Jack Tars and White Oaks. In France in 1789 there was the official Third Estate, the bourgeoisie, who wanted an end of privilege and despotism; but there were also the peasants and the peasant revolution of the summer of 1789, and there were the urban "small people" or sans-culottes whose voices were heard with particular insistence in 1793 and 1794.

In the Canadian rebellion in Quebec (and as there are French Canadians present I shall have to tread cautiously), in the Canadian rebellion of 1837-38, Papineau and the middle-class lawyers of Montreal wanted a largely political solution, autonomy for the French-speaking majority, but the habitants wanted something else, such as the end of feudal dues and tithes and the whole seigneurial system. In the French revolutions of 1830 and 1848, a new antithesis developed between classes with the growth of an industrial society. It was no longer the old sans-culottes of the century

143

before, but the real, or self-styled, prolétaires of an emerging
industrial age who were now ranged against an industrial bourgeoisie. In 1830 there was a temporary alliance to throw out
Charles X and to restore the Charter, but once the Trois Glorieuses
were over, the workers continued the struggle for a program of
their own. In 1848 the antithesis was sharper still. The bourgeoisie, disillusioned with the Orleanist monarchy, moved from
reform to republic, but the workers, now organised, in clubs with
their own banners and slogans and leaders, demanded a République
démocratique et sociale, which was not the same as what the
bourgeois were after at all.

In Germany and the Habsburg Empire there was a similar
dual revolution in 1848. In Austria, as in parts of Germany, the
peasants wished to end feudalism and servile dues. In Germany
there were the moderate political aims of the Prussian industrialists of the Rhineland and the professors of the Frankfurt Parliament at one end of the scale; but, on the other, there were the
more far-reaching social and political aims of the Berlin craftsmen and the peasants in Silesia and Baden.

So in every case there was a revolution within the revolution, one closely connected with the other yet distinctive; there
were two sets of protagonists, acting in unison for an immediate
goal, yet whose partnership was unstable, contradictory, and in-
variably came to a parting of the ways. In fact, to the senior
partner the relationship was at best a necessary evil and the junior
partner a Frankenstein monster likely to get out of hand. A
necessary evil, for how else get rid of Charles I or George III of
England or Louis Philippe of France? How else overthrow the
Bastille and feudalism or drive kings from their thrones without
the active involvement of the people in the streets? But how and
when to dissolve the partnership once the job was done would of
course depend on the circumstances at hand. Cromwell executed
the Leveller leaders soon after Charles's execution in April 1649
and he muzzled the less dangerous lower-class sectaries in the
1650s. In America, the middle-class leaders (as described in
Pauline Maier's recent book on the American Revolution), the
Loyal Nine and the Sons of Liberty, appear, after the Stamp Act
riots, to be as much concerned to control the city "mob" as to
settle accounts with George III. In the great French Revolution,
owing both to pressure from below and to the succession of intractable problems facing the bourgeoisie, the partnership was closer
and lasted longer--in fact, from the summer of 1789 to the summer
of 1794.

In 1830 the opposite happened. As I said, the revolution
itself--the Trois Glorieuses of 27 to 29 July--ended quickly with

the proclamation of Louis Philippe; but the "revolution" within the revolution, which had hardly time to develop in July 1830, was carried far beyond this point. In France, again, in 1848 the partners of February fought it out to a bloody conclusion on the barricades in June. In Germany the bourgeoisie was not prepared to take any chances at all, and it seems likely that the Frankfurt parliamentarians surrendered to Frederick William IV and the princes as easily as they did because they were afraid of stirring up the peasants and urban workers any more than they had done already.

A word of caution here. We sometimes assume that "people" in revolutions mean the people as a whole. Yet even in the case of such dramatic and cataclysmic revolutions as the French, the Russian, and the Chinese, there was never a challenge from the population as a whole. In the English revolution the peasants played hardly any part at all. (Those who did, the so-called Clubmen, were willing to enlist their services on either side, and the role of the servants, the wage earners was negligible compared to that of the independent craftsmen and yeomen.)

In America the negroes on the plantations had hardly begun to give voice to their own claims in the revolution of the 1770s; this came later. In the French Revolution the main shock troops and lower class challengers were the peasants and the urban sans-culottes, but by no means all of them and some conspicuously more so than others. In the countryside the vagrants and poorest villagers played a comparatively minor role even in food riots; and, in spite of the prominence accorded to some of these by Richard Cobb in a recent book, their activities were a nuisance to the new authorities, but were of little significance to the course and conduct of the Revolution itself. In the cities similarly the poorest workers and the large manufactories workers played little part in events. This last point is perhaps of some interest, for in the first French revolution you have the apparent paradox that the larger the business undertaking, the less likely were the workers employed in it to play an active revolutionary role. For at this time, as Jaurès noted in his Histoire socialiste three-quarters of a century ago, the main industrial base for revolution lay in the small workshop and not in the large manufactory that had recently come into being. Still less impressive was the part played by the submerged 20 percent or so of the population, the gens sans aveu, the very poor, the people on poor relief in the hôpitaux or ateliers de charité. Relatively untouched by the Revolution, they played next to no part in the events, and their condition remained as wretched after as it had been before. And this was by no means peculiar to France: those whom the Englishman Daniel Defoe called the "miserable" class and whom he distinguished from both the "working trades" and "the poor" played no significant part in any of the revolutions of which I am speaking.

Now, in the revolutions of 1830 and 1848, you have, as I said, a shift from the sans-culottes to the wage earners and prolétaires; so that you find mécaniciens, engineers and railway workers actively engaged, particularly in the Paris "days" of June 1848. Yet these are not the lumpen-proletarians or "nomads" of whom Louis Chevalier writes so eloquently in his Laboring and Dangerous Classes and who, he suggests, played a large part in the riots and revolutions of nineteenth-century Paris. I do not believe that this was the case and it may appear to be another paradox that research has tended to show that the shock troops of revolution, in the nineteenth as in the eighteenth century, were drawn from a stable rather than from an unstable and footloose population. And I suspect that, in spite of what Franz Fanon wrote about the revolutionary potentialities of the African bidon-ville, further enquiry will show the same to be true of the twentieth century as well.

Now I come to the role of ideology. Corresponding to the revolution within the revolution there must be some form of ideology. Every revolution--whether "from above" or "from below"-- needs an ideology or Weltanschauung to give some degree of unity and coherence to an otherwise diversified movement. The nucleus of a political ideology may be formed by the structured program of a mass political party, but this had hardly begun to happen during the period--the "pre-industrial" period--of which I speak. Or it may be formed by a looser set of political concepts, Leitmotifs or what the French call idées-force, accompanied by a few simply stated political aims which acquire a greater degree of precision and sophistication as the revolution goes on. And, broadly speaking, this was so in the centuries in question.

Thus, in the English Revolution, the prevailing ideology was compounded of both theological and political concepts, but there was no clearly formulated body of political ideas. Christopher Hill, among others, has shown that this ideology, unlike that of several later revolutions, tended to be backward rather than forward looking in the sense that it was rooted in traditional beliefs rather than reaching out for something new. It contains such concepts as the Rule of the Elect and the Puritan Ethic, crossed with others like the Freedom and Privilege of Parliament which is constantly asserted against Divine Right and the Tyranny of Kings--a combination of ideas that derive on the one hand from the Protestant Reformation and, on the other, from the English Common Law and Magna Carta. Now, some of this ideological mixture was in-

herited by Americans in preparing for their own revolution over a
century later, but their dominant ideology was far more secular,
and the mixture was by no means the same as before. A study of
Bernard Bailyn's work on the intellectual origins of the American
Revolution will reveal the great influence of the ideas of Locke,
Milton and Shaftesbury in England and from what have been called
the eighteenth-century Commonwealth, influences which certainly
appear in the Declaration of Independence of 1776. In the French
Revolution there is a similar ideological purpose served by the
writers of the Enlightenment--Montesquieu, Rousseau and the
Encyclopedists--which are given political expression in the Declaration of the Rights of Man in its varying formulations between
1789 and 1795. And, basically, these same principles, as formulated in 1789 or in 1793, reappear in a new guise in the later French
revolutions of 1830 and 1848.

Now this dominant revolutionary ideology is to some extent
the ideology of all, both of leaders and followers, that is of revolutionaries at both ends of the social scale. In England, in the 1640s
and 1650s, the lower-class sectaries based their own thinking,
however wild and "way-out" it might seem, on the common stock
of Protestant and Puritan ideas. In France we find concepts like
le tiers état, la nation, le contrat social and les droits de l'homme
repeated in popular speech, as early as April 1789 in Paris and, as
we learn from Arthur Young's travels round France, somewhat
later in the provinces. Similarly, Bernard Bailyn and Pauline
Maier are no doubt right to insist that American city rioters of the
1760s and 1770s were also concerned with traditional English
"liberties," the "tyranny" of ministers, and the "conspiracy"
widely believed to be subverting "liberties" previously enjoyed by
Americans under the British Crown. In much the same way, Parisian crowds in 1830 identified with the liberals' call for the Charter
and in 1848 with the Provisional Government's proclamation of the
Republic. In 1848 also, crowds in Berlin and Vienna wished to
overthrow the old despotic constitution, and crowds in Naples,
Rome, Milan and Turin identified with liberal-bourgeois demands
to liberalize the constitution and drive their Austrian overlords
from Italian soil.

Thus leaders and followers appeared to act as one, and the
people in the streets and villages adopted the aims, slogans and
ideas of the men at the top. But that was never the whole story,
and as there was always a revolution within the revolution so there
nearly always developed another, supplementary, ideology as well.
For the lower-class challenge, provided the revolution lasted long
enough, was always infused by an ideology of its own. Thus, in the
English Revolution, as Christopher Hill shows in his recent, fas-

cinating, study of <u>The World Turned Upside Down,</u> there was a two-fold development.   On the one hand there was the political, largely secular, program of the Levellers and Diggers; and, on the other, there were the theologically clothed, yet often irreligious and even atheistic, beliefs of the Ranters, the Seekers and others who rejected Hell and Sin and even promoted such thoroughly un-Puritan activities as swearing, drinking and fornication. We do not expect Puritans to fornicate; but these not only did but gloried in it and said that it was going "back to Nature," or as some said, "All comes by Nature" and not by the Bible or by the teachings of the Puritan divines.

        Now, in America, this exploration of revolution "from below" has not yet gone very far. But some work has been done. For example, Jesse Lemisch has challenged the view that the ideology of the crowd was the same as that of its leaders and, in his study of "Jack Tar in the Streets," he argues that the particular grievances of the sailors over impressment and customs officers' exactions gave them ideas on liberty that were not the same as those of their leaders.   And it is because of this that they were able to give a peculiar twist to events such as the Stamp Act riots and the later riots in New York, Boston, Philadelphia and other towns whose outcome was shaped by the ideology, or mentality, of the people in the streets as much as by the wishes of their leaders. Yet, as I say, this type of investigation has not gone far, and a great deal more work requires to be done before it can be said with confidence that the crowd in the American Revolution was a conservative or a radical one. One must not assume that it generally behaved in a radical way just because it did so in the case of "Jack Tar" without looking at a number of other, similar events more closely.   It is true that in France the <u>sans-culottes,</u> the popular shock troops of revolution in Paris and elsewhere, were essentially radical and moved leftwards as the revolution progressed.   But it was not true of people similar to them in other cities in France nor was it true, of course, of the Vendean peasants in their counterrevolutionary movement after 1793.

        The French Revolution has become a natural model for investigations of this kind. There are various reasons for this. Not only were the events in France more dramatic and thorough-going than they were elsewhere, but the French revolutionaries left a multiplicity of records; and these combined with the pioneering studies of Lefebvre and Soboul have made it possible to find out a great deal more about what happened in the villages and streets and in French popular assemblies than we do in the case of the American and English revolutions.

For one thing, we know that in the French Revolution the peasants had their own views about la féodalité, what feudalism meant in the years between 1789 and 1793. And I suppose all historians are agreed that it was essentially the upsurge of the peasants in the early days of 1789 that led to what was called the abolition of feudalism in August of that year. The process was only completed, however, when the peasants won their complete freedom from the remaining feudal taxes, duties, and levies with the Jacobin laws of the summer of 1793.

We also know that, in Paris, the term tiers-état when used by the sans-culottes no longer had the same meaning as that given by the bourgeoisie of the National Assembly. When in the Paris riots of April 1789 the people of the Faubourg Saint-Antoine destroyed the houses of two manufacturers, Réveillon and Henriot, they shouted "Vive le tiers état!" But what did they mean by "tiers état"? Obviously they did not mean the two manufacturers in question, although the men were well-known representatives of the local Third Estate, but people like themselves--workers, craftsmen and sans-culottes. It is one of many examples during the Revolution of the people borrowing slogans and concepts from the bourgeoisie adapting them to their own use, and giving them a meaning of their own. Similarly, words like "liberté" and "égalité" had one meaning for the bourgeoisie and members of the National Assembly and another for the people in the markets and city streets. For the latter "liberty" certainly did not include the right of the merchant to buy and sell as he pleased: the frequency of food riots and the demand for a general control on prices amply bear this out. For them, too, "equality" was not merely a matter of having the right to vote, equal access to jobs, and equal justice but an equal share in the distribution of all social benefits which even Robespierre's amended version of the Declaration of Rights in April 1793 did not envisage. It might also mean a restriction of the rights of property: no one, asserted a Paris Section in September 1793, should own more than one farm, one workshop or one store.

Popular sovereignty, too, came to acquire for the sans-culottes a meaning which their Jacobin leaders and teachers had never intended. As Soboul has shown, the Paris Sections, dominated as they were by the sans-culottes after the summer of 1793, believed in direct democracy; that is, in the "permanence of their assemblies, in the appel nominal, in open voting, in the constant accountability of deputies and, above all, in the people's "sacred right of insurrection" whenever government infringed their rights. It was natural that such views could not commend themselves to even the most advanced of the Jacobin leaders and they led to the inevitable parting of the ways between Jacobins and sans-culottes in the summer of 1794.

The revolution of 1830 was, as we have seen, extremely short-lived so that nothing like this full flowering of a popular ideology could possibly have taken place. But it was also a sort of delayed action bomb, and some of the most interesting and significant events associated with that revolution took place after the revolution itself had come to an end. This was most certainly the case with the "popular" revolution, and there was far more going on in the way of street demonstrations, strikes and popular agitation in 1831 and 1832 than there was in 1830. In fact, almost as soon as the Trois Glorieuses were over, the workers began to turn the word "liberty" (as the sans-culottes had done before them) to their own account, and it was to shouts of "Vive la Liberté" that they began to demand a living wage and the right to work, organize, and even destroy machinery that put them out of work. To the employers and government this was not only disconcerting, but seemed altogether perverse; but, as Edgar Newman of the New Mexico State University has shown in an excellent paper, to the workers it made perfectly good sense.

By the time of the revolution of 1848 this type of popular independence and sophistication had reached a far higher stage. By now many workers had read Buonarroti's Conspiracy of the Equals (first published in Brussels in 1828) as well as the socialist, or near-socialist, writings of Cabet, Fourier, Saint-Simon, Louis Blanc and others. They were already organised in clubs and, as soon as the revolution started (and this was quite different from the sans-culottes' experience in 1789), were ready with their own demands for the right to work, the reorganisation of industry through "social workshops," and a Social and Democratic Republic. But, far from achieving these aims, over 11,000 of them were rounded up and sent to prisons and transportation after fighting on the barricades. Nor was the experience limited to Paris. John Merriman's recent study of "L'Affaire de Limoges" shows us that at Limoges the workers, even before they did so in Paris, took the city over through their sociétés populaires and held it for several days. In both cases, then, the popular challenge ended in failure, but the challenge showed a remarkable degree of independence which, it seems reasonable to suppose, had only been made possible by the emergence of this new type of popular ideology.

Allow me to return briefly to the Lower Canadian rebellion of the 1830s. The habitants' aims went much further than those of Papineau and the lawyers of Montreal; they said they had taken up arms to abolish tithe and destroy the seigneurial system. This is a factor to which, in my view, some French Canadian historians have paid too little attention. It is, of course, true enough that the rebellion (even if we add together the two outbreaks of 1837 and

1838) lasted a very short time and that ideas like these did not have time to circulate widely.   Yet our other examples seem to suggest that such a divergence between the aims of leaders and followers becomes magnified as a revolution develops so that it is perhaps reasonable to suppose that this would also have happened to the aims of the Lower Canadian habitants if their revolution had lasted longer and not been stifled almost at birth.

About this time factor, I believe the following point is of some importance.   There is between one revolution and the next, and between one phase and the next within the same revolution as well, the likelihood that a higher degree of political sophistication may develop. For example, the lower-class French revolutionaries of 1789 were far more politically sophisticated than the English a century and a half before; and there is an even larger gulf separating the sans-culottes of 1793 from their equivalents of 1789.   On the other hand, there may be a substantial setback with the reaction that often follows the end of a revolution; this was notoriously the case in France after 1795 when there was a lull in the popular movement until the end of the 1820s.   Yet the setback in ideological development was certainly not total, and the lower-class revolutionaries of 1830 and 1848 took off at a higher level of political sophistication than their forebears of 1789.

The next question I want to pose is "How does this popular ideology develop?"   In my view (and this is highly contentious and I do not expect you to take what I say about this as authoritative in any sense whatever), in my view, popular ideology is composed of two elements, one of which is superimposed on the other.   On the one hand there is the inherent, intrinsic, mother's-milk type of ideology which you come into the world with or you imbibe so early in your infancy you might have been born with it.   It arises within the direct experience of a class.   On the other hand, there are the derived ideas, such as the political programs or concepts formulated by and borrowed from other social groups: such as the Rights of Man, the sanctity of property, nationalism, the Cult of the Supreme Being, Babouvism, socialism, Marxism and the like. These are all structured systems of ideas which have to be derived and learned; they cannot just automatically filter through, as it were, and come to be in your blood.

I am not suggesting there is a wall between these two.   What I am calling the derived ideas cannot be absorbed and taken in if the ground is not already prepared.   For example, the French revolutionary ideas of 1789 and 1793 penetrated quite easily into Northern Italy, Poland, Naples and the Rhineland, but not across the Pyrenees into Spain, yet Spain is far nearer to France than Poland.   It was history rather than geography that stood in the way.   As I said, in order to assimilate new ideas which can have revolutionary effects, the ground has to be prepared in advance. Moreover, it is one thing for ideas to cross frontiers and find a receptive audience among the people at the top; it is quite another--and a far longer process is involved--for them to circulate among the people at large.

Another point to note is that these derived ideas are quite often an articulation in a more sophisticated form of inherent popular beliefs. Marx, for example, learned a great deal from the struggles and outlook of the early English factory workers and without these could not have written Das Kapital so that this is an instance of the interaction between direct experience and a structured system of ideas each of which serves to stimulate the other. In fact, you get a mixture, or coexistence, of the two--of both what I have called the intrinsic and the derived ideas--in all revolutionary and popular movements, though the proportions naturally vary from case to case. (In the twentieth century, for example, when the slogans and programs of mass political parties have played a part that they have never been able to play before, the mixture has inevitably been somewhat different from the period of which I am speaking.)

Let us look more closely at this problem, and, to start with, at the intrinsic, inherent or antecedent ideas which are often the expression of what Smelser calls "generalised beliefs." For example, there are the traditional rights of the peasant to land, of the small consumer to cheap bread and of the wage earner to a just wage, which are voiced in eighteenth- and early nineteenth-century rural and urban riots both in and out of revolution. In these there is expressed a deep concern for justice, for a just share in property, a just wage, or a just price. A just price for the small consumer is what Edward Thompson is talking about when he writes of "the moral economy of the poor"; and this is also what is involved in the French small consumers' protest known as taxation populaire, or price control by riot.

There is something of this, too, in the notion of the freeborn Englishman, in slogans like "Wilkes and Liberty" and their equivalents in revolutionary America, in the long-held tradition that King Alfred the Saxon was the great upholder of English liberties and that these had been subverted by a "Norman Yoke" fastened on Englishmen's necks by William the Bastard and his French banditti in that year of disaster, 1066. Such notions survived in one form or another well into the 1830s in England and Wales. In America, too, we can perhaps find something of this type of folk culture in the ceremonial of Pope-burning and burning one's enemies in effigy (which, of course, also came from England), not to mention planting trees of liberty; and all of this is no doubt the ceremonial expression of an attachment to community, or Gemeinschaft, whether that community takes the form of the village, the commune, the guild, the compagnonnage, fraternity, conventicle or chapter. In fact, the attachment to community is an extremely important element in the ideology of the poor or menu peuple and its disruption may provoke a violent response of which there is ample evidence in the response of Parisians and French villagers to the events of 1789.

Closely allied to this instinct for justice is the levelling instinct or desire to bridge the gulf between the rich and poor. In the French grain riots of 1775, for example, there was the case of the man arrested for saying to an army officer, "The price of bread is too high for the poor, but it is not too high for people like you." This is the expression of a very elementary class awareness, of rich against poor and not yet of workers against their employers. This awareness had reached a slightly more advanced stage in England, where, in 1780 during the Gordon Riots, a man asked why he helped to pull down a non-Catholic house replied, "Catholic or not, no gentleman should be allowed to live on more than a thousand pounds a year." These, as I say, are expressions of the levelling instinct of the poor, which is not quite yet the language of class against class, but it is certainly not the language of deference--a term, incidentally, that many social historians are freely using at present.

Talking of deference, we have also to note as a part of this popular ideology the attachment to the king as the father and protector of his people, which was particularly strong in Eastern Europe, in Russia and the Habsburg Empire, but also found expression in French peasant rebellions of the seventeenth and eighteenth centuries. Such terms as "Vive le Roi et le pain à deux sous" are frequently heard at this time. It is true that there were exceptions to this popular veneration for monarchy as when Louis XIII was burned in effigy in 1630. But this revulsion was something quite unusual or short-lived, as was the rejoicing over the death of Louis XV in 1774, for as soon as Louis XVI followed him on the throne, he was greeted with enormous enthusiasm and jubilation. It is also well known that French peasants who burned down châteaux and destroyed manorial rolls in the summer of 1789 often claimed to be doing so at the express command of the king. For it was widely believed that the king was bound to protect his people against the innovations and depredations of the landowners and aristocracy who by this time had become Public Enemy No. 1.

In addition, there was the chiliastic belief in a sudden transformation which could lead to a paradise on earth or, possibly, in heaven. As an example of the first, there was the "Great Hope" raised in France by the summoning of the Estates General which, it was fervently believed, would cure the people's ills and wrongs. On the other hand, there was the paradise preached by the Wesleyan Methodists in England, ostensibly confined to heaven but inevitably leaving the door open--whatever John Wesley himself thought about it--to a transformation on earth as well.

Religion could also play the part of a popular cult. In the French Revolution, there was the adoption by the people in the villages and streets of a cult like that of the "Martyrs of Liberty" which Soboul writes about. In this case, religion was taken over and used by the people to glorify the current revolutionary martyrs, Marat and Lepeletier, and many others less well known but closer to the people themselves. Moreover, in countries where Protestant sects proliferated as in England or Germany or America, it was not uncommon for a sect (perhaps an offshoot of the more official Lutheranism, Puritanism or Wesleyanism) to serve as the progenitor of popular protest or rebellion.

Now, as I suggested before, such ideas as these, though they might generate action that led to a radical change, tended during this period to be backward rather than forward-looking and to focus on the restoration of lost rights rather than on the substitution of something new. The real pacemakers in the deliberate promotion of change were not the common people but royal and city officials, enlightened monarchs, capitalists, "improving" landlords or grain merchants, who enclosed fields, built roads, forced up grain prices, thus often disrupting the old communities and upsetting the traditional pattern of life and driving the people onto the defensive and to demand the restoration of the life that they knew. For this reason, it is not uncommon to find the people--the townsmen and peasants--looking for allies among conservative elements, such as old-style aristocrats and country gentry, against "forward-looking" officials and the up-and-coming radical bourgeoisie. Such alliances tend, of course, to be directed against the developing commercial society and the spread of capitalist values. The outbreak of a "bourgeois" revolution (like the French of 1789) may well lead to a change of partners, but this phenomenon may help to explain why the sans-culottes of the French Revolution were both anti-aristocratic and anti-bourgeois at the same time.

I have spent some time on these "inherent" ideas because I believe they are important and have been too long neglected. The "derived" ideas are perhaps more obvious and may be dealt with more briefly. I will not take up time by attempting to make any precise definition, but by such ideas I mean--broadly--the political slogans or ideas or programs that the people learn or derive from other social groups. Of course, in the revolutions of this period there are no ready-made political programs or political parties; at best, they emerge from the revolution rather than help to create it, and this may be a long process as in England after 1640, America after 1775 and France after 1789. But even if there were no structured programs and parties, there were, from the outset, political slogans such as "No taxation without representation," "Vive le tiers état," "Long live the Charter" or "Vive la République démocratique et sociale." These served to crystallise demands and give them a political focus. Admittedly, slogans may be mouthed without any high degree of political sophistication, but they contain the germs of a higher political wisdom, and the emergence of slogans of this kind marks an important stage in the political education of the menu peuple.

Additional to these are the political symbols which may take the form of symbolic terms like Monsieur et Madame Veto, or even Le Boulanger et la Boulangere (depending on the circumstance), for Louix XVI and Marie Antoinette in the early stage of the revolution in France. Other important popular, or near-popular, symbols at this time were the autel de la patrie set up for ceremonial occasions in the Champ de Mars, and the guillotine which, in addition to being an effective instrument for chopping off heads, was also seen as the great leveller which reduced all men to less than life-size. Then there was the day-to-day political vocabulary, or idees-force, which might be used approvingly like citoyen, nation and tiers etat, or be applied to an enemy like aristo, sangsue or accapareur. Such terms, whether used in a negative or a positive sense, played an important role in the political education of the people at large.

At a higher level, there were the more sophisticated manifestos or statements of aims, such as the Declaration of Independence in America and the Declaration of the Rights of Man in France which took various forms as the revolution advanced or receded. More sophisticated still were the succession of constitutions (particularly numerous in France between 1789 and 1799) which the revolutions generated; but these, unlike the manifestos, were not calls to action but intended to formulate and consolidate the gains (or setbacks, according to the interests involved) made at each stage of the revolution.

I want now to return briefly to the time factor to which I made only a passing reference before. As I said, ideas take time to germinate, to take root, and to circulate widely: this is true even in revolutions when everything happens more quickly than in more settled times, and I also said before that some revolutions in this period were so short that an identifiable popular ideology had no time to develop.

I will therefore attempt to illustrate this evolution of a popular ideology from two examples drawn (once more) from the great revolution in France. The last great popular outbreak in France before the events of 1789 was the grain riot of 1775. Now, whether you follow its course in Paris or in the half-dozen provinces to which it spread, you will find not the whisper of anything like popular sovereignty or the Rights of Man, and no sign of an attack on monarchy, on feudal rights, or of any of the particular targets of popular anger that emerged in the summer of 1789. These are essentially riots for bread, grain and flour, and for physical survival. The targets are the large or "middling" farmers and merchants, sometimes the curé and the seigneur, but only if they have stores of grain which they are believed to be hiding or withholding from the market. Thus all grain dealers and accapareurs, whether noble or bourgeois, are put in the same bag. This is important because it shows that there is here no sign of an ideology derived from outside, only a concern for the just price which must be enforced by popular action through the traditional taxation populaire. It was only in early 1789 that these other, "derived," notions began to intrude. Note the difference between that and what happened between 1792 and 1795. Already in 1789 (as I said before) bourgeois-derived notions began to circulate among the poor, but it was not until after 1792 that the small people of Paris began to formulate a set of social and political ideas which, although borrowed in their original form, they could call their own. The peak of the sans-culotte movement was undoubtedly reached towards the end of 1793, but the high point in their political initiative and political sophistication was probably reached after rather than before the fall of Robespierre in the late summer of 1794. For the two uprisings of germinal and prairal of the Year Three (March-May 1795) were the only two popular uprisings of the whole revolution in which one can say that the sans-culottes both took the initiative and saw the action through; and it was they and not the small group of Jacobin deputies still remaining in the Assembly who called the tune. Until then, in their numerous uprisings, the sans-culottes, in spite of their growing independence and sophistication, had always played second fiddle to one or other of the radical groups among the bourgeoisie. If we compare these two stages in the revolution, we can trace both the escalation of popular ideology and the types of activity it helped to promote.

And now a brief word on how and by what means these ideas became assimilated, for in all revolutions it is of some importance to pick out the media whereby the slogans and ideas are handed on. In the English Revolution of the 1640s--if we except, for the moment, the printed tracts and journals which are common to them all--this transmission took place through the pulpit, the army and meetings of the elect. In peasant revolutions, as in France in 1789, villages and market towns naturally assume a place of first importance. In contemporary cities, however, like Paris (where large-scale industry was as yet virtually unknown), it was in the small workshop that the artisan, the independent craftsman and journeyman acquired the slogans and discussed the new revolutionary ideas. In addition, there were the wine shops, markets and baker's shops, all of which served as a forum for debate and often acted as a launching pad for popular agitation and revolt.

This is perhaps obvious enough. What does not always appear to be so obvious is that the message that comes through the channels of transmission is not always the same as the one that goes in. The point is that in every revolution--and at other times, as well--the ideas that are derived and transmitted suffer a sea-change in the process of transmission and assimilation. I already mentioned that the term tiers-état had a meaning for the sans-culottes that was not the same as what it had for the Abbe Sieyès and his colleagues of the National Assembly. In a famous pamphlet, Sieyès asked the question, "What is the Third Estate?" and replied: "The Nation." Well, you may say, he says: "The Nation," so he means that each man has the same rights as any other. However, when it came for Sieyès and the Assembly to decide who was to have the vote, the nation found itself divided in two: the "active" citizens who were given the vote and the poorer or "passive" citizens who were not. Clearly, the Assembly's notion of tiers-état was, for practical purposes at least, not the same as that of the man in the street.

This happened early in the revolution, at a time when the sans-culottes were only beginning to learn the new political vocabulary and to turn it to their own use. By 1793, as I have said often enough already, the whole process of learning and transmission and adaptation of ideas--not to mention the people's own direct experience--had gone a great deal further. It was now no longer a question of half-a-dozen concepts recently acquired, but of an ideology of revolution which, though owing so much to their middle-class teachers, had in the process become virtually the people's own.

A final question is what happens to such ideas in the long run? Does it mean, for instance, that after the defeat of the sans-culottes in the reaction of 1795, all this political experience was lost and it had to start all over again in the next round of revolutions beginning in 1830? No, obviously not. What is certain enough is that the reaction that followed was a very real reaction, real enough to ensure that there should, both during the Napoleonic Empire and the Restoration, be no repetition of the popular experience of 1792 to 1795. But what is also true is that the popular revolutionary tradition, having led an underground existence, survived and reemerged with the same type of ideology, though recast to respond to the changes in society, in the subsequent revolutions in France in 1830 and 1848 and, at a higher level still, in the Paris Commune of 1871.

We then have, in addition to survival of ideas on fraternity and the rights of man, a new set of derived ideas which replace or reinforce or become grafted onto the old principles of 1789 and 1793. The communist-egalitarian ideas of Babeuf, which could not have found a large following among the small-property minded sans-culottes of 1796, were resurrected and found a more receptive audience in the new conditions of a developing industrial society in 1830. For, by this time, the same sort of people had begun to see themselves as prolétaires and no longer (as in 1789 or 1793) as independent craftsmen or journeymen who might still aspire to become masters themselves or own their own shops. But they are not only Babeuf's ideas; they are also those of Saint-Simon, Fourier, Cabet and many others. Thus a new set of derived ideas became superimposed on those of a generation before.

But the recipients of ideas, as I have suggested already, like the ideas themselves, undergo a sea-change. We have new social groups and classes becoming involved, no longer just the old workshop craftsmen, but new industrial workers as industry develops. Even in old cities like Paris where the factory system took a long time to appear small craftsmen were beginning, as I have said before, to call themselves prolétaires so that by 1848 wage earners or proletarians (both real and self-styled) were already acting as purveyors of a popular revolutionary ideology which was by no means the same as that of 1795. And with these developments there came a shift in the balance of the inherent and derived ideas which, I am arguing, were the two main components of popular ideology, with the balance becoming gradually tilted towards the more formal and structured systems and programs of political ideas and the old backward-looking ideology tending to become eclipsed or to take a back place.

But I realize I am now entering a territory of which I have little certain knowledge; so I had better leave it at that.

THE SCIENTIFIC REVOLUTION AND COUNTERREVOLUTION

Bernard G. Harvey

Too often history is taught--at least to me it was--as a chronicle of kings and battles, but never of ideas or of philosophies. Like most of my colleagues in the "hard" sciences, I am an historical illiterate, but nevertheless I welcome this opportunity to talk back to the scientifically illiterate historians at whose feet I sat in a bygone age and in a distant country. They were proud of their illiteracy, my teachers, for knowing no sicence they confused it with technology and therefore concluded that science was concerned with things and not with ideas. But now, in the United States of the 1970s, the problems raised by science translated into technology--atomic warfare, pollution, the energy crisis--need for their resolution a broad vision that includes an understanding of science as well as an historical and philosophical (perhaps a religious) perspective. Scientists get their doctorates and historians their faculty appointments by making tiny contributions to their respective fields. The generalist who knows less quantum mechanics, but more history, than a physicist and more physics, but less history, than a historian is likely to fall between two stools and pass his days assembling Fords or hamburgers.

The theme of our conference is "France and North America: The Revolutionary Experience." The scientific revolution, which is my topic today, did not take place in a short period of time so that most people would call it an evolution in man's knowledge of the universe. However, I prefer a mathematical notation: when the rate of change of human knowledge, dk/dt, exceeds a certain critical rate, it may be defined as revolutionary. Such a rapid change can--and has in the sciences--continue for several centuries, unlike political revolutions, which always seem to produce an immediate counterrevolution so that the rapid change cannot continue. In mathematics, they are called delta functions--infinitely large but persisting for (almost) zero time. The scientific revolution has lasted for three centuries and it is still going on. Some generations have hardly noticed it; others--particularly our own--have seen their lives transformed from conditions something close to the Middle Ages to the rootless industrial society of American suburbia.

Permit me to digress for a moment to illustrate this change. In my childhood I spent many happy weeks in the village of my family, a stable society of farmers, artisans, and gentry. Around the winter fire and oil lamp I remember hearing stories of the mummers--the players of the medieval morality plays--who on cold and starry evenings presented their debased eighteenth-century version of the Christmas story. I remember learning village dialect words that much later turned up in an Anglo-Saxon dictionary. Our toy balloons were pig's bladders; our winter sport was delivering bread to isolated houses over snowy fields and hedgerows. And yet this village was not as stable as it seemed. Its inhabitants now buy bread from the co-op, work in the big city only twelve miles away, have cousins in Australia, Canada, yes and even in California. But just after World War I, the influences of the Roman road nearby, the Elizabethan houses, the eighteenth-century social structure of judge, squire and parson were overwhelming; today it has disappeared under an avalanche of scientific and technological progress which we must understand and control if we are to survive as a sane society.

This scientific revolution, which started in the seventeenth century, long before the American and French political revolution, undoubtedly contributed to the ways of thought that brought about those abrupt changes in political institutions. Early civilizations--Chinese, Egyptian, Greek, Roman and Central and South American--had no science as we now know it; they had many detailed astronomical observations and many beliefs about the history and nature of the universe. I do not say "beliefs" in any derogatory sense, for they undoubtedly satisfied hundreds of generations of intelligent men and supplied them with all the technological support that they needed to lead fruitful lives and to create great civilizations and works of art. But until the modern scientific age, beliefs about nature, often enshrined in myth or religion, were challenged rarely and then only at considerable risk.

Medieval European science was Christianized Aristotle and Ptolemy, with its crystal spheres and the purple Empyrean from which rebellious angels had fallen. Below were Earth and roasting Hell, the medieval equivalent of our twentieth-century prisons. The theories about the structure of the universe were not unsupported by astronomical observations, but much more important, they were incorporated into religious dogma. To this day, students of the Old Testament will persecute--when they can get away with it--teachers of Darwinism. Paul Krüger, prime minister of South Africa during the Boer War, believed that the earth was flat, and many of his compatriots are still notorious for their tenacious adherence to the worst ideas of Western Christendom.

For the last few centuries, it has been difficult to remember that nearly one thousand years of European Christian history passed without an accurate knowledge of the great Greek and Roman classical legacy. Many classical works were known in the west through defective translations from Greek to Arabic to Latin, but in 1453, when Constantinople was taken by the Turks, thousands of classical documents were carried to Italy by fleeing scholars. This date, more than any other, marks the beginning of the new age of restless search and discovery that continues to our day.

Science, then, began to be studied for its own sake, without religious overtones. Rabelais proclaimed that "Physics gave birth to beauty and harmony"; Erasmus referred to "Mother Nature, the ingenious worker"; and François I founded the Collège de France in 1530. But the first great revolutionary surge was the work of one man, Copernicus, in 1512. There is, as far as I know, no detailed and rational explanation for the sudden genesis of those cosmological ideas on someone who was still, in many respects, a medieval man believing in a universe bounded by a finite sphere of stars. The theory that the earth moved around the sun, however, pushed back the distance of that sphere of stars by a factor of 2,000 because the fixed stars do not appear to move relatively to one another as the earth makes its enormous annual journey around the sun and must therefore be a long way from us. Copernicus's ideas spread very slowly--there were no sixteenth-century scientific journals with instant delivery to all parts of the civilized world. Later in the century, though, Giordano Bruno argued for an _infinite_ universe with many worlds, none of them at the center, for of course an infinite universe has no center. He was burned by the Inquisition in 1600 in Rome. In the sixteenth century, coal mining began in France.

Many objections raised against Copernicus's ideas now seem childish to us. It was argued, for instance, if the earth moved, a stone thrown into the air would be left behind. But the heavens themselves conspired to show the doubters that there is no immutability by exhibiting a nova in 1572 and a great new comet in 1577.

The seventeenth century opened with some prophetic words by the English scientist Gilbert: "Science is a new style of philosophizing dedicated not to lettered clowns, grammatists, sophists, spouters, but to you alone, true philosophers, ingenious minds, who not only in books but in things themselves look for knowledge." This was perhaps the opening shot in the war between the sciences and the arts, a war that certainly still raged in my youth. It was an odd sort of war because the scientists rarely felt impelled to shoot back, and feeling sure that they were masters of the situation they were quite immune to the verbal barbs of the "grammatists, sophists and spouters."

In the seventeenth century, the great mathematical language of science was developed. In 1623, Galileo stated that "Nature is written in mathematical language. Knowledge is power of creation," and by creation, he meant experiment. Previously, knowledge had been gained by contemplation and by observation of eternal verities because it was believed that experiments, being contrived and artificial, could neither imitate Nature nor throw any light upon her. The destruction of this belief and the development of the mathematical language were crucial to the unfolding of science as we know it. The seventeenth century saw the development of symbolic algebra, the theory of equations, logarithms (Napier), number theory (Fermat) and of course the elegant structure of the infinitesimal calculus developed by Newton and Leibnitz. Science rapidly adopted the new language, and the theories of Copernicus and Kepler were synthesized by Newton into the grand structure of classical mechanics with which twentieth-century man is almost instinctively familiar, even when he has never heard of Newton's Laws.

Science was not then organized as it is now, for the ancient universities remained firmly enlisted in the ranks of the "sophists and spouters." In fact, in my own university of Oxford, the physical chemistry laboratory remained in a dismal cellar of one of the colleges until 1940 when the university provided an elegant building. (I wish that I could report that the quality of the work thereupon improved.) In the seventeenth century, scientific ideas spread slowly--many scientists were afraid to publish ideas that might be disapproved in Rome. Popular knowledge of the new thoughts was gained only slowly, and science, in contrast with our times, had little impact upon technology. But slowly the modern institutions emerged--The Paris Observatory and The Academie des Sciences created by Louis XIV, the Royal Society and the Greenwich Observatory by Charles II.

Long before science changed men's material lives, it had a revolutionary effect upon their minds. For centuries, the Church had monopolized beliefs about subjects that we now call biology, astronomy or cosmology. Instead of welcoming the new knowledge, it often resisted it from fear that, proved wrong in one matter, dogma would be suspect in all. And thus it happened that the strength of ancient tradition and authority was eroded and the way was opened for rationalists and revolutionaries. Of course, science was not the only beneficiary of the change: the artist too were liberated and nourished by the classical revival. Secular music came into its own: the underground songs of the Carmina Burana could be sung openly. But science increasingly described and explained the universe in which men lead their lives, and put into their minds a method of investigation and reasoning that seemed to be successful wherever it was applied. The great success of the method stems, in fact, from its totally undogmatic approach. With infinite labor, scientists observe and measure nature and then weave webs of theory that attempt to correlate disparate phenomena and to interpret them as the results of the most basic forces known at the time. No sooner is this work completed than the offensive team takes over and with positive joy attempts to show that the beautiful web is full of holes. When a scientist speaks dogmatically or defends his views emotionally, he is being untrue to his science. Afraid to rhapsodize about the beauty of the scientific edifice for fear that his esthetic appreciation will be mistaken for uncritical belief--the first of the deadly sins of science--the scientist earns a reputation as a cold, unpoetic thinker.

In an uncanny way, events seemed to conspire to produce the great scientific and technological explosion of the nineteenth and twentieth centuries. This explosion required the social stability of the great nation states--especially England and France initially--the growth of mercantilism which made raw materials available from all parts of the world and produced profits that the nineteenth century, taking advantage of new financial techniques, invested into the creation of the great urban industries. And so finally science and technology became the twin pillars of late nineteenth-century mechanized society. This indeed was a revolution whose consequences were as great--and perhaps more enduring--than those of the eighteenth-century political upheavals. For the scientific revolution has spread across the world to societies that were unaffected by the American and French revolutions. It has spawned its own Marxist political revolutions whose idealistic purpose is to liberate the industrial worker from the chains recently imposed upon him.

The American Revolution was based upon the promise of political liberty, but the Jeffersonian ideal of a democracy of the educated middle classes hardly survived the demands of plantation and factory for more and more workers. And just as the laboring classes, through the political power of their trades unions, begin to enjoy the fruits of their incredible productivity, industry and science play a grim joke upon them by automating them out of existence.

I am reminded of a short story by an author whose name escapes me. He relates that by the year 2100, all factories were so automated that the workers were given permanent vacation with pay. But they soon became tired of golf and fishing so that the factories were equipped with large windows to allow the workers to watch the machines doing their old jobs. This soon became tedious, however, and the technocrats who ran the country began to worry about a counterrevolution. They therefore had large factories built in which the workers could assemble marvelous complex machines. The purpose of these engines was kept a secret, but the workers were not concerned about the end result of their labor as long as it was well paid. The secret of the technocrats was that the machines each night disassembled themselves, put their parts into the appropriate boxes and returned them to the start of the assembly line. The only difference between that situation and ours is that we are ecologically less sound--our machines rust away so that the parts are hardly worth salvaging.

By the early 1970s, it has become clear that the exponential growth of science-based industry can no longer continue. Even if expansion stopped today in the developed countries, we would soon have a crisis of raw materials as the "backward" countries caught up with us. The great historical era of scientific and industrial growth must surely come to a halt and maybe even reverse itself.

We can visualize a world in which we deliberately slow down while retaining the best science has given us--medical care, for example. But as long as the whole world remembers the techniques of scientific and industrial growth, it is hard to imagine such a static world remaining stable. For somewhere, surely, a nation or group would be certain to try to gain an advantage over its neighbors, and the whole dismal cycle would start over again. Perhaps we, the industrial nations, will become tired and sink into rural oblivion while younger nations arise to repeat our errors.

There are many young people among us who already show symptoms of battle fatigue. They refuse to participate in the scientific-industrial society, preferring a subsistence existence in urban or rural slums. Their philosophies are anti-intellectual and anti-scientific. They do not recognize that science exists apart from technology. How could they: "By their fruits ye shall know them." They adopt the most irrational beliefs and religions they can find, rejecting two millenia of Christian philosophy and finding consolation in astrology, devil worship, or drugs.

While it is hard to imagine that the dropouts from our industrial society could summon the coherence of purpose or indeed the will to become the new revolutionaries, they nevertheless represent the first symptoms of a disease that sooner or later will afflict the whole body politic. It is even harder to imagine the people of the world, or even of a single nation, developing the coherence of purpose and the will to slow down the rate of development adiabatically so that the population and men's minds can adjust smoothly.

Nevertheless, it must be done if we are not to revert to the lives of desert nomads. We need leaders with the qualities of Renaissance men, skilled in history and the law, but understanding the contribution that science can make to the new order. And we need scientists who are historians and philosophers and leaders too so that we can chart a course among the rocks, throwing overboard what is worthless and retaining what we will need when the storm is passed.

If we do not succeed in this great attempt to reorganize our world, we are likely to die in a nuclear holocaust, fighting for the last drop of Arabian oil to fuel our Cadillacs.

———————

THEATRE AND REVOLUTION
(AN IMPROVISED LECTURE)

Mario Fratti

When I was invited to give a lecture on revolution and theatre, I felt I should check the word <u>revolution</u> in the dictionary. Very often we are brainwashed into misunderstanding words--into believing that words have a meaning absolutely different from the real one. For instance, the word <u>Bolshevism</u> immediately suggests fierce Russian soldiers slaughtering innocent women, though <u>Bolshevik</u>, in fact, only means <u>majority</u>. We have forgotten that meaning as we have forgotten that <u>Menshevik</u> means <u>minority</u>. The word <u>revolution</u> in America today suggest Black Panthers brandishing machine guns in Harlem. This is an absurdity. Revolution means something else, something constructive. Roget's <u>Thesaurus</u> gives "turning or change" as synonyms; Webster defines it as "rotation or change," and the <u>American Heritage Dictionary</u> as "orbital motion, turning, or change." The original meaning of <u>revolution</u> is thus basically a moral, constructive desire for change.

Taking the word in that sense, it becomes immediately obvious that for at least 2500 years, theatre has been concerned with revolution. Many valuable and important revolutionary plays have been written since Euripides' <u>Trojan Women</u>, a most revolutionary work in that it is an indictment of war, and every indictment of war is an attack on the establishment, the leader, the general, and the army. Aristophanes wrote biting revolutionary comedies such as <u>Lysistrata</u> in which the women, who are always wiser and more intelligent than men, go on strike, sexually, to remind men that love is more important than war. "Make love, not war," was the message of Aristophanes, just as revolutionary today as it was in the fourth century before Christ.

It is interesting to note in passing that free theatre, revolutionary theatre, important theatre, exists only in democratic societies such as the Athens in which Aristophanes lived. Greece today is no longer democratic, and thus Aristophanes is outlawed by the present Greek government. That totalitarian governments fear free theatre was evident two hundred years after Aristophanes condemned war in Lysistrata when Cornelius Nevius, a Roman, wrote the first Latin play. Nevius, a man with a dream, attacked the Roman military establishment and was immediately imprisoned and exiled. In Greece, revolutionary writers and theatre were allowed; in Rome they were not. Still today Latin countries such as Italy, Spain, Portugal, or South America, do not allow good, solid, moral theatre, for their governments fear constructive, revolutionary theatre.

Remembering that revolution means recognition of the need for change, we can go through the history of the drama and find that good playwrights have usually been, in one way or another, revolutionaries. Ariosto in his Negromante, for instance, attacks hypocritical behavior as does Aretino in The Hypocrit. Those plays are obviously revolutionary since they strip off the masks that most people wear, and the response to revolutionary plays has often been censorship.

The existence of censorship, in fact, led the Italians to devise a most revolutionary form of theatre, the Commedia dell' Arte. Commedia dell'Arte may be defined in many ways, but I like to think of it as emerging from the Machiavellian aspects of the Italian character. Italians, who have had to struggle to survive, invented a new type of theatre to evade the censors. Still today in some countries a playwright must submit his script to the censor who might mutilate the play. To avoid this danger, Italians decided to work ad lib. The actors were given certain characters to play and, according to the feeling of the audience whose faces they studied, improvised one type of play or another.

Recently I was strolling around San Francisco where a mime theatre was improvising Commedia dell'Arte. Having noticed an Arlechino which reminded me of my Venice, I stayed as a large crowd gathered. It was a surprising and beautiful experience. All of a sudden, someone in the troupe gave a signal-- when they felt that the audience was listening--and the actors immediately changed the subject. It was fun to see fathers panicking and trying to pull the children away. They had been tricked into that square by Commedia dell'Arte. They expected entertainment and when they were given something meaningful, they just ran away. It is interesting to note, by the way, that in 1680, Commedia dell'Arte was legally forbidden in Italy, and actors could be arrested for improvising. A theatre so completely untrammeled was a menace to an authoritarian regime.

Many classic playwrights were basically revolutionary playwrights whose plays clamored for justice and change. Ruzzante, for example, advocated change as he portrayed poor men as victims of the army and wrote brilliant plays which are being rediscovered now. Lope de Vega's Fuente Ovejuna is also a revolutionary play in which a crime has been committed. The authorities want to find the criminal, but the citizens answer: "We are the criminals, we committed the crime," as they unite against injustice in a beautiful play performed rather frequently of late even in New York. Voltaire also wrote an interesting revolutionary play Mahomet in which he preaches religious tolerance. Friedrich Schiller's Die Räuber, written when he was young, is a romantic drama about the young generation who cannot stand injustice and tries to rebel. Friedrich Hebbel's Maria Magdalena, the first working-class play, presents an innocent protagonist driven to suicide by a society which makes her a prisoner.

The need for a theatre was acknowledged in Italy in the middle of the nineteenth century when the government decided to create a real theatre, a real company, which produced about 600 plays. But in 1855, Cavour, a prime minister praised in so many textbooks, realized that this theatre was dangerous and terminated the subsidies immediately. His action led to the suicide of Bon, a most interesting actor and playwright in an age of many committed actors like Gustav Modena, for instance, who was condemned to death for taking an active part in the Italian movement for freedom.

Today, what do we call revolutionary? What kind of theatre could be considered revolutionary? What kind of theatre can teach the young, can illuminate? After World War I and the Russian Revolution of 1917, a new awareness developed, new problems were faced, and a new type of theatre appeared, one tolerated only in free societies. From 1917 to 1937, the only two free societies were the American and the Soviet, and a fantastic revival of the arts took place both in the Soviet Union and in America. Beautiful plays were written in the Soviet Union, plays which really should be translated here. The playwrights faced all possible subjects-- unemployment, prostitution, bureaucracy, freedom, fear of the state--with absolute freedom. Unfortunately, as you know, in 1937, Stalin became mad, obsessed with the idea of being surrounded by capitalistic plots. Persecution began and art declined.

It is important to remember the theatre may be a weapon and may be used as such by governments. For instance, the Fascists in Italy decided that the theatre could be a useful weapon and began writing plays. Even Mussolini wrote a play in which, of course, he tried to prove the superiority of the Roman race, a real fascist point of view. The play was obviously a failure; it did not work. When a government tries to use the theatre as a weapon, their plays do not work because they cannot be revolutionary. The establishment, by nature, cannot advocate change. Government-controlled theatre advocates only acceptance, blind acceptance.

Fortunately, there is another free society, America, in which the theatre is flourishing beautifully. Besides the writers everybody knows, the classics--Elmer Rice, Clifford Odets, Lillian Hellman, and Arthur Miller--there is a generation of playwrights who began writing after 1945, and who are saying important things in the theatre.

What have the key issues been in revolutionary theatre from 1945 to today? What pitfalls must we try to avoid? The most dangerous pitfall today, I believe, is the cliché. We are surrounded by clichés. The playwright must dig into the conscience of men and eliminate the masks they wear continuously. All of us, brainwashed into a strange, grotesque, false behavior, wear masks. The playwright who guessed this, and wrote some revolutionary masterpieces about it, is Luigi Pirandello whose plays are collected under the title Naked Masks.

Pirandello discovered that in modern society, a Latin society especially, men wear masks in order to survive. Yesterday his Henry IV opened in New York and it is one of the best plays ever written. The play, composed in Italy in 1922, was staged in America in 1924 and failed. It was ahead of its time and the main actor was Arnold Korf, a man with a strong German accent. The critics misunderstood the play. It was, therefore, a failure. Fortunately, Rex Harrison is reviving this important revolutionary play. It concerns a man who has been rejected by a woman. He has not been trained to accept defeat and rejection and therefore cannot cope with the situation. He pretends he is insane and for twenty years isolates himself, pretending to be in another world and waiting for an excuse to come out. When the daughter of his fiancee appears, tragedy explodes.

Bertolt Brecht is another revolutionary playwright. Persecuted in his country, Brecht came to America where he did not succeed. He went back to Germany where his plays finally became recognized for their special message. One of his greatest plays, Mother Courage, is a masterpiece, basically because of the character of the mother who thinks that war may be useful. How many among us believe that war may bring advantages, war may bring novelty, may bring money, may bring wealth? The protagonist of the play thinks so, as do many of us. What makes the play beautiful is that because of war her world crumbles around her and she loses absolutely everything. The protagonist is not an aware human trying to teach the audience a lesson. She is an unaware character who, by making mistakes, gives lessons to an audience. The moral of this is: "never be didactic!" Some of Brecht's plays fail because sometimes he uses a didactic approach. Another one of his plays, The Good Woman of Setzuan, has an interesting Pirandellian theme, the wearing of masks. The protagonist must pretend that she has a double personality--a good one and a bad one because if she were only good, others would take advantage of her and would destroy her. The point of the play is that we unfortunately must sometimes use two different approaches to a problem.

Besides Brecht, there were some sparks of hope in the Soviet theatre. Pagodin wrote some interesting plays including one, The Kremlin Chimes, which treats the problem of an engineer who cannot accept the new society and instead of being part of it, fights against it. It was a courageous play. So was The Aristocrats.

Now, today in America, are there any good playwrights, asking for change, fighting for change? America, as a matter of fact, has the best playwrights, because Americans have a very special tolerance. For instance, a few years ago, Barbara Garson wrote a play, MacBird!, in which she absurdly accused President Johnson of having murdered President Kennedy. Any other country in the world would have forbidden such a play, but here it was allowed. It is smart to have a free flow of ideas. The free exchange of ideas creates a climate in which good playwrights can flourish.

Who are those playwrights? In Europe, if you ask about American theatre they will tell you that the two greatest playwrights are Arthur Miller and Barrie Stavis. In America everyone knows Miller but hardly anyone has heard of Barrie Stavis. Yet he is an important, a careful playwright who writes only one play every five years. He has written some very important plays, Lamp at Midnight, which is the life of Galileo, Harper's Ferry, The Man Who Never Died, and Coat of Many Colors. He is not well known because he unfortunately writes plays with huge casts. The American theatre is, as you know, a commercial enterprise, in which the producer looks for a small cast and an entertaining script so that he can save money and make money. Barrie Stavis, therefore, is not staged. He is a victim, in a way, of the establishment. He is beginning to be staged more in universities, and that is good because here are to be found the future actors and the future directors.

Besides the established playwrights, are there any promising young ones? Unfortunately, there are none among the whites. White playwrights have some kind of hang-up and often write avantgarde plays influenced by Ionesco or Beckett. Under these influences, they do not know what they want to say or where they want to go, and the white theatre is consequently rather disappointing. But there is a most interesting phenomena in New York--the black theatre.

It is a unique phenomena which should be carefully studied. If there is theatre in America which can really be called revolutionary theatre, it is the black theatre. For one thing, the black playwrights talk to their people in their own language. To educate an audience, one must use its language. The Spanish drama, the French drama, and the Italian drama are all written by professors. The plays are literary, well-written, but disappointing, theatrically. The black theatre uses what is called black English, a form of dialect which both amuses and allows a black audience to identify with the characters. I see all the black plays staged in New York, mostly at the St. Mark's Playhouse and there find one's self among a few silent whites and maybe two hundred blacks. The reaction of that audience is something to behold. The spectators really feel it; they really understand it; they really are aware.

The most interesting of the black playwrights, I think, is Ed Bullins. He writes their language and shows them their own life. Moreover, he has a keen sense of humor, something the blacks appreciate. An audience with a sense of humor is important for a playwright. Italians have no sense of humor. In Italy a playwright who criticizes Italians gets booed. The blacks, on the contrary, accept criticism if it is done with humor. Last year, for instance, Van Peebles had an extraordinary musical produced, Ain't Supposed to Die a Natural Death, the best musical I have seen in the last ten years. It is, to be sure, monstrous in a way. Van Peebles showed the blacks as they are. He showed pimps, prostitutes, thieves, drug addicts. As a black man, of course, he can take liberties because he is talking about himself, his life, his background. But the play was shocking, and some in the black audience were wondering "What is he trying to do? What is he trying to prove?" Finally the old black lady in the play came downstage and confronted the white audience. "You whites have made us into this." The audience reacted violently to this accusation at the end of a powerful play, a play one cannot forget in an hour. That reaction, too, is revolutionary. A play that is enjoyed and forgotten is just a silly evening of entertainment. But a play like The Crucible, which forces one for hours to think about hypocrisy, his acceptance, his passivity, that is a good play, that is revolutionary theatre.

Revolutionary theatre does not necessarily need novel, startling, gimmicky techniques. The Drama Review, the former Tulane Drama Review, tells us that revolutionary theatre is synonymous with guerrilla theatre, groups of students who run about the streets, brandishing fake machine guns and screaming: "We need revolution." That is not theatre; it is a cliché.

A revolutionary idea is something else. Sometimes in New York, pornography is passed off as a defiance of the establishment. To equate pornography and revolutionary theatre is really a dirty trick. Pornography is just cheap commercialism, another attempt to sell tickets. Nudity is not needed to make people think. But it can be useful, sometimes. For instance, a few weeks ago, I was warned that something would happen that night in Washington Square, and something did. A group of people were selling a slave, a beautiful black girl, half naked. An audience gathered, people listened, and men looked with interest. The sale was so realistic that after twenty-five minutes a man asked, "Can I pay with a check?" He signed a check, $300.00, and really thought he had bought the girl. The group even allowed him to touch her wrist; and then of course he realized it had been a play. The group was dramatizing an interesting point: people can be sold and bought in New York. The Village Voice just two or three weeks ago mentioned that children eleven or twelve years old are for sale. Yet it took something like this theatrical performance--the sale of a black slave--to make us aware that such sales do take place.

In this case, guerrilla theatre was useful. And in this case, the nudity was pertinent to the point made. But generally I see no future for revolutionary theatre in this type of guerrilla theatre. After all, who saw that performance? Thirty-five or so unemployed people who happened to pass by. I was the only critic there and that was because somebody had called me. But not only is this type of theatre limited because few people see it, it is limited because it is too direct, too blunt. Revolutionary theatre should be a subliminal effort to change a bourgeois audience.

The composition of the audience is an important factor. Nowadays, who goes to the theatre? With tickets costing about ten or fifteen dollars, the audience is largely made up of the rich, the bourgeois, to whom the playwright must convey a moral message. He must, therefore, make them realize how low we have sunk, how uncommitted, passive, cowardly we have become. Today, we tolerate everything. We accept any crime. We once accused Nazi Germany of accepting any type of crime, but we have learned that it is easy to tolerate crime, to remain passive and uninvolved.

The temptation today is to withdraw in oneself or just not listen, not participate. When I first came to New York I saw a man fall and I went to pick him up. Bystanders immediately stopped me: "Don't do anything or he might sue you." Helping someone who has been wounded can be dangerous and should be avoided. Kitty Genovese, a young woman, was murdered while forty people watched and nobody intervened. The theatre audience today is largely composed of people of that sort: passive, indifferent, apathetic. The playwright must, therefore, write a new type of revolutionary theatre. We do not need nudity or drugs; we need awareness.

How do you create awareness? By standing up, by committing yourself, by living, by being a part of society. Revolutionary playwriting has these qualities. I wrote a play called Che Guevara which I hope is a revolutionary play. In it I celebrate a man who was honest. Che Guevara had won a revolution in Cuba; and instead of settling down to enjoy it, as most successful revolutionaries do, he went to Bolivia to export revolution. It was noble for Che Guevara to go to South America and commit his symbolic suicide. He knew that revolution could not be exported. And I, who share that point of view, want his words, and his failure, to be remembered not only in revolutionary textbooks, but also in the theatre. Something read in a book may be forgotten, but something heard in the theatre will not. In the theatre, we sit with others and something happens; it is a ritual. We are born to live together and to work together. When together we watch a play which dramatizes the fact that revolution cannot be exported, we are also getting, I hope, a constructive message. I want to tell the spectator that it is his duty as a human being to improve his own society. He cannot export his ideology, his way of life, his policemen, his armies, but he can work in his society, save his society, improve his society. That is the duty of every human being.

Because of what it says, I think Che Guevara is revolutionary. I also use what I consider a most interesting gimmick. One dead guerrillero, El Loro, a symbol of eternal life, quotes the best lines of great Americans and great Europeans. He quotes Jack and Robert Kennedy, Malcolm X, Martin Luther King, Rosa Luxembourg, and this gimmick is intended to dramatize the fact that the best men, the moral men who most desire constructive change, often are eliminated. Martin Luther King had a dream and died for it. All of us, white and black, brown and yellow, have a duty to have a dream. Writers, playwrights, poets, if they happen to be a little more aware than other people, if they have the gift of seeing more, must try to communicate this awareness to the audience, for only awareness will save the world.

REVOLUTION AND THE ROMANTIC SENSIBILITY

Gita May

There are of course many definitions of Romanticism, and the topic I selected attempts, albeit tentatively, to link two phenomena: on the one hand Revolution, a social and political occurrence which manifests itself in an unmistakable and violent way, and on the other hand Romanticism, a complex aggregate of psychological, literary and social tendencies.

Historians of ideas and of French literature have long recognized the existence of a Romantic mood which, interestingly enough, co-existed with the more rationalistic and ideological efforts of the writers of the Age of Enlightenment.[1] The terms

---

[1]Cf. Daniel Mornet, Le Sentiment de la nature en France de J.-J. Rousseau à Bernardin de Saint-Pierre (Paris, 1907), Le Romantisme en France au XVIIIe siècle (Paris, 1912) and Les Origines intellectuelles de la Révolution française; 1715-1787 (Paris, 1933); Pierre Trahard, Les Maîtres de la sensibilité française au XVIIIe siècle; 1715-1789 (Paris, 1931-1933), 4 vols. and La Sensibilité révolutionnaire; 1789-1794 (Paris, 1936); André Mongold, Histoire intérieure du préromantisme (Grenoble, 1929), 2 vols., reissued in 1965 by J. Corti, Paris; Arthur M. Wilson, "Sensibility in France in the Eighteenth Century: A Study in Word History," French Quarterly, XIII, 1931, 35-46; Robert Mauzi, L'Idée du bonheur au XVIIIe siècle (Paris, 1960); Jean Fabre, Lumières et Romantisme (Paris, 1963); Gita May, De Jean-Jacques Rousseau à Madame Roland: Essai sur la sensibilité pré-

"preromantic" or "preromanticism" are frequently used as a convenient means of avoiding the confusion with the full-blown Romantic movement of the nineteenth century. Let us note, in this connection, that romantique appears quite late in France as a neologism, and its first use has been traced to Jean-Jacques Rousseau's fifth "Promenade" of the Rêveries du promeneur solitaire (1777).[2]

Eighteenth-century romanticism is generally characterized by a certain affective state, perhaps best conveyed by the vague but richly suggestive French word: sensibilité. To be an homme sensible or a femme sensible in the eighteenth century was to be a feeling, compassionate man or woman. It implied a capacity to feel deeply, to be at once susceptible to aesthetic and ethical values--that is, to appreciate keenly both beauty and goodness. More and more, as the century advanced toward its climax of 1789, it implied as many contemporary texts illustrate,[3] a basic dissatisfaction with the way things were, a growing aptitude to compensate through the powers of one's imagination, for present unhappiness or deprivation. No one better than Rousseau has described the exquisite and ineffable joys that his ever active imagination provided when reality failed to live up to his expectations or when exterior circumstances combined with his own miscalculations, errors in judgment or naivete forced him into untenable situations.[4]

To be sure, sensitive souls did not have to wait for Rousseau to come on the scene to make their presence felt in French letters. As Gustave Lanson pointed out in an important essay on Nivelle de La Chaussée, sensibilité in the sense that the term would be understood in the eighteenth century already made

---

romantique et révolutionnaire (Geneva, 1964); George R. Havens, "Pre-Romanticism in France," L'Esprit créateur, VI, No. 2 (1966), 63-76' Henri Peyre, "Le Romantisme davant les romantiques," in Qu'est-ce que le romantisme? (Paris, 1971), pp. 9-44.

[2]Cf. Alexis François, "Romantique," Annales J.-J. Rousseau, V (1909), 212-230.

[3]For further information on this point, cf. supra, note 1.

[4]For some of the most perceptive comments on Rousseau's psychological problems, cf. Ronald Grimsley, Jean-Jacques Rousseau: A Study in Self-Awareness (Bangor, 1961) and Lester G. Crocker, Jean-Jacques Rousseau; The Quest, 1712-1758 and Jean-Jacques Rousseau; The Prophetic Voice, 1758-1778 (New York, 1968 and 1973).

its appearance during the waning years of the reign of Louis XIV, at the end of the seventeenth century. [5]

Sensibilité, in the sense that the term is understood in eighteenth-century language, signifies not only the capacity to feel, and to feel deeply, but, perhaps more importantly, the ability to translate, to display these emotions in an unmistakable fashion. Hence, the widespread eighteenth-century propensity for ever ready and abundant tears, a clear means of communication if there ever was one. Racine's tragic heroines and Mme de Lafayette's Princess de Clèves, among other seventeenth-century compelling figures, suffer agonizingly, but cling steadfastly to a comportment of reserve and dignity. Their eighteenth-century counterparts, on the other hand, whether they be Prévost's Manon Lescaut, Diderot's Suzanne Simonin, Rousseau's Julie d'Houdetot, or even Voltaire's Mlle de Saint-Yves (the hapless heroine of that uncharacteristically sentimental conte, L'Ingénu), are forever ready to dissolve into oceans of tears.

To be endowed with sensibilité, in the eighteenth century, meant to be born with a superior soul, a tender heart and a virtuous nature. What distinguishes the eighteenth century from the seventeenth and paves the way for the Romantic rehabilitation of the passions at the expense of reason is the pride eighteenth-century men and women, both real and fictional, took in displaying those emotions they deemed socially and morally desirable. This psychological exhibitionism becomes especially noticeable during the decade between 1760 and 1770, in the works of Diderot, Rousseau as well as in the correspondence of Julie de Lespinasse and Mme Roland, among others. Be it mentioned in passing, that this capacity to suffer, to shed torrents of tears, to be openly emotional, was never associated with effeteness. A sharp-minded man like Voltaire and a decidedly forceful thinker like Diderot felt absolutely no compunction in manifesting their emotions unreservedly and in a fashion which, today, would be considered embarrassingly effeminate (even for women).

This trend is already well illustrated in l'abbé Prévost's novels. In Manon Lescaut (1731), he writes in a style which is still quite classical. Yet Des Grieux gives free expression to his stormy passions and, unlike a Racinian victim of love, experiences hardly any guilt in allowing his psyche to be overwhelmingly dominated by his irrational attachment for a woman. As for the same

---

[5]Cf. "La Sensibilité; Nivelle de la Chaussée et la comédie larmoyante," in Gustave Lanson, Essais de méthode de critique et d'histoire littéraire, ed. Henri Peyre (Paris, 1965), pp. 377-384.

author's many-volumed novel, today generally forgotten, Le Philosophe anglais ou Histoire de M. Cleveland (1731-1739), it was read with keen interest and great admiration by Rousseau, Diderot and others. In Cleveland, moreover, readers could find lyrical descriptions of the "natural" life of the Abaquis, those invented Indians of Prévost's imaginary America. The theme of the naturally virtuous and noble savage was to be treated not only by Rousseau and Diderot, but also by Voltaire in his sentimental conte, L'Ingénu. [6]

Scholars have also traced the growing interest in outdoor nature. Already Daniel Mornet delineated the easily recognizable features of this new preoccupation. [7] Formal French gardens were little by little relegated in favor of the casually placed trees, the rocks and grottoes, the winding streams of the "English garden." What is no doubt more significant than these exterior manifestations of a new sensibility is the fact that a new emotion, that of terror, connected with nature began to penetrate the consciousness of writers, theorists and artists. The sentiments and reveries inspired by untamed nature, by its powerful, somber, overwhelming aspects such as mountains, precipices, stormy oceans, gradually made their way into the writings of the major eighteenth-century authors. [8] The hypnotic effect of water, whether it be in the form of the sea, a lake or a thunderous waterfall, was already depicted by Diderot, Rousseau and less famous writers in terms that foreshadow Chateaubriand and Lamartine.

Nature and its variegated manifestations were also reflected by James Thomson in his Seasons (1726-1730), which were

---

[6]For a recent discussion of primitivism in the eighteenth century, cf. Peter Gay, The Enlightenment: An Interpretation, vol. II, The Science of Freedom (New York, 1969), pp. 92-96, 196-197. Also cf. Gilbert Chinard, L'Amérique et le rêve exotique dans la littérature française au XVIIe et au XVIIIe siècle (Paris, 1934) and Arthur O. Lovejoy, "The Supposed Primitivism of Rousseau's Discourse on Inequality," in Essays in the History of Ideas (New York, 1960), pp. 14-37.

[7]Cf. supra, note 1.

[8]Cf. Gita May, "Diderot and Burke: A Study in Aesthetic Affinity," PMLA, LXXV (1960), 527-539. For an excellent treatment of this new esthetic with regard to English writers, cf. Marjorie H. Nicolson, Moutain Gloom and Mountain Glory: The Development of the Aesthetics of the Infinite (New York, 1959).

greatly admired in France and translated by Mme Bontemps and more successfully by Saint-Lambert. [9] Young's Night Thoughts (1742-1744) were translated by Le Tourneur who also adapted Shakespeare for the French public whose interest in the Bard had steadily grown since Voltaire had first introduced him in his Lettres philosophiques, or Lettres anglaises (written in London in 1726 - 1730 and published in France in 1734). And there was also Ossian, which Macpherson successfully foisted upon the credulous public as the work of a third-century Gaelic poet. With its northern landscapes--howling winds, pale moon and dark mists--Ossian was to lead to Mme de Staël's exaltation of northern climes which coincided with imaginative, sensitive and melancholy men and women of the preromantic age. With Bernardin de Saint-Pierre, exotic nature came into its own.

It was the eighteenth century, too, which revealed Shakespeare to France. The timid and prosy French translations by La Place, Le Tourneur and Ducis nevertheless contributed to the growing popularity of the Bard in France and to the gradual discrediting of the classical rules of the unities. [10] Simultaneously, in the field of comedy, less hampered than tragedy by fixed rules and patterns, La Chaussée's sentimental and weepy plays, Diderot's didactic and self-conscious drames, Sedaine's more effective depiction of bourgeois life and values in Le Philosophe sans le savoir (1765) and Beaumarchais' witty and racy comedies, Le Barbier de Séville (1775) and Le Mariage de Figaro (1784) have this in common that they exalt those qualities of intellect, resourcefulness and character that are independent of an individual's station in society.

This brings us to the other aspect of our paper: the preromantic sensibility and the Revolution.

Much has been written about the influence, or non-influence, of the Encyclopedists and Rousseau on the French Revolu-

---

[9]Cf. Paul Van Tieghem, Le Sentiment de la nature dans le préromantisme européen (Paris, 1960).

[10]Cf. Fernand Baldensperger, "Esquisse d'une histoire de Shakespeare in France," in Etudes d'histoire littéraire, 2e série (Paris, 1910); C. A. Haines, Shakespeare in France (London, 1925); George R. Havens, Voltaire and English Critics of Shakespeare (New York, 1944); J. J. Jusserand, Shakespeare en France sous l'ancien régime (Paris, 1898)'; Philippe Van Tieghem, "Shakespeare et le théâtre élizabéthain en France avant le romantisme," in Les Influences étrangères sur la littérature française (Paris, 1961), pp. 113-119.

tion. Daniel Mornet, in a classical, if by now somewhat dated
study, <u>Les Origines intellectuelles de la Révolution française</u>
(Paris, 1933), stressed the impact of Rousseau's famous political
treatise, <u>Le Contrat social</u>, but at the same time minimized the
influence of Rousseau's immensely popular novel, <u>La Nouvelle
Héloïse.</u>[11]

When the Revolution broke out in 1789, the generation that
inherited the philosophical and moral creed of the Encyclopedists
greeted the event with overwhelming enthusiasm. Through reading
and study, and often in open opposition to their immediate environ-
ment, the members of the revolutionary generation had worked out
a concept of life and society that was directly molded by the ideals
of the <u>philosophes</u>: civil equality and religious toleration, the dignity of the individual and his liberation from oppressing institutions
and traditions, the right to earthly happiness and well-being together with the freedom of intellectual investigation. [12] Whether it
be Robespierre or Brissot--who were to confront one another so
bitterly during the revolutionary turmoil, each stemming from
different sectors of French society--they had readily identified with
a set of beliefs that fired the entire Third Estate into action against
the representatives of entrenched privilege. An entire generation,
from Lafayette to Danton, had read the same works, works that
shaped the minds of Desmoulins, Danton, Marat and a score of
other leaders of the Revolution. Sons and daughters of great nobles
and petty bourgeois alike had been imbibing the same spirit and
were all in favor of political innovation. Even some courtiers

---

[11]For a more recent treatment of this problem, cf. Joan
McDonald, <u>Rousseau and the French Revolution</u> (London, 1965).
Mrs. McDonald agrees with Mornet insofar as she establishes a
sharp distinction between what she considers the negligible influence on the French Revolution of Rousseau's political ideas, as
presented principally in <u>Le Contrat social</u>, and the extraordinary
impact on the leaders of the Revolution of a Rousseau myth and
mystique.

[12]In my two studies, <u>De Jean-Jacques Rousseau à Madame
Roland; Essai sur la sensibilité préromantique et révolutionnaire</u>
(Geneva, 1964) and <u>Madame Roland and the Age of Revolution</u> (New
York, 1970), I have focused on one case that is highly illustrative
of the mentality of the early revolutionaries. Madame Roland's
intellectual and emotional evolution is especially instructive in that
she left a voluminous body of writings of a highly personal and
revelatory nature.

were affected by the Enlightenment and viewed reforms with favor because they bore old, deepseated grudges against an absolute monarchy that had stripped them of their ancestral rights. Many members of the highest nobility had lost faith not only in the king but also in the church and therefore welcomed the philosophes' repeated assaults against despotism and fanaticism. Mirabeau, Lafayette, Larochefoucauld-Liancourt, Lally-Tollendal, Clermont-Tonnerre, and, of course, the Duke of Orléans, cousin of Louis XVI, were some of the more striking figures among these forward-looking nobles. And Condorcet himself, one of the last surviving representatives of the Enlightenment and eventually a victim of the Terror, was a marquis.

But if the Revolution did not arise solely among the alienated members of a society that recognized only prerogatives of birth and wealth, it was the younger generation of the bourgeois and the small nobility that felt the kind of solidarity and frustration resulting from firsthand humiliations and the keen awareness of social injustice. The books they avidly read only confirmed their deeply-felt malaise. They were stirred by more than abstract theories and the ideas they adopted reenforced beliefs born from personal experience. Madame Roland would never forget being relegated to the servants' quarters after accepting an invitation to the mansion of a rich fermier général. Neither would she ever fail to mention the fact that, as a young girl, she had witnessed the open condescension with which her beloved grandmother had been treated by a lady of rank. Such painful memories would be recounted in detail in her autobiography, and not even the prospect of the guillotine could efface their bitter sting. [13]

In the final analysis, it was Jean-Jacques Rousseau, more than any other writer or philosophe of the Age of Enlightenment, who threw a blazing light on the hidden causes of the malaise that tormented the young Robespierre, Brissot, Buzot, Madame Roland and others who were to play an active role as revolutionaries. Rousseau renewed their faith in mankind and made them see that their aspirations and resentments were wholly justified. In a language that they readily understood and to which they responded with both their heart and mind he gave eloquent expression to those repressed longings common to a whole class of serious intellectuals who felt hampered by their circumstances and who, on their own, had discovered and become committed to the philosophy of the Enlightenment. It is no mere coincidence that, at approximately the

---

[13]Cf. Mémoires de Madame Roland, ed. Cl. Perroud (Paris, 1905), II, 75.

same time, obscure youths and students who would one day become
famous, were experiencing a similarly decisive revelation. To
Rousseau who, more boldly than any Encyclopedist, beheld and
pointed out the social wrongs masked by intellectual, social and
artistic brilliance, the future leaders of the Revolution turned for
spiritual guidance.

It was Rousseau, more than Montesquieu, Diderot or even
Voltaire, who shaped their moral being and, sometimes unbeknown
to themselves, determined some of their most important acts both
in their private and political lives. To be sure, many of his ideas
they had already encountered in one or another form in the course
of their readings. But he presented these ideas with such compelling eloquence and force that they somehow acquired the conviction that he was addressing himself directly and personally to each
one of them, that he alone had truly perceived their most private
and pressing longings and dreams.

And this is where a direct connection between the preromantic sensibility and revolutionary ideology can be established.

La Nouvelle Héloise, with its brooding romanticism and
sentimental atmosphere, its vivid depiction of passion pitted
against familial and social duty, its idyllic scenes of marriage,
country life, motherhood, and its lengthy digressions on manners
and morals, made an unforgettable impression upon the reading
public of the time. A scholar belonging to the more traditional and
historically minded school of criticism such as Daniel Mornet
found it hard to explain this predilection for a novel--an admittedly
frivolous genre, as it was generally viewed in the eighteenth
century--on the part of a generation for which politics was to become a way of life. More recently, however, La Nouvelle Héloïse
has come into its own, as a total work that functions on many
levels. As Lionel Gossman convincingly demonstrated, a work of
fiction by "one of the greatest political theorists of all time and a
relentless and outspoken social critic and reformer cannot without
some distortion be divorced from social and political reality or
from its author's concern with and reflections on that reality. "[14]

It has also been established by historians of ideas that the
ideology which was predominant in the minds of the early revolutionaries combined the many streams of the Enlightenment movement. And we also know that Rousseau, although not wholly of the
Enlightenment, was nevertheless an inseparable part of it. To be
sure, the course of his life was one of growing estrangement from

---

[14]Cf. "The Worlds of La Nouvelle Héloïse," in Studies on
Voltaire and the Eighteenth Century, XLI, 237.

his fellow philosophes, and the most tragic chapter in his turbulent career was no doubt the change of his friendship with the Encyclopedists, especially with Diderot, into mutual hostility.[15] Peter Gay, in the second volume of his important study of the Enlightenment, made this perspicuous comment on the basic causes for the quarrel that divided Rousseau from his intellectual peers: "They were," he writes, "partly the fault of his style, an instrument much admired in his day, even by his critics, but a sharp knife that could cut in two directions."[16] But it is precisely this vehemence of expression, this emotional rhetoric which, while puzzling and repelling a Voltaire or a Hume, had a powerful, indeed irresistible, appeal for a Robespierre.[17] There was in Rousseau a combination of factors--personality, ideas, style--which made his elders and contemporaries feel uneasy, yet caused his revolutionary disciples to regard him as a prophet, martyr and patron saint.

---

[15]Cf. Jean Fabre, "Deux Frères ennemis: Diderot et Jean-Jacques," in Lumières et Romantisme (Paris, 1963), pp. 19-65.

[16]Peter Gay, The Science of Freedom (New York, 1969), p. 529.

[17]The various and contradictory ways in which this highly inflammatory yet frequently vague and ambiguous rhetoric had upon successive generations of readers are well delineated in Ernst Cassirer, The Question of Jean-Jacques Rousseau, tr. and ed. Peter Gay (New York, 1954). For the impact of Rousseau on the American revolutionaries, cf. Paul Spurlin, Rousseau in America; 1760-1801 (Alabama, 1969).

REVOLUTION, RELIGION, AND MORALS:
CONTINUITY AND CONTEMPORANEITY

John W. Padberg, S. J.

The impact of the French Revolution on religion, especially organized religion as represented by the Catholic Church, was deep. It was almost overwhelming during the Revolution itself and during the reactions to it. Religion played its part again during the nineteenth-century quarrels concerning the forms of government France should assume and the place the heritage of the Revolution should occupy in those governments and during the upheavals that accompanied these quarrels. During the more peaceful and in a way more profound changes of the twentieth century, religious thought and practice were again called into play.

In this presentation--all too short for everything that ought to be done--I shall attempt first, to set religion in France in the context of the Revolution itself and to describe briefly what happened to it both externally and internally; second, to contrast this very briefly with the experience of our own American Revolution, briefly, because the subject is too vast to go into here and because I simply am not an expert in the American scene; third, to pick out several of the subsequent revolutions in France and see how religion fared in them, again with brief references to the North American experience; fourth, to compare and contrast some of the continuities in all of these experiences of religion and revolution and then to make one final suggestion about the characteristic that both must share to interact fruitfully in the future.

The French Revolution and the revolutionary experience were born out of concrete French circumstances at a particular time and place, but they were equally born out of the eighteenth-century concern for the rights of man, for reform of ancient institutions, for the progress of enlightenment versus superstition, for the rule of reason. It must also be said that this rule of reason could and in some instances did harden into a rationalism as dogmatic as any creed, that enlightenment itself became invested with an untouchable character, that new or reformed institutions became as rigid as the old ones, and that the rights of man became curiously circumscribed when it was suggested that they be applied to inequalities inherent in a class society.

The Revolution was also born out of the incipient romanticism of its age. It came partly from notions of return to the simplicity of nature, of the spontaneity of expression, exaltation of feeling, and suspicion of organization which were part of the romantic syndrome. These congeries of attitudes helped the Revolution insofar as they opposed the force of tradition and custom, ancient rights and duties, a hierarchically organized world view as well as religious traditions, teachings, and practices. But when all this has been said about the intellectual and emotional antecedents and circumstances of the Revolution, it is still true that it happened at a particular time and place, and each of its manifestations was modified by that time and place. The Revolution itself underwent a formalization and a systematization, or, in Max Weber's famous terms, a routinization of charisma. And that routinization itself enters into the complexus which makes up the revolutionary experience.

It is said that Malesherbes, Louis XVI's reform minister, advised the king in 1788 to ponder the situation of Charles I of England. "Your position, Sire, is the same as his: the issue is joined between the royal power, as it has been exercised in the past, and the demands of the citizens. Fortunately [distinguishing this from the English experience] religious quarrels are not involved." "Ah," answered the king, "that's right; it is most fortunate, for there won't be the same bitterness."[1] Although Louis and Malesherbes may have been correct at the time, events did not so turn out: religious quarrels did become involved and thus envenomed the Revolution to an extent hard to realize today.

In the France of the eighteenth century, the Church was so woven into the texture of the state that throne and altar were linked inextricably in the minds both of the defenders and of the enemies of the Church. The clergy was the first order in the state; the

---

[1]Cf. John McManners, The French Revolution and the Church (New York, 1969), p. 1.

Church, in its various forms, owned between six and ten percent of the land, and its revenues were great, much of it spent on charity or education. On the other hand, the Crown controlled church patronage; the Gallican Articles supposedly excluded direct interference from Rome. The Church was held to have the role of moral leadership in the nation and enjoyed protection of the state (as well as the sole right to public worship) to make that leadership at least externally effective on its side, the state enjoyed the benevolent regard of the Church towards its institutions. In practical terms this was "an arrangement giving power and prestige to both sides at no cost to either--except to the spiritual mission of the Church."[2]

Despite the philosophes, despite Voltaire's desire to "crush the infamous thing," and despite the anticlerical tendencies among a significant part of the French people, France was still in general a conformist Catholic country with a significantly high level of external religious practice. It is difficult for us to assess either the internal quality of that practice or the degree of religious fervor or conscious, positive allegiance to the Church.

The Revolution changed the situation as it sundered Church from nation. But no one envisioned such a possibility on May 4, 1789, when the deputies to the Estates General, the Archbishop of Paris carrying the Blessed Sacrament, and the king in his coronation mantle, marched in procession to the Church of St. Louis at Versailles. When the National Assembly came into being and started to exercise its powers, the deputies were in the great majority sincere Catholics, and the Assembly declared that it was going to found the new order upon "the sacred basis of religion." Alas, this was not to be.

It is impossible to go into the details of how France divided on the religious question. If there was one single moment at which things began to go wrong, it was the Constituent Assembly's imposition of the oath to the Civil Constitution of the Clergy, November 27, 1790, which ended the unity of the nation and ushered in civil war. The real sticking point, even for those in the Church who wanted to accept the changes, was that the Assembly was acting unilaterally, imposing these changes, and enormous ones at that, without consulting the Church.

From this point on, events went from bad to worse, with the progressive alienation of much of the French clergy, the adamant stand of Rome against the Civil Constitution, the imposition

---

[2]McManners, The French Revolution and the Church, p. 5.

of the oath, the confusion among ordinary lay Catholics, the beginnings of persecution in January 1791, the several decrees against non-juring priests (November 29, 1791; May 26, 1792; August 14, 1792), the origins of the revolutionary religion, the prison massacres of September 1792, the beginning of the Terror, the deliberate attempts at the de-Christianization of France, the Feast of Reason in Notre-Dame in November 1793, and the cult of the Supreme Being in May and June of 1794. With Thermidor and finally with Brumaire, a settlement could be started.

The Directory period is not one noted for its grandeur in any way, and religion and religious life could only hope for some breathing space. Napoleon saw that the revolutionary settlement and the re-knitting of a divided France depended on a settlement with the Church, hence the Concordat. Napoleon was a realist who saw the Church as an institution with power over Frenchmen's minds and hearts and he wanted to turn that power to his service. Many of his remarks are quite illustrative of this attitude, one will suffice as example: "The people must have a religion; this religion must be in the control of the government." He was convinced that inequality of fortune was inevitable in society, and that only religious belief in a future life could make the poor accept their condition. Shades of the revolutionary Marx or of the aristocratic Count de Mole who during the Restoration began an address: "Religion, sublime preserver of the public order!" As Napoleon remarked, "If I ruled a people of Jews, I'd rebuild the Temple of Solomon."[3]

By 1802 the intellectual fashion too was turning back toward Catholicism. From Bonald to Madame de Staël to Rivarol and finally to Chateaubriand and his Génie du Christianisme, there was ample evidence of the conviction that morality needed sentiment, and most assuredly religious sentiment, as its basis. This was not always exactly a return to Catholicism as the one, true religion, but a return to something which would compensate for the radical deficiency of philosophy which, as Rivarol remarked, "cannot speak to the heart. . . . Even if we consider religions as nothing more than organized superstitions, they would still be beneficial to the human race; for in the heart of man there is a religious fibre that nothing can extirpate."[4]

Finally, in the negotiations for the Concordat between Napoleon and Pius VII, a new element entered into the consideration

---

[3]McManners, The French Revolution and the Church, p. 140, 142.

[4]Ibid., 146.

of organized religion's relations to the nineteenth-century revolutions, the greatly increased prestige of the Papacy and the increasing centralization in Rome of decision-making in religious matters. The Gallican church which had once proudly proclaimed its special place and its independence vis-a-vis Rome was not there to negotiate about its own existence; the Roman pontiff alone negotiated terms for the French church.

It would be useful, but far too long an exercise for this presentation, to compare the 1789 revolution in France and its relationship to religion with the 1776 revolution in America and its relationship to religion. For instance, there were established churches here in the colonies, but no one established church as in France. What difference did that make? The revolutionists in America did not think that setting up a Novus Ordo Seclorum, a "new order of the ages" as stated on the obverse of the Great Seal pictured on the back of the dollar bill necessarily meant tearing down the superstition-ridden old order of the ages. Why not? The civil religion of America which Will Herberg has convincingly discussed for the past twenty years and which the sociologist Robert Bellah has perceptively described allows, nay encourages, the traditional religions of Protestantism, Catholicism, Judaism. That civil religion which began with the American Revolution has been encouraged in a directly non-competitive growth over the past two centuries. No counterpart to this compatibility is found in the French revolutionary experience. Civil religion has flourished in the United States in amity with the traditional creeds; in France, a "civil religion" has almost always involved antagonism to the traditional creeds, especially Catholicism.

As Alexis de Tocqueville said perceptively more than a century ago, in France he had always seen the spirit of religion and the spirit of freedom marching in opposite directions. But in America he found them intimately united and reigning together over the same country.

Not only in France was the Church in turmoil, if not in ruins; throughout Europe the old order had been swept away, and religion in its manifold institutional forms was in utter disarray. For example, where there had been several thousand Benedictine houses before the Revolution, only about twenty were still functioning by 1815. The Christian religion in many of its recognizable forms lay in ruins. It is to the credit of its nineteenth-century versions that it rose almost phoenix-like from the ashes of destruction although the resurrection was not as sudden as that of a phoenix.

At the time of the Restoration, there occurred in France a recrudescence of the bitter anticlericalism and antichristianity

which were to characterize much of French nineteenth-century life
and which were to survive the revolutions of that era. The country
was to be divided into the "two Frances" of legend, one which supported the Revolution and all its implications, (supposedly including
a virulent hatred of religion as represented in Christianity and
especially in the Catholic Church), the other rejecting the Revolution and its traditions and embracing the notion of a truly regener-
ated France, firm in its sane traditions (supposedly including a
special place in its life for the Church).

Two interesting examples of the nineteenth-century anticlericalism (in this case especially anti-Jesuitism) will suffice.
One is the refrain from one of the Béranger's songs:

> Hommes noirs, d'où sortez vous?
> Nous sortons de dessous terre,
> Moitié renards, moitié loups,
> Notre règle est un mystère. [5]

The other is a letter from the Jesuit Archives addressed to the
inmates of the Montrouge Novitiate, outside Paris:

> Tremble, satellites of Loyola; your last hour is
> going to sound. Vile rabble, filthy corrupters of
> youth, monsters of treachery, tremble; hypocrites,
> criminals, the colossus of your power is going to
> collapse and it will crush you under the ruins.
> Cursed race, enemies of your fatherland, you will
> perish. Burdened by your crimes, your name will
> be held in abhorence by all future peoples...40,000
> defenders of our liberties have sworn your destruc-
> tion...40 more days and Montrouge will be no
> more!

>   signed: Geoffroy--friend of the Constitution
>   Jouvillier--friend of Liberty
>   Métrouvel--friend of Equality
>   Gordeau--friend of the Republic
>   Tournilly--enemy of Traitors.

The "Friends of Fraternity" are conspicuous by their absence.

---

[5]Cf. Guillaume Bertier de Sauvigny, La Restauration
(Paris, 1955), p. 279.

On the other hand, the conservatively and ardently religious sang stoutly at religious services:

> Vive la France
> Vive le Roi
> Toujours en France
> Les Bourbons et la Foi. [6]

Beginning in 1815, under a cooly skeptical Louis XVIII and an ardently clerical Charles X, there occurred a restoration of the Catholic state and the reconstruction of the Church. Despite the Voltairianism of much of the middle class, a large part of society, especially the upper classes and the country or peasant class, underwent a religious revival.

Nonetheless, throne and altar were so closely linked in reality--and even more so in the popular mind--that when one of them was toppled in the revolution of 1830, the other collapsed also. Perhaps more than any other modern revolution in France the 1830 upheaval directed its fury against the institutional Church. Almost a thousand years of Church records were destroyed when the revolutionaries sacked the archbishop's residence and archives alongside Notre Dame. The attitude of the people is clearly revealed in the remark of a Hungarian diplomat posted in France at the time: "The role of schemers, knaves, scoundrels in the comedies or melodramas are always represented by the Jesuits. Also, the worst insult that you can offer to anyone is to call him a Jesuit." [7] Yet, the anti-religious agitation died down surprisingly fast, and, in what was at first a rather infelicitous set of circumstances, a first attempt was made to reconcile the Church and modern society by men such as Lacordaire, Montalembert, Dupanloup and especially Lamennais who published the journal L'Avenir. Had their movement been successful, it would have meant truly a revolution in the Church. Unfortunately, it failed, partly because of organized religion's lack of understanding of the positive goods produced and propagated by the Revolution. Because of widespread exasperation with the state, the principles and practices of ultramontanism gained an ever-wider support.

A popular pope, the hero of the liberals in his first year, Pius IX ascended the papal throne in 1846. But the Christian romanticism of his early years soon changed with his first experience of the 1848 revolution. After 1848 Catholic authoritarianism

---

[6] Cf. John W. Padberg, S. J., Colleges in Controversy (Cambridge, Massachusetts, 1969), pp. 7, 8.

[7] Comte Rodolphe Apponyi, "Autour de la Revolution de 1830," Revue des Deux Mondes, 71 (October 15, 1912), 798.

won the day, both in the Roman Curia and in the French Church
which increasingly supported the maneuvers of Prince-President
Louis-Napoleon Bonaparte, soon to be Napoleon III. The Church,
in the person of the archbishop of Lyons, blessed liberty trees
with holy water during the 1848 revolution, but by 1851 it was enjoy-
ing a honeymoon with Louis-Napoleon. This close relationship with
the emperor was praised by the right-wing journalist Louis
Veuillot, editor of L'Univers, and opposed by the increasingly
isolated Catholic liberals.

Louis Veuillot had proclaimed in 1858: "Our zeal for the
Empire is one with our zeal for religion."[8] But the involvement of
Napoleon III in the vagaries of the Roman Question from 1858 on
increasingly led the most religious among the French people to
oppose the policies of the Second Empire. The Empire was accom-
modating the temporal power the Papacy had wielded for more
than one thousand years, since the Donation of Pepin in 752.

For its part, the Church hardened its position both in
France and in Rome. This die-hard opposition to the modern
world and to the "pernicious" principles of the Revolution was
symbolized by the 1864 Encyclical Quanta Cura and the Syllabus of
Errors published in the same year. Ultramontanism, which triumphed in both over the principles of 1789, had its ultimate victory
at the Vatican Council of 1869 when papal infallibility was proclaimed as a dogma.

If these moves represented as some thought a revolution
in the internal life of the Church, the final loss of Rome--the last
temporal domain of the Church--was an external change of the first
magnitude. That loss came in 1870 when the French troops which
had protected papal power were withdrawn to participate in the disastrous Franco-Prussian War. Napoleon's defeat went largely un-
mourned by religious Frenchmen, but the Commune found another
reception. In the eyes of the bien-pensant Catholic population, the
Commune appeared a full-scale revolution, a direct attack on religion and morals, symbolized by its supposed excesses, most of all
the murder of the archbishop of Paris and of some innocent priests
held captive. This civil war which was a social war was seen by
some as a war against God and the faith.

It is interesting to compare French religious history from
1815 to 1870, the aftermath of the French Revolution, with the religious history of the United States from 1789 to 1865, in the aftermath of the American Revolution. The various churches of the
erstwhile colonies continued living their own lives, some of them
even for a time remained established even occasionally after the

---

[8]Adrien Dansette, Religious History of Modern France
(New York, 1961), I, 283.

adoption of the First Amendment which prohibited religious establishment by the federal government but not by the states. The religious patterns of the United States did not appreciably change under the new government. Religious tensions appeared with the beginning of massive immigrations, and the presence of numerous Catholics among the immigrants helped to awaken the Know-Nothing movement and the American Protective Association. The Civil War resulted in consequences which might be called revolutionary, but altered little or not at all the fundamental religious picture of the United States despite the separation of some groups into northern and southern branches.

We might ask ourselves the reasons for the relatively small impact that internal strife and change had on religion in the United States in these first six or seven decades of the nineteenth century. American Catholicism was too absorbed in settling its newly arrived members and in setting up the infrastructure of a nationwide parochial life to pay much attention to the potentially damaging implications that Quanta Cura and the Syllabus held for its life in a land of theoretically total religious toleration. One searches in vain for the reaction of American Catholics to these papal moves. There were alarmed Protestant outcries, but less numerous and less strident than might have been expected if the nation had not been undergoing the agonies of the Civil War.

The advent of the Third Republic brought again to the forefront the accommodation the "religion of the French people" to the principles of the French Revolution. It is impossible to detail the religious political crises of the Third Republic and the Church, each of which seemed at the time a revolutionary move or at least a prelude to revolution in the life of the state or the life of the Church.

> To assume anything automatic in the Church's hostility to philosophical and political views differing from its own would be to give an entirely false impression of the religious position in the nineteenth century. From the Revolution onwards, the important question for the Church, creating a deep and lasting division within the Catholic world, was whether to condemn the innovations out of hand or whether to come to terms with them. [9]

---

[9]Dansette, Religious History of Modern France, I, 356.

One problem concerned the return of the monarchy and the firm allegiance it commanded on the part of the Church. The problem presented by rights of religious teaching orders and the existence of independent religious schools was complicated by the problem of educational reform. Finally some of the religious orders were expelled when the teaching profession was extensively secularized, a revolutionary move for a country where for centuries the schools had been controlled by members of religious orders. This move was regarded as a Satanic, Masonic, Republican plot.[10] Yet the Papacy made the unprecedented attempt to effect a ralliement which would have gained the republic the neutrality, if not the support, of the French Church. This ralliement eventually failed, but some liberal French Catholics remained convinced that one could support the Republic and still be a fervent practitioner of the faith.

These men were bolstered in their convictions by the example of the flourishing American Catholic Church. If American Catholic liberalism could work, could not its analogue be successful in France? In June 1892, John Ireland, archbishop of St. Paul, Minnesota, said in Paris that "the Church in America is certainly that of the people....In the United States, we have a great feeling of loyalty towards the Republic."[11] Some members of the French clergy took up enthusiastically a melange of theories and manners called "Americanism." But this "Americanism" which was easily acceptable in the United States, aroused horror among the conservative French who found it unorthodox. A book extolling the doctrine was put on the Index, and Leo XIII expressed to Cardinal Gibbons his criticism of a set of opinions "going under the name of Americanism." The American bishops denied that the criticized opinions were being taught in the United States and agreed with Archbishop Ireland that "Americanism...was unknown in America until the news of its condemnation was cabled from Rome."[12] They and the American Church essentially continued as though nothing had happened.

From 1893 to 1898 a spirit of accommodation developed between the Republic and the "religion of the French," but it was

---

[10]For an interesting account of how some Catholics believed wholeheartedly in the conjunction of Satanism and Freemasonry and in their influence on Republican policies, see Eugen Weber's Satan Franc-maçon (Paris, 1964).

[11]Dansette, Religious History of Modern France, II, 145.

[12]Ibid., II, 148.

shattered by l'affaire, the famous--or infamous--Dreyfus Affair. A group of militant and vocal anti-Dreyfusard Catholics compromised the whole Church, unfortunately the confrontation between their intransigent clericalism and the equally intransigent anticlericalism of the radical Dreyfusards snuffed out the flickering flame of reconciliation between official religion and official republicanism. In the wake of the Dreyfusard's triumph, militantly anticlerical Republicans decided to proceed against the Church. Their first target was the teaching orders which had returned after the 1880 expulsion. In the name of the revolutionary principles of 1789 and for the sake of a strong state, Waldeck-Rousseau decided to limit the religious orders and submit them to the restrictive provisions of the Law of Associations. The law, passed in 1901, was harsher than he had foreseen. When the ardently anticlerical Emile Combes succeeded him, a campaign for the defense of the Republic turned into an openly anti-religious offensive, again in the name of the principles of 1789. The religious orders were finally ousted in 1904, and their schools and property confiscated by the state.

In 1905, the final separation of church and state ended the Napoleonic Concordat which had kept an uneasy peace between the religious establishment and the heirs of the Revolution. It also ended the ancient union of the French Church and the sovereign political power which dated back to the Merovingian era. The separation, the last blow aimed at the ancien régime, put the final seal on the movement of laicisation and secularisation begun in 1789.[13] Ecclesiastical intransigence was epitomized by Pius X's condemnation of the separation and its supporters. Gradually, however, a modus vivendi was once more worked out between church and state.

If the heirs of the spirit of 1789 expected the Church to wither away or religious practice to disappear, they were disappointed. The Church sustained an enormous financial loss, but found itself free, free from the encumbrances of the Concordat, free from the necessity to fit its institutional structure into that of the bureaucracy of the state.

Religious practice continued with remarkable equanimity. Furthermore, from the late 1890s to the First World War saw the development of social Catholicism and Christian Democratic Movement through Marc Sangnier's Le Sillon. A veritable intellectual renaissance began in religious thought, to bring into harmony the

---

[13]Cf. the collection of material in La Séparation de l'Eglise et de d'Etat, ed. by Jean-Marie Meyer (Paris, 1966).

unchanging demands of religious faith and the contemporary developments in knowledge as well as the intellectual problems resulting from the nineteenth-century intellectual revolution. "Modernism" describes the whole range of efforts to bring the church into harmony with contemporary society. It was more particularly a movement of religious intellectuals, rather heterogeneous and never as coherent as its opponents claimed, to interpret religious teaching and religious dogma in the light of current modern findings in philosophy, history, linguistic, and biblical exegesis. Tragedy struck the movement when Pius X condemned it, but its long-range fruits did much to move the French clergy and some of the laity away from the watertight traditionalist compartment in which they had existed. Traumatic is the only word which can describe both the movement and the countermovement it provoked among traditionalists, but, for all the pain and suffering, it began to move French religious thought into the twentieth century and into the mainstream of change brought about by the intellectual revolutions of the nineteenth century.

In the United States, from the Civil War to the First World War, religious questions indeed did agitate certain parts of the population, but as a whole organized Protestantism saw the destiny of the country as the fulfillment of God's promises to this new nation while organized Catholicism had all it could do simply building the churches, schools, and charitable institutions necessary for the ever-swelling tide of Catholic immigrants. Neither religious group experienced to the same degree as in France, either in theory or in practice, the turmoil of church-state quarrels, the question of the form of government flowing from their interpretation of the political revolution which had established the country, or the intellectual upheavals brought on by the new findings of historians, philosophers, and scriptural scholars.

World War I in France brought about the Union Sacrée and a notable improvement in the political-religious climate which continued through the interwar years. There was almost a second ralliement, despite the objections of some of the French hierarchy and despite the reversion to a rigid anti-church attitude during the Herriot ministry of the 1920s. Most interesting of all was the growth of left-wing Catholicism composed of people who took increasingly serious the social teachings of the church. In the light of these social teachings rather than of the anti-religious implications of the so-called revolutionary principles, they wanted to form a political union of left-wing Catholics and organize a popular democratic party of Catholic origin.

There was, on the other side of the ledger, and had been since earlier in the century, the Action Française, fiercely dedicated to the extirpation of the fruits of the Revolution of 1789, to the end of the Republican regime, and to an "integral nationalism" which, based on a strong state and a supportive religion, would return France to its ancient grandeur. Pius XI condemned the Action Française in 1926, despite the reservations of many French bishops. At almost the opposite end of the spectrum was the review Esprit, soon to be founded by Emmanuel Mounier and destined to have a profound liberal influence on French religious thought through and beyond the Second World War.

It has often been asked whether France was dechristianized under the Third Republic as the legitimate inheritor of the revolutionary tradition and as the logical outcome of an acceptance of the Revolution. That question cannot be answered in a simple way. Any answer must include the changing relationships between church and state, the regulations and laws on the involvement with education, the attitudes of the various political parties, the practices of the French people, and the currents of religious thought and action.

Whatever the case may be, and various studies have been done on the question, the turbulent years immediately before World War II embittered both opponents and partisans of the Popular Front. To the ardently religious, the Front appeared as the harbinger of a new revolution; to the Socialists and Communists it was at last the culmination of the implications of all the previous revolutions. When the Vichy government came to power after the calamity of 1940, it, too, was hailed as the inaugurator of its own national revolution, and at least some of its partisans saw it as such. To some of them, the Vichy regime vindicated the true France against the partisans of the Revolution.

The troubled Fourth Republic was born from the Allied victory in World War II and took its early steps in the atmosphere of the Cold War. It was a time when the inherently conservative French equated revolution and communist takeover while the poor and dispossessed equated such a takeover with the fulfillment of the political and social promises of the French Revolution.

De Gaulle's advent to power, after the failure of the Fourth Republic and the emergence of the Fifth, was greeted by some as an example of the recurrent need of the French for a strongman government. But underneath the stability which de Gaulle brought to the government were forces making for real change in France. The economic stagnation of the immediate postwar years was over; the material expectations of the French were rising; the children of the past war baby boom now university students. The French student population shared in the "arribismo," the desire to rise, to become someone, to take one's destiny in one's own hands. Much of this ferment erupted in "les événements" of May 1968, a protest against what was seen, rightly or not, as a way of life characterized by routine, hypocrisy, misdirection or priorities, joylessness, and the overwhelming power of the "system." Without being aware of it, the "événements" were rooted also in the Enlightenment belief in the inherent perfectibility of man and in the view held by Rousseau and the Romantics of the natural goodness of man corrupted by society and social structures. The American counterparts of the French students shared the same philosophical assumptions. As one of the graffiti on the walls of the Censier branch of the University of Paris put it, "Ici, on spontane."[14]

Another of the graffiti, this time in the grand amphitheater of the Sorbonne, asked "Savez-vous qu'il existait encore des chrétiens?"[15] But these Christians, these adherents of religion, had themselves been seeing and perhaps undergoing a revolution in the Church since Vatican II. They were not necessarily aware of the theological bases for the changes, but if they were practicing Christians, they could under no circumstances be unaware of the changes. Again, one of the graffiti of the May days could apply to the members of the Church as the liberating messages of Vatican II and the postconciliar actions of the Church began to make an impact. "Etre libre en 1968, c'est participer."[16] Participation was everywhere demanded.

For more than a century and a half in France, religion, especially in its organized form, had engaged in a running battle with the Revolution and with the regimes which had tried to legitimize their rule in its name. In the United States, the civil religion started after the Revolution had grown through the years in amity with institutional Catholicism, Protestantism, and Judaism. Will Herberg has explained that this civil religion is not a syncretistic system composed of beliefs found in all or a few religions, but an organic structure of ideals, values, and beliefs that constitutes a faith common to Americans as Americans. Genuinely operative in their lives, it is a faith that markedly influences, and is influenced by, the professed religions of America. In France a mutual suspicion, fear, hatred has characterized relations between the state and organized religion. In the United States, an all too facile and unexamined accommodation allowed church and state to

---

[14]Julien Besançon, Les Murs ont la Parole: Journal Mural (Paris, 1968), p. 13.

[15]Ibid., p. 16.

[16]Ibid., p. 27.

flourish. That accommodation may be one of our problems: in France, the partisans of revolution have claimed the role of prophet against the existent society, but in America the sincerely religious have not always been eager to take on that role.

In both the French and North American experiences of revolution and religion there have been threads of continuity. If, in our contemporary world, either or both revolution and religion are to interact, if they are to call people to rise to the best in themselves, to hope and plan for a future which each sees as the fulfillment of man's potentialities, then, more than ever in the past, both revolution and religion will have to heed another one of the May 1968 graffiti--this one from the Ecole des Sciences Politiques in Paris. This one says simply to its readers, including the adherents of religion and/or revolution who wonder about the future of their interaction as they strive to learn from their pasts: "L' imagination prend le pouvoir."[17]

---

[17]Besançon, Les Murs ont la Parole: Journal Mural, 146-147.

THE EXPLOSION OF 1968:
REVOLUTION OR PSYCHODRAMA?

Henry Ehrmann

I am very glad to see that obviously the topic I have been asked to discuss still packs them in. At least in southwestern Louisiana interest in the events of May 1968 in France obviously has not flagged. I do not intend to give an account of those events. Innumerable accounts have been given--some good, some less good. What I intend to do is to place the events within the French tradition which has been discussed throughout this symposium. I want to investigate whether, and to which extent, these events partake of the exemplary character which Karl Marx saw in the French Revolution of 1789, which he considered rightly as a paradigm, as a scenario, so to speak, of all bourgeois revolutions. I also want to ask what is more important about the May 1968 events: that they revitalized, even if only for one historical moment, past French traditions, including half a dozen of almost forgotten isms: or that they were one of the first violent episodes in the crisis of civilization of which, during the events, none other than General de Gaulle and his court philosopher André Malraux spoke in the midst of crisis.

Rigorous historical analysis and sociological probing would probably justify separating the student revolts which shook Paris as well as some, though not all, provincial universities from the strike movements which encompasses seven to eight million French workers, and which affected, it has been calculated, at least one-third of all of the French households in some way. They can be separated because it can be claimed that the students acted as detonators for the workers movement, or, as some of the student leaders would say, the students opened the breach into which the strike movement rushed. Nonetheless, I propose to treat the two movements together. However, I do so not because they actually merged--they generally did not. In most factories the students were forbidden entry; most street demonstrations--not all, but most--were separate, here the unions, there the students. I treat them together because the short-lived simultaneity of the two movements--they overlapped after all--gave in my opinion the explosions their significance.

The two movements influenced each other, changing attitudes on both sides, and even if the two movements proceeded separately, their superimposition was undoubtedly what brought the regime seemingly near collapse. I also think they should be considered together because we must, of course, conclude that the inability of both the students and the workers to move further with their rebellion and to prevent the restoration of the Gaullist Republic--I am not speaking about counterrevolution, that is connected with traits of the French society in which both movements lived, by which they were both affected. Especially, I would like to discuss the particular and secular difficulty of Frenchmen to overcome on the one side excessive centralization, not only of administrative but also of political life, and on the other side the opposite phenomenon, the exceeding fragmentation which makes it as difficult as does centralization to affect social change.

What were the grievances of the movement in terms of the French Revolution? What were the Cahiers de Doléances of 1968? They are not to be found in archives, departmental or national. These Doléances were shouted in the streets and written in the form of the famous graffiti on walls not built to receive them. Why no grievances put down in writing, as had been possible in the eighteenth century? Because the channels for processing grievances had been all but blocked by the government of the French Republic. But when the channels are blocked, what Crane Brinton calls the revolutionary cramps become of course more painful and more violent.

That the fuse should blow in the universities and secondary schools was not astonishing. These institutions had really become, and may be still today, hothouses of societal contradictions, ruled still essentially by the excessive hierarchization and centralization which Napoleon had introduced, a hierarchization which proved particularly inappropriate for the explosions of student numbers at all levels. A democratization of the educational system has undoubtedly taken place in France as it had in Germany but the institutions were not ready for that. The regime in France had announced reforms, but they always offered too little too late.

In this field, even de Gaulle's wonted ministerial stability did not work. There had been seven or eight ministers of national education, which is an indication that there was uncertainty about the form educational reforms should take. To give an example, problem solving has been long recognized as the most creative form of learning, but nothing of that was taking place at the secondary or university levels. Perhaps some of it had been introduced at the level of the Grandes Ecoles which, typically enough, were caught in the explosions last. There was on the part of the students justified indignation about the relevance of what was being taught, but the indignation was even greater about how things were taught, about material conditions, but also about the style of teaching.

In the months preceding the explosions there had been contracts (to which little attention was being paid) between a few politically conscious students, mostly Trotskyites and Maoists, and young workers in the provinces. Those young workers, recently arrived from the countryside, had as yet been insufficiently integrated into the plants and into the trade unions. The unions were rather indifferent to generational conflicts which they saw as nothing but an appendage of the class conflict. If our society, as Herbert Marcuse has said, is characterized by the increasing integration of all, including the workers, into the existing situation, it is then characteristic, that young workers, in the situation I have just described, and students should be the least integrated in modern society.

The industrial working class as a whole was aware of continuing social injustices in the midst of rapid modernization. That during the last decades France had modernized and urbanized more rapidly than other countries had something to do with the delays in creating social justice. The inequities of the wage and the tax structures were greater than elsewhere in the Common Market countries. Statistics showed these inequities, but the experience of daily life also made them very clear. Moreover, the elections of 1967 had given a very small majority to the Gaullists so that the regime tried to circumvent parliamentary channels, even for major pieces of legislation. It enacted, for instance, by governmental decree and without discussion, important reforms of the social security system which, of course, is of concern to almost everybody in modern times.

Then depersonalization of political life was also present in the factory. White collar workers as well as professionals discovered the dehumanization of existence, and Frenchmen do have a strong sense of the human quality of life. There was the special case of the many workers and employees of the radio and television services, the government controlled ORTF, which was so dominated by the government that one spoke during those days of another Bastille to be taken. Actually it was the striking ORTF workers who held out longest, far into June.

Above the grievances, there was an universally expressed desire to be heard, an impatience with being ignored. This desire had long been frustrated by the absence of any valid student organization, a lack which was partly a consequence of the regime's attitude and partly the fault of the students who fought each other in innumerable little groups, never going anywhere. The labor unions had become more and more bureaucratized. Unions were only interested in questions of bread and butter, except for the former Catholic trade union movement which no longer was Catholic, but which was more concerned than other union movements with questions of human existence.

If these were the grievances, then for all its heterogeneity and for its complete decentralization, at least during the first weeks, the movement gave almost perfect expression to these grievances. The movement was finding empirically the adequate form. You might be familiar with the writings of the French sociologist Durkheim. Durkheim, in a study on suicide, speaks about the phenomenon of anomie, a situation in which all rules, all règles, break down and where a universal rage mixes reformist, revolutionary, and anarchistic characteristics. To some extent, I believe that the situation resembled the anomie described by Durkheim. It's probably no accident that de Gaulle's prime minister, Pompidou, spoke about "collective suicide" just as Durkheim had tried to analyze suicide by the phenomenon of anomie. Even more interesting was de Gaulle's reiterated statement that he found the situation insaisissable (difficult to grasp). For a man who usually thought of politics in military terms, he must have felt that he was in the position of a military chief of staff who had lost contact with the field and whose field commanders no longer gave him a correct picture of what was happening.

It may be fascinating to seek the intellectual sources of the movement. I also think that it is largely irrelevant, for as the Catholic journal Esprit said, the movement was probably the least theory-inspired of all revolutions. And you may remember that yesterday Professor Rudé said that without a theory, without an ideology, there is no revolution because there is no guiding idea.

I have just mentioned the name of Herbert Marcuse. Another French journal published, shortly after the events, a special issue about "Marcuse, cet inconnu." Marcuse was really unknown in France except maybe through R. Dutschke, the respected German leader of the SDS who had been a student of his. But, there was a concurrence between the theories of many of the student rebels and possibly of the young workers, and Marcuse's analysis of the present political discontent, ending up in _Angst_, as the Germans would call the "anxiety" which the French rebels felt.

What about Marxism? I might astonish a few and anger others when I say that Marxism has never made a deep impact on major French social movements except in the form of the Soviet-Russian and at times Stalinist version of Marxism as it was propagated through the Communist party and the trade unions. There was an interesting but tiny movement, the so-called _situationisme_ which students in Strasburg started about a year before the events. They tried to merge Marxism with more modern ideas and came forward with an interesting pamphlet which tried to express the grievances in some Brechtian, or better Peter Weissian, forms. But that again was a tiny aspect of the movement. The Maoists and Trotskyites were quite clearly surprised by the events though the police probably thought otherwise.

I heard yesterday some of my colleague historians speaking with awe about the value of eighteenth- and nineteenth-century police reports. I can only hope that these are less paranoid than the police reports of the twentieth century must be. Otherwise, they are probably as misleading as the police reports will be when they become available in another fifty years because they will tell you that the rebellion of May was caused by a certain Mao sending instructions and money to the French students.

Anarchism, especially the aesthetic version called surrealism, was certainly most prominent in various expressions, especially those of the so-called "March 22 group," March 22 being the date when the trouble really started in Nanterre. This kind of anarchism, 1968 version, did indeed negate all authority: father; family; university; university professors (however liberal, however left wing); the state (of course); but also intermediate organizations, parties, trade unions, and even the revolutionary organizations that were springing up. There was much symbolism in the appearance of the black flag of anarchy which most social movements had put into the museum of the far past.

Take the only book written by one of the major participants, namely, the famous Daniel Cohn-Bendit. That book criticizes Lenin and Trotsky because of their characteristic Bolshevik organization but especially because they crushed the sailors' rebellion at Kronstadt and the uprising organized during the first years of the revolution by a largely unknown Ukranian anarchist. The point has sometimes been made that there was something Leninist in the student movement because it was trying to outfit the workers who only had a trade unionist consciousness with more general political ideas. But, the student movement of 1968 had nothing of the Bolshevik party organization or its leading ideas. What mattered to the movement was not a program, but action and perhaps some models for action from the past. There the graffiti are of great interest. "Revolutionaries," one of them said, "are men without programs. Let us push together, but not think together." An even more radical graffito said, "I have something to say, but I do not know what."

The key concept of the movement, which was not unknown in the factories was that untranslatable <u>contestation</u> which meant a permanent opposition to all authority, on any ground. Whether this opposition was completely spontaneous or planned on the spot, from one hour to the next, it needed little organization, no program, and objected to ready-made solutions. The rebels declared that they did not have solutions for what would come afterwards and that they had only contempt for them. But they discovered, or so they thought, that in action the students and the workers were achieving a unity that had almost always escaped them in discussions. In discussions they talked each other apart. In action they went together from one level to the next and attracted an ever wider following of people who in the process discovered their alienation and wanted to participate in some form of common action. They discovered togetherness as an emotional value in a society which dreads, as one French sociologist had put it, "the face-to-face relationship." To overcome this inhibition was an important experience for the movement in all camps.

After all, ten years of opposition to the Gaullist regime had brought no results; elections, referendums, small strikes, nothing had made the Gaullist regime budge. But now suddenly the regime revealed its weakness and made headlong concessions to both the students and to the workers. This was exhilarating to the radicals and gave them a possibly exaggerated feeling, both about their problems and their potentialities.

As far as models are concerned, it was again typical that there should be a two-fold inspiration. The Russian events, especially of 1905, were one model which had gone from strikes to a general strike, to a political general strike, to an insurrectional general strike, and finally, at least in the 1917 version, into revolution. Of course, French events never even got as far as the events of 1905. In fact workers lived most of the time what I would consider an idealized version of the Popular Front strikes of 1936 which also had ushered in an age of important social reforms. The other model, at least for many students, was Che Guevara. Why? Not because students knew much about his guerilla tactics which indeed did not make much sense on the Boulevard St. Michel.

What impressed those who knew anything about him was his skepti-
cism in the midst of action. He had said that today's struggles
were "sans issue," would not lead anywhere, but that they had to
continue since some day people would wake up. Many of the 1968
rebels approved. It is quite typical there was a certain prominence
given to a group that called itself Freud-Che Guevara, for this
again represents a symbiosis of psychological and political trends.

Let me also speak briefly about the significance of a student leader about whom you have heard, namely Cohn-Bendit. He
said of himself, "I am not a leader, I am only a loudspeaker."
Loud he was. His torrential eloquence was appropriate to that
ever-fluent situation. He seemed generally surprised about himself and the turn of events. He was utterly, obscenely critical of
organized powers to the right and to the left; he insulted de Gaulle
just as much as the Stalinists and thereby earned rapidly the hostility of the communist functionaries of the trade union movement.
But in the streets, he served as a symbol. When the communists
mentioned his foreign background, the students went out with banners saying: "Nous sommes tous des juifs allemands." They
wanted to express their anti-segregationist feelings, opposed to
the segregation of races as well as of nations.

But temperamentally, too, Cohn-Bendit was well suited,
it seems to me, for what was happening in typical French fashion:
a merging of revolution and festival. There was, after all in the
great French Revolution, the famous Fête des Fédérations. The
Commune has been described recently by a French historian as
one of the great festivals, if not of the nation, then of the people of
Paris. When Cohn-Bendit was asked: "What would you have done
if during that fateful night the police had not taken the barricade?",
he said he would have danced on the barricade. The emphasis on
joie was quite important. That, incidentally, I have observed myself already during the strike movement of 1936. But joie has a
verb form which is jouir. I do not know whether your French is
good enought to know the double sense of that verb, but the participants knew it, and it did not exactly please the French bourgeoisie
which, famous cliches notwithstanding, is just as Victorian as all
other bourgeoisies.

The rebels did not hesitate to call themselves "Enragés,"
again another reference to traditions. At least in the 1968 version
they found merits in being "mad." Like madness a revolution
would change people and thereby would be of therapeutic value.
Indeed I would say that the experience of contestation might be
likened to a psychoanalytical treatment which brings new truth into
personal life, or at least a new idiom of truth, overcoming hypoc-

risy about yourself or about society. The same phenomenon was also characteristic, if in less intellectual forms, of the workers. This is what the union delegates discovered to their surprise when they came back from negotiations with the government and at which they thought they had obtained excellent conditions. The workers, young and old, received them with cat calls because better minimum wages and better representation of trade unions in shops were not what the movement was about. They wanted something more radical, something new, that new sense of truth which could not be gotten by the negotiations which had taken place.

Looked at from this perspective, you will understand why I consider the question "Was the movement political or cultural?" as being not very meaningful. It was indeed a juncture of cultural and political rebellions, just as it was a juncture of some kind of new-fangled Marxism and anarchism. But is it not true that the famous Chinese cultural revolution was not essentially political either? Politization of a much greater number of students than had ever been politicized before was a fact. And for them a point of departure were the cultural grievances about which I have spoken. But were the students right when they said "For us culture and revolution are the same thing because true culture is always contestation"? And while the workers' contestation was less cultural, and more political, it was also political in a different and novel way. Another French author characterized the events as a "faceless revolution" and concluded that everything happened as though the political process had been paralyzed, as if the country had simultaneously become apolitical and entered the revolution.

It must also have become clear why I am really not quite prepared to answer the questions "Was it psychodrama or revolution?" Revolution and psychodrama may intertwine. The term psychodrama, incidentally, was invented by a conservative observer, Raymond Aron, who explained the events entirely as a form of psychological aggressiveness unleashed by the pacification, by the tranquility of collective life, by the boredom of life in an economy of abundance. I would not accept this as a sufficient explanation. But one thing was true: it was the psychodrama that was played out quite fully, and when the curtain fell, the revolution, if revolution there ever had been, was over.

The reasons for the failure, I believe, are largely embedded in what I have said. To discuss them in detail would necessitate that chronicling of events I do not want to give. I would have to go into the tactics of de Gaulle, and we still do not know all of his maneuvers. I would have to evaluate the tactics of the communist leadership as well as the vacuousness of the noncommunist left. Instead I will comment somewhat more on the significance of that failure of revolutions in our time.

The events show that everybody, from all sides of the political spectrum, had probably underrated the fragility of the political system. As in all revolutions, in all uprisings, the confusion, the perplexity, and the ensuing stupidity of the elites in power were something to behold. But that, in my opinion, is very true of all revolutions. University professors and university officials, who in all countries excel by what I just called stupidity, made all the mistakes one could make. Pompidou, de Gaulle, a large fraction of the highest civil servants, all made tactical mistakes and contributed their part to that serious impasse which a conscious revolutionary power, seeking power, might have exploited, possibly with success. But that is an "iffy" proposition because I have shown that such a force just did not exist. One might even wonder whether it wanted to exist, whether students or workers were interested in taking power. Father Padberg this morning quoted another graffito: "L'imagination prend le pouvoir." That is a fine conclusion for a learned address. But imagination cannot take power. Power has to be taken by something more than imagination. There were, toward the end, beginnings of a new form of a revolutionary organization in the so-called "action committees." They were slightly reminiscent of the Soviets, but when pushed farther, had no clearer goals than the other organizations. It too was a movement for movement's sake. In this sense Aron was right when he said that the critical function becomes nihilism when it denounces society as a whole without presenting an alternative. And you know what nihilism means: nihil, nothing. For an excellent description of nihilist movements, I recommend that beautiful if frightening novel by Dostoevski, The Possessed.

Further, in all true revolutions, there is a more or less prolonged period of dual power where new blocks of power are being formed and try to tear at the existing power structure and its monopoly of force. Typical maybe in this respect was one city, not Paris but Nantes. In Nantes there is a huge, nationalized, airplane factory, and there, for particular and local reasons, the surrounding countryside briefly joined the workers' movement. Now in Nantes, for a few days the central strike committee took over some of the economic and administrative life of the city, which is what happens in revolutions. But, also in Nantes everything dissolved literally into thin air as soon as de Gaulle regained the initiative and announced new elections while a million of middle-class Gaullists marched down to the Arc-de-Triomphe in Paris.

At this point it is almost unavoidable to quote a much over-quoted Tocqueville passage but which fits beautifully: "At one moment," he says, "the Frenchman is up in arms against authority and the next we find him serving the powers that be with a zeal such as the most servile races never display. So long as no one thinks of resisting, you can lead him on a thread, but once a revolutionary movement is afoot, nothing can restrain him from taking part in it. That is why our rulers are so often taken by surprise; they fear the nation either too much or not enough."

Besides returning Gaullists as a stronger group in parliament than before, the elections meant a return from that fragmentation which I have described to the former centralization. The rebels did not know what to do with a fragmentized non-power and left, indeed almost returned, it to the government and the executive rather than to that "house without windows," as the French parliament is often called and whose role would be as insignificant after 1968 as it had been before. The rebels left it to the government to bring it about, not the total renovation about which the days of joy had dreamed, but at least some of the most needed reforms. If Pompidou won the elections by arousing the fear of Communist totalitarianism, he committed a great historical injustice because the Communists had not in the least been interested in taking power. But, while politicians are permitted to commit historical injustices, historians (and political scientists) must assess the true significance of the events they set out to describe.

In my opinion no social movement is entirely "lost" to history. The years following the uprising of 1848 were those of a counterrevolution under Napoleon III. Reaction, if not counter-revolution, are quite regularly a phenomenon born out of an ineffective attempt at revolution. Yet historians are right when they tell us that the events of that "mad year"--1848--are far from being lost to history. The events of May-June 1968 must be considered an episode in the crisis of modern civilization and as such they laid bare many of the elements of that crisis. Those musically trained know what is considered an "episode" in a musical score: a certain number of bars, allowed to intervene from time to time before the main theme is resumed.

The main theme of public life in France is forever a playing-out of the traditional concepts of freedom and authority. Since they have time and again proven inadequate for bringing about needed social change, such change, when it comes, is either imposed from above or fought over in pitched battle. In between, society appears "blocked," stalemated, as President Pompidou's first prime minister, Jacques Chaban-Delmas, put it very well.

Yet he too was unable to remove the "blocks"; for having tried, he himself was removed from office.

For the time being May 1968 has become another of the country's divisive historical memories. To many Frenchmen, it appears still as a threat (and was played upon as such by the government during the elections of March 1973). To others, it remains an inspiring myth. What the friends of France everywhere might regret is that the events are rarely evaluated as an object lesson in the possible benefits of cooperation, of acting together. What has not been eradicated is the long-established habit of leaving decisions to superiors, and above all to the government, which can then be blamed for interfering with the pursuit of happiness by individual Frenchmen.

The French writer, Charles Péguy, once wrote: "It's annoying, says God: when the day comes when there are no more Frenchmen, there are some things I do which no one will any longer understand." And, looking at the events of 1968 as well as at many other events in the country's fascinating history, one is tempted to add that there are some things Frenchmen do which only God can understand. *

---

*For those who wish to read farther into the many-sided aspects of the 1968 events there exists now an excellent guide to the overflow production of opinion and analysis: France: The Events of May-June 1968, A Critical Bibliography by Laurence Wylie, Franklin D. Chu and Mary Terrall (Council for European Studies, University of Pittsburgh, 1973).

WHITHER REVOLUTION?

Amos Simpson

In his address earlier this week Professor Albert Soboul said that the scholar must not be cold. He must be passionate. He must come from a particular time and a particular country, or he is flat. Our participants in this week's symposium all came from our own particular time and from various particular countries, and I think we can all agree, they were not flat. We remember the ringing words with which Professor Mario Fratti ended his address: "Awareness will save the world."

A glance at our program sets the stage. Professors Mathé Allain and Glenn Conrad organized the symposium into phases of study for each day: the background of revolution; the revolutions themselves; their impact on taste and sensibility, on art, architecture, science, theatre, religion and morals; and on mass response then and now. Their planning, and the outstanding quality of the participants, produced a week's study which has not only stimulated and excited us, but has indeed broadened our understanding of change--revolutionary as well as evolutionary--in our own era.

Professor Robert Holtman's keynote address combined eloquence with a near-clairvoyant appreciation of what has transpired since that time. In a delightful preliminary introduction on the nature of history, he established firmly what such a conference should be. History, he said, deals with change. And change is the essence of revolution. Here he warned that beyond that point there might be little agreement on the definition of revolution. He was right.

213

Professor Soboul insisted on a rigidly and narrowly defined experience which is determined by the totality of change of institutions in a short period of time.   Thus he would deny the term to what many of us call the American Revolution--A War for Independence, or even a civil war, but not a revolution, because the basic and existing institutions within this country were not immediately changed by the event.

In philosophic terms Professor Robert Caponigri appeared to agree. He argued that revolution is a transaction (change) at the constitutional level and necessitates an alteration of the legitimizing principle. Yet the clear influence of Edmund Burke's thought on Professor Caponigri gives one pause, because Burke believed that constitutions grow and are not mere abstractions. Therefore, the revolution which changes the constitution must already have come about by evolution--and nobody knew it.

Professor Fratti's view of revolution is considerably more relaxed. To him the term signifies little more than constructive change, and as such has been the pursuit of people of good will for the past two thousand five hundred years, and will continue at least until all people have a sufficiency of food and a roof over their heads. But all did agree that the revolutionary experience marks more or less rapid change in the most basic elements in our lives.

Yet misery never causes revolutions, according to Professor Holtman. They are caused rather by the sudden halt in the improvement of conditions. Many factors may contribute to a revolutionary situation: war, weakness of government, a disloyal or misused army, development of new leadership outside the existing establishment and unable to break in, or even the witnessing of a successful revolution elsewhere. Revolution breeds revolution.

Professor Gérard Laurent admitted that the French Revolution sparked the upheaval which took place in the prosperous colony of Santo Domingo. Yet he argued as well that a revolution is born from local causes and results from the contradictions within each society's own milieu.

Richard Bienvenu added the powerful force of myth. Whether the French revolutionaries were or were not carrying out the ideas of the Enlightenment, they thought they were, and therefore drew heavily from what they made the Enlightenment to be in their own minds. Interestingly enough, without having heard Bienvenu, Professor George Rudé lent him strong support. Every revolution, he said, contains within itself another revolution. The larger of the two has a dominant ideology which is in part the ideology of all involved and which is essential to success. But the revolution inside the revolution has its own ideology which is quite different from the dominant one and often causes contradictions and conflict.

For example, in the French Revolution the dominant ideology vested the term "Third Estate" with the meaning of nation, or more exactly, the bourgeoisie. But the sans-culottes transformed its meaning into a term exclusive to themselves. In the same way "liberty," "equality," and "popular sovereignty" all had clearly documented and quite different meanings to the middle class on the one hand and to the workers on the other. Yet both factions acted on their own interpretations of the slogans. It is this factor which causes revolution to tend to escalate to the left rather than to the right, and which causes the Thermidorian reaction, and sometimes the failure of the revolution itself.

While holding with the principles of modern history that revolution cannot be exported and must be born from local causes, Gérard Laurent agreed that a revolution evolves gradually toward the final outburst. In his discussion of the Santo Domingo revolution, he argued that revolution is the logical consequence of social conflict, unequal distribution of wealth, and explosive situations created by a spirit of exploitation and inequity. Accepting the Declaration of the Rights of Man on their own terms, and grateful to the Convention for making them free men, the former slaves of Santo Domingo might have remained a part of France, but the policies of the counterrevolution appeared to destroy many of the social gains they had made, and they determined on total rejection of France.

Professors Donaghay and Caponigri agreed that there are ways in which governments may avoid revolution. The former documented the role which finances play in producing a revolutionary situation. Had the French government not been in such desperate financial straits, it might have been able to deal more effectively with the growing demand for reform, in which case the masses would have been far less inclined to support the bourgeois leadership in overthrowing the government. Professor Caponigri believes that the most viable form of constitution is that which is not purely abstract or concrete, but which operates on historical consciousness (I should think that Fratti's "awareness" is applicable here) and therefore is capable of "self-generating change."

In discussing the impact of revolution on art, Albert Griffith carried forward Bienvenu's idea of the changing interpretations of men's work. There is a two-way interplay, he said, between history and art. Art alters history by organizing a new mode of examining it. Meaning emerges as data are filtered through the historian's sensibilities. The term American Revolution, for example, is really an abstraction. Facts determine meaning, but meaning is determined by what is seen. And men in different times and places see quite different things. Thus Walt Whitman saw a particular America, overt and democratic, and today our vision of America is formed partly by what we think Whitman saw.

Presumably the artists and leaders of social thought during the Enlightenment would have agreed. Keith Marshall documented the development of art as propaganda, as Diderot and others demanded that it be useful and moral. The result was a new naturalism and a frank appeal to the emotions. French leaders used neoclassical art to teach what they thought was historical in order to sanctify what they were doing. One can trace transition of thought by examining the changes in art. David's Death of Marat, Mr. Marshall called the French Revolution's Pietà.

Violent revolution, as in the French political revolution, is an attempt to institute radical social change. And unquestionably the French Revolution did provoke drastic change--but not in the ways the revolutionaries themselves had hoped. In other words, the expressed economic and political goals of the French revolutionaries were not achieved during the upheaval, but their endeavors unleashed a tidal wave of change which reached not only France but the entire western world for decades after.

In the panel discussion Professors Holtman and Hyslop pointed out that the major significance of the French Revolution is to be found in the nationalism which it generated in France and which Napoleon's conquests evoked in the other parts of the European continent. Dr. Holtman argued that the French Revolution produced a revolution of rising expectations, and thereby he reinforced Professor Soboul's contention that the French Revolution has a universal and general significance.

Soboul called the French Revolution a necessary stage in the transition from feudalism to capitalism, and Professor Marie Donaghay established that the financial and economic conditions which moved France toward political revolution forced her at the same time to adopt the industrial revolution already begun in England. More vividly, Bernard Harvey argued that the scientific revolution came into the industrial revolution by way of the political revolution. Political revolution contributed to that rather unfortunate alliance between science and technology, and, in his words, "Things conspired to bring about the industrial revolution." The social consequences were overwhelming. The growing need for literate workers led to universal education, and as education spread, it strengthened the desire of politically excluded groups to participate in determining the course of their own and their government's development.

But education takes many forms. Roy Graham's paper and slide presentation showed how revolutionary changes in France's architecture came to the United States by way of émigrés, having a profound impact on the development of truthfulness in architecture, appropriateness of role, and the concept of function. But more importantly, the ideals of order, harmony, progress, and perfectibility expressed in architecture created an environmental milieu which reinforced intellectual strains in developing American thought and became an integral part of the American democratic ideal. David Chase pointed out that democratic ideals also found expression in landscape architecture, as the private gardens of the aristocratic great were transmuted into the establishment of municipal parks for the use of the general public.

There are many areas of influence which are difficult to analyze, but Professor Gita May did an outstanding job in her effort to portray the significance of widespread emotional change--the change in mood which developed the capacity to feel deeply, both happiness and misery. Such a capacity, Professor May asserted, was a new attitude. It even became fashionable to communicate deeply felt emotions, and an entire set of simple symbols developed to assist in the process. Diderot, virile and tough-minded, could weep. While it is difficult to quantify these judgements, Professor May argued that Rousseau's romantic novel, La Nouvelle Héloise, had far greater influence in awakening a revolutionary consciousness than did his Social Contract. They express the same ideas, but the novel fired the people's imagination--the entire reading public knew it, and it fitted their experience. Professor May argued that abstract ideas do not produce revolutions. Experience brings people to commitment. This is the quality found in La Nouvelle Héloïse.

And it is this same quality to which Mario Fratti addressed himself. Revolutionary theatre normally can be written and produced only in an open society. In 1855 the great Cavour said that theatre is dangerous, and apparently the present government of Greece agrees, for it has banned Aristophanes. Even governments recognize theatre as a weapon and sometimes attempt to use it to generate support for unpopular regimes. Thus even Benito Mussolini wrote a play. It didn't work. But theatre makes people think, reflect, look at themselves in a mirror, and educates them to a realization of their potential. Then they can begin to work within their own society to bring about constructive change.

Religion, of course, affects revolutionary change and is in turn affected by it. The rejection in France of the superstition attached to religion, according to Father Padberg, contributed to the development of dogmatic rationalism and established religion in the revolutionary context. But the financial losses and the oath to the civil constitution caused a rupture between church and state, and the effort to destroy the Roman Catholic Church in France. In the United States, because there was no one established church, the revolutionaries saw no need to destroy the old order to establish a new one.   Subsequently there has developed in this country a civil religion which accepts belief in a supreme being, but tends to emphasize how good God has been to the United States.   In France things have not proceeded so smoothly; but since the separation of church and state in 1905, the church has been freed, and after World War I the growth of a left-wing Catholicism has shown evidence of a possible reconciliation.

There is no revolution without leadership, so that we must study those individuals who have played large roles in bringing on revolution.   But George Rudé emphasized that revolutions do not occur without a mass participating, so that attention must be paid to those largely without names or identity.   The mass impact has a different thrust at different times.   It can be radical or reactionary.   In the French Revolution the sans-culottes pushed the revolution toward more radical solutions.   Twice, Soboul argues, the masses drove toward economic and social equality.   But in Germany in 1848, fear of mass demands led the middle classes represented at Frankfurt to yield without struggle to Frederick William IV.

And then, as Dr. Rudé pointed out, there are many who do not participate, but who are, nonetheless, affected by the changes which do occur.   Their sophistication grows as change occurs and prepares the seedbed for further change.   Obviously then, change is not only accelerating but ultimately unavoidable.   Whether we look at revolution in terms of its more narrow definition--that is, a short term cataclysm--or in the broader sense of sweeping social, political, and economic alteration, we face the inevitability of change.

So what does all this mean for our own time?   As we have heard several times this week, it is not our job to prophesy, but we do have a responsibility to examine trends and to continue to function as critics of our society.   Holtman said that there is no inevitability in history (other than the inevitability of change)--and that is the more true if we, as scholars, do our job.

Many writers have suggested that the next left-wing revolution will take place in the United States.   They see the increasing alienation of the blacks, the Indians, and other minority groups, their growing tendency to separatism, and fear that conditions may deteriorate into revolution.   Men quake that even women have gotten into the act.

Professor Henry Ehrmann in his discussion of the 1968 student revolt in France provided a rather significant clue, it seems to me, on whether such fears are realistic.   He argued that while a certain unity of <u>action</u> developed between workers and students, they bored each other to distraction when they tried to talk together. In the long run, Ehrmann said, the revolt underscored the stupidity and rigidity of the Establishment, and that was the ultimate goal, if any genuine goal. The rebels did not want power. They wanted to make themselves heard, to make their grievances known. But the old urge to power was lacking in such graphic graffiti as "I have something to say, but I don't know what it is."

I believe that in western, industrialized states where the secret ballot exists old-style revolution is no longer necessary and possibly can not even happen. All of the necessary procedures actually exist to bring about change peacefully through the elective process, and political parties, even industries--wonder of wonders, even universities--<u>do</u> respond to mass demands. The effort by minority groups to establish their aims by violence now flies in the face of reality. The primary effect is, therefore, what we term backlash. And that pushes us toward right-wing, rather than left-wing revolution.

Actually there have been more right-wing than left-wing revolutions in the twentieth century. Most recently one thinks of Greece, South Korea, the Philippines. But our tradition of freedom and individual human dignity is too firmly established for us to accept with equanimity to an authoritarian government. Even President Nixon may begin to learn that.

The middle-class demands of the eighteenth century were met in the nineteenth; and they generated both the demands of the masses (the crowds) and their consciousness of potential power. Those demands, however, are being met today with a rapidity almost sufficient to Soboul's time demands--and for the most part peacefully. In this sense, we are today experiencing revolution. In some respects the revolution has already taken place. Shirley Chisolm and Julian Bond are in Congress. Adam Clayton Powell is not.

Popular songs, movies, and television shows have not only made manifest existing inhumanities and injustices, but have helped to provoke an evolution in contemporary structures of existence which has bewildered many with its rapidity. Returning POW's after only five or six years out of touch with America's social realities are returning home to face as complete a change in manner of dress, accepted patterns of behavior, and interpretations of morality as did Rip Van Winkle after his twenty-year sleep. Actually, it's much more than that.

Professor Soboul reports that in 1973 the French Revolution is alive and well in Lafayette, Louisiana. A classic example of bourgeois revolution, it was more, much more. As a peasant and popular revolution it tried twice to go beyond its bourgeois limits, and continues as a prophetic example, and a source of today's revolutionary thought and action. Even the memory of it is revolutionary. In Professor Soboul's words, "it still exhilarates us." And so it does, and has, especially during this week of study of "France and North America: The Revolutionary Experience."

APPENDIX

THE FRENCH REVOLUTION IN CONTEMPORARY WORLD HISTORY

Albert Soboul

The revolution of 1789-1794, which signalled the coming of modern, bourgeois, capitalistic society into French history, was characterized essentially by the realization of the country's national unity based on the destruction of the seignorial regime and of the privileged feudal orders. The purpose of that Revolution, says Tocqueville in L'Ancien Régime et la Révolution, "was to abolish everywhere the remaining medieval institutions."[1] That the French Revolution finally succeeded in establishing a liberal democracy underlines even more its historical significance. From this double point of view, and from the point of view of world history which is our concern here, the Revolution deserves to be considered the classic model of bourgeois revolution.

Two series of problems therefore arise from a comparative study of the French Revolution. There are first of all problems of a general nature concerning the transition from feudalism to modern capitalism, transities which as Marx points out in the third book of Capital, can take place in two ways: one totally destroys the former economic and social system "the true revolutionary way"; the other preserves the former mode of production within the new capitalistic society--that is the way of compromise.[2]

---

[1] Alexis de Tocqueville, L'Ancien Régime et la Révolution in Oeuvres Completes, Vol. II (Paris, 1972), 99.

[2] Karl Marx, "Aperçu historique sur le capital marchand,"

There are also problems of a specialized nature, which result from the specific structure of French society at the end of the ancien régime and take into account the individual characteristics of the French Revolution as compared to the various types of bourgeois revolution.[3]

From this double viewpoint, the French Revolution cannot be isolated from that of Europe. In every country of the continent, the formation of modern society began within the old economic and social systems with their feudal remnants, then proceeded at their expense. In all European countries this evolution was carried out, to various degrees, for the benefit of the bourgeoisie. The French Revolution was not the first to benefit the bourgeoisie: the Dutch revolutions of the sixteenth century, the two English revolutions of the seventeenth century, the American Revolution of the eighteenth century marked stages in this evolution. But one must account for the classic character of the French Revolution.

I

1.--The French Revolution was the most striking of bourgeois revolutions, the dramatic nature of its class struggles having eclipsed the preceding revolutions. This situation probably arose from the obstinacy of the aristocracy which clung to its feudal privileges and refused any concession as well as from the opposite stubbornness of the masses. The bourgeoisie did not wish the downfall of the aristocracy, but was forced to pursue the destruction of the older order by refusal of compromise and counterrevolution. The bourgeoisie, however, could accomplish that aim only by alliance with urban and rural masses which had to be satisfied:

---

in Le Capital, Vol. VI (Paris, Editions sociales, 1966), 342. On the problem of transition from feudalism to capitalism, see Paul Marlor Sweezy et al., The Transition from Feudalism to Capitalism: A Symposium (London, 1954); Rodney Hilton, "Y eut-il une crise générale de la féodalité?" Annales, VI (1951), 23-30; Guiliano Procacci, Georges Lefebvre and Albert Soboul, "Une discussion historique: du féodalisme au capitalism," La Pensée, XIII (1956), 10-32.

[3]These are the problems raised more particularly by Georges Lefebvre in "La Révolution française dans l'histoire du monde," Annales, III (1948), reprinted in Études sur la Révolution française (Paris, 1954), 317-326.

the ground was cleared by popular revolution and the Reign of Terror, feudalism was completely destroyed, and democracy was established.

From feudalism to capitalism, the French Revolution took "the truly revolutionary way." By clearing away all feudal remnants, by freeing the peasants from seignorial rights, ecclesiastical tithes and, to a certain extent, from communal restrictions, by destroying corporate monopolies and unifying the national market, the French Revolution marked a decisive stage in the development of capitalism. By abolishing feudal landed property, the Revolution freed the small producers and made possible the differentiation of the peasant masses and their polarization between capital and labor. From this differentiation resulted entirely new production relations, since capital, freed from feudal subjection, made the labor force commercial. The autonomy of capitalistic production was thus secured in the agricultural as well as in the industrial sector. For this transition to capitalist society two conditions appear necessary in the light of the French Revolution: the breakdown of feudal landed property and the enfranchisement of the peasants. The agrarian question occupies a central position in the bourgeois revolution.

The active wing of that revolution was not the commercial bougeoisie since insofar as it was exclusively a trade intermediary it came to terms with the old society: from 1789 to 1793, from the Monarchiens to the Feuillants and then the Girondins, the commercial bourgeoisie inclined to compromise. The active wing was composed of the mass of small direct producers whose surplus labor or surplus product was monopolized by the feudal aristocracy, supported by the judicial system and the state's enforcement of the ancien régime. The political instrument of change was the Jacobin dictatorship which brought to power the small and middle bourgeoisie supported by the masses. The ideal of those social classes was a democracy of small autonomous producers--peasants and independent artisans--working and exchanging freely. The peasant popular revolution was at the very heart of the bourgeois revolution and pushed it forward. [4]

The victory over feudalism and the ancien régime did not mean the immediate appearance of new social relations. The

---

[4] For the theoretical aspects of the problem, see Maurice H. Dobb, Studies in the Development of Capitalism (London, 1946) and H. K. Takahashi, Shimin ka-kumei-no hozo [Structures of Bourgeois Society] (Tokyo, 1951) reviewed by Charles Haguenauer, Revue Historique, CCXVII (1955), 345.

transition to capitalism was not a simple process by which capitalistic elements developed within the older society until they were strong enough to break through; it took much longer for capitalism to become definitely established in France, its progress having been slow during the revolutionary period when industries remained rather small and commercial capital remained dormant.[5] Nevertheless, the destruction of feudal landed property and of the regulatory corporate system uncompromisingly paved the way for bourgeois relations of production and distribution, a revolutionary transformation, par excellence.

The French Revolution overthrew economic and social structures and at the same time broke the state structure of the ancien régime, sweeping away the vestiges of an older autonomy, destroying local privileges and provincial particuliarism. Thus it made possible, from the Directory to the Empire, the establishment of a new state which served the interests and the needs of the modern bourgeoisie.

From this double point of view, the French Revolution was far from being a myth, as some have claimed.[6] It is true that feudalism in the medieval meaning of the word no longer meant anything in 1789. But for bourgeois and especially peasant contemporaries, this abstract term denoted a reality they knew well (feudal rights, seignorial authority) and which finally crumbled. It is true that the revolutionary assemblies were essentially composed of professional men and government officials instead of industrialists. In the Constituent Assembly two-thirds of the deputies belonged to the liberal professions and thirteen per cent only to the business world--merchants, bankers, manufacturers, capitalists big and small. Among the 1539 members of the Constituent Assembly and the Convention, 629 exercised public functions, 289 of whom had owned offices before the Revolution. One cannot, however, use

---

[5]One must emphasize the economic progress during the Napoleonic period, so closely related to the revolutionary period. See Ernest Labrousse, "Du bilan du monde en 1815. Eléments d'un bilan économique: La croissance dans la guerre," Comité international des sciences historiques. XVIIe Congrès, Vienna, 1965. Rapports, Vol. I, Grands Thèmes, 473.

[6]Alfred Cobban, The Myth of the French Revolution (London, 1955). By the same author, along the same lines, The Social Interpretation of the French Revolution (Cambridge, 1964). See Georges Lefebvre, "Le mythe de la Révolution française," Annales historique de la Révolution française, XXVII (1956), 337-345.

those facts as an argument against the importance of the French Revolution in establishing capitalism. Besides the fact that manufacturers, financiers and négociants were represented by a very active minority, besides the importance of pressure groups such as commerce deputies and the Massiac club which safeguarded the interests of planters, shipowners, and refiners,[7] the essential fact remains that the older system of production and exchange was destroyed and that the French Revolution proclaimed a total freedom of enterprise and profit, thereby opening the way to capitalism. The history of the nineteenth century, particularly the history of the working class, shows that that was no myth.

The French Revolution was a necessary stage in the general transition from feudalism to capitalism, but it nevertheless preserves, compared with similar revolutions, its own characteristics determined by the specific structure of French society at the end of the ancien régime.

Those characteristics have been denied. The French Revolution, according to this view, was but "one aspect of a western revolution, or more exactly an Atlantic revolution which began in the English colonies of America, a little after 1763, was continued by the revolutions in Switzerland, the Netherlands, Ireland, before reaching France between 1787 and 1789. From France it bounced back to the Netherlands, invaded the Rhineland, Switzerland, Italy...."[8] The French Revolution would then be integrated into

---

[7]See in particular J. Letaconnoux, "Le Comité des députés extraordinaires des manufactures et du commerce et l'oeuvre économique de l'Assemblée Constituante (1789-1791)," Annales révolutionnaires, VI (1913), 149-208; Gabriel Debien, Les Colons de Saint-Domingue et la Révolution. Essai sur le club Massiac (août 1789-août 1792) (Paris, 1953).

[8]Jacques Godechot, La Grande Nation. L'expansion révolutionnaire de la France dans le monde (1789-1799), Vol. I (Paris, 1956), 209. This concept of a "western" or "Atlantic" revolution was first advanced by Robert R. Palmer, "The World Revolution of the West," Political Science Quarterly, LXIX (1954), 1-14. It was picked up and developed by Jacques Godechot and Robert R. Palmer, "Le problème de l'Atlantique de XVIIIe au XXe siècle," X Congresso internazionale di scienze storiche. Relazione, Vol. V (Florence, 1955), 175-239; Robert R. Palmer, The Age of the Democratic Revolution: A Political History of Europe and America, 1760-1800, Vol. I: The Challenge (Princeton, 1959); Jacques Godechot, Les Révolutions (1770-1799) (Paris, 1963). An overall

"the great Atlantic revolution." Undoubtedly, one cannot underestimate the importance of the ocean in the renewal of trade and in the exploitation of colonies by the West. But that is not what the author quoted is talking about, nor does he intend to show that the French Revolution was but an episode in a general phase of history which, after the Dutch, English and American revolutions, helped associate or bring the bourgeoisie to power. The French Revolution is not the geographic terminal of this revolution as the ambiguous adjectives "Atlantic" and "Western" would suggest. In the nineteenth century the bourgeoisie rose wherever capitalist economy established itself. The bourgeois revolution was universal. On the other hand, to put on the same plane the French Revolution and "the revolutions in Switzerland, the Netherlands, and Ireland" minimizes strangely the depth and the dimension of the former and the sudden change it represented. Such a conception would nullify half a century of revolutionary historiography from Jean Jaurès to Georges Lefebvre by removing any specific content, economic (anti-feudal and capitalist), social (anti-aristocratic and bourgeois) and national (one and indivisible).

Yet, Tocqueville had cause to pause when he asked "why analogous principles and similar political theories only led to a change in government in the United States, but led to a total subversion of society in France?" To pose the problem in those terms is to go beyond the superficial aspect of political and institutional history to try to reach the economic and social realities in their national individuality.

The French Revolution ended up occupying a singular place in the history of the contemporary world.

2.--As a revolution of freedom, it invoked, like the American Revolution, natural law and conferred on its accomplishment a universal character neglected by the English revolution. But who could deny that the declaration of 1789 emphasized that character much more than the American declarations? Let us add that it went farther toward freedom. It guaranteed liberty of conscience and granted civil rights to Protestants and Jews. Furthermore, by

---

view will be found in Jacques Godechot and Robert R. Palmer, "Révolution française ou révolution occidentale," Bulletin de la société d'histoire moderne (July, 1960), 1-10. Bibliography in Jacques Godechot "Révolution française ou révolution occidentale?" L'Information historique (1960), 6. This concept was criticized by Georges Lefebvre in Annales historique de la Révolution française, XXIX (1957), 272.

creating a civil state on September 20, 1792, the Revolution acknowledged the citizen's right to belong to no religion. The Revolution freed the whites, but also, by the law of 16 Pluviôse, Year II (February 4, 1794), it abolished black slavery in all colonies.

As a revolution of equality the French Revolution went far beyond the preceding revolutions. Neither in England nor in the United States had emphasis been placed on equality since the aristocracy and the bourgeoisie became associated in power. The aristocracy and the aristocratic resistance, the counterrevolution, and the war forced the French bourgeoisie to give primacy to equality of rights. Thus it was able to rally the people and achieve victory. Thus appeared in the Year II the draft of a regime of social democracy characterized by a compromise between bourgeois ideas and popular wishes. The masses knew what fate awaited them; that is why they were hostile to the economic freedom which paved the way for concentration of wealth and capitalism. Their ideal at the end of the eighteenth century was for every peasant to be a landowner, for every artisan to be independent, for the wage earner to be protected against the might of the rich.

After August 10, 1792, and the fall of the monarchy, the revolutionary bourgeoisie which had instituted universal manhood suffrage and sealed an alliance with the sans-culottes, had to go beyond a theoretical equality of rights and progress toward the equality of enjoyments the sans-culottes demanded. Hence, there resulted an orientation of economic life to bring prices into line with salaries and insure everyone's daily bread. Taxation and regulation were instituted by the law of general maximum (September 29, 1793) and war industries were nationalized, as was foreign trade. Hence there also resulted the attempt at public schools open to all established by the law of the 29 Frimaire, Year II (December 19, 1793). Hence the beginning of social security created by the law of bienfaisance nationale of the 22nd of Floréal, Year II (May 11, 1793). The egalitarian republic of the Year II filled the property-owning bourgeoisie with indignation and fear. After the 9th of Thermidore it seems banished forever. But there did remain from then on in the consciences of men this conviction that freedom without equality is but the privilege of a few, that liberty and equality are inseparable, that political equality itself might be only an illusion when social inequality reigns. "Liberty is but a vain phantom when a class of man can starve another with impunity," stated the enragé Jacques Roux, June 25, 1793, from the rostrum of the Convention, "Liberty is but a vain phantom when the rich, owing to his monopoly, exercises the right of life and death over his brethern. "[9]

Revolution of unity, the French Revolution completed the nation which became one and indivisible.[10] The Capetian monarchy had given the nation a territorial and administrative framework, but had failed to complete the task. In 1789, national unity was not perfect. The nation remained territorially divided through the incoherence of administrative division and the persistence of feudal subdividing. The diversity of weights and measures as well as internal customs made a national market impossible. Furthermore, the nation was divided socially, since Ancien Régime society was hierarchical and partly corporate. As Georges Lefebvre pointed out, corporate implies privileged; inequality reigned while the nation, already formed by governmental unity, had had its cohesion reinforced during the eighteenth century by the manifold links woven by material progress, the expansion of the French language, the development of culture, and the brilliance of the Enlightenment.

Once orders, states, and corporate bodies were abolished, the French were free and equal in rights and constituted the nation one and indivisible. The rationalization of institutions carried out by the Constituent Assembly, the return to centralization brought about by the revolutionary government, the administrative effort of the Directory, the rebuilding of the state by Napoleon completed the task of the Ancien Régime monarchy by destroying autonomies and particularisms and by setting up the institutional framework of a unified state. At the same time, civil equality, the federative movement of 1790, the development of a network of societies affiliated with the Jacobin anti-federalism, and the grouping (or réunions centrales) of popular societies in 1793 aroused and strengthened the consciousness of a nation one and indivisible. The progress of the French language contributed to this national consciousness which was reinforced by new economic bonds. With tolls and internal customs destroyed and with customs barriers pushed back to the political border, the national market became unified, being moreover protected from foreign competition by a protectionist tariff. The French Revolution gave national sovereignty a strength and an efficiency it had never experienced before.

---

[9]J. Roux, Adresse présentée à la Convention nationale au nom de la section des Gravilliers...(A.N., W 20, d. 1073).

[10]On the whole problem, see Albert Soboul, "De l'Ancien Régime à l'Empire: problème national et réalités sociales," L'Information historique, (1960), 59-64, 96-104.

Meanwhile, a new international public law was being born. Trying to formulate its principles while discussing the problems of the German princes who owned land in Alsace, Merlin de Douai, on October 28, 1790, opposed the dynastic state and the nation, understood as a voluntary association: "There is, between you and your Alsatian brethren, no legitimate right of union except the social pact entered into last year by all Frenchmen, old and new, in this Assembly." Merlin de Douai was alluding to the decision of the Third Estate, on June 17, 1789, to proclaim itself a national assembly, and to the decision of that assembly, the following July 9th, to declare itself the Constituent Assembly. He was alluding also to the federative pact of July 14, 1790. A single question, "infinitely simple," exists: one must decide whether "It is from diplomatic parchments that the Alsatian people draws the advantage of being French.... It matters not to the people of Alsace, it matters not to the French people that there were agreements which were intended to unite them in the days of despotism. The Alsatian people united with the French because it wanted to. Its will alone, and not the Treaty of Munster, justified the union."[11] Alsace manifested its will by participating in the Federation of July 14, 1790. International public law was revolutionized just like national public law: nations had now the right to free themselves and to dispose of themselves.

The traits we have just sketched show the true worth of the French Revolution and its value as an example to the contemporary world. It is true that it was the armies of the Republic, then those of Napoleon, more than the force of ideas which overturned the ancien régime in the countries they occupied. By abolishing serfdom, freeing peasants from feudal dues and ecclesiastical tithes, and putting main morte lands back into circulation, the French Revolution cleared the way for the development of capitalism. Though nothing remains of the continental empire Napoleon wanted to create, he abolished the ancien régime everywhere he had time to do so. In this sense, his rule continued the Revolution and he was the soldier of the Revolution as ancien régime rulers never ceased reproaching him. [12]

---

[11]Le Moniteur universel, October 30, 1790, 1254-1255.

[12]See Albert Soboul, "Le bilan du monde en 1815. Esquisse d'une bilan social," Comité international des sciences historiques, XIIe Congrès, Vienne, 1965. Rapports, Vol. I. Grand Thèmes, 517.

After Napoleon, the prestige of the Revolution did not fade. Looking back, it seems to have been born from both reason and enthusiasm. A powerful, emotional impact became attached to its memory, the storming of the Bastille remaining the symbol of popular uprising, the Marseillaise remaining the war song of liberty and independence. In this sense, the French Revolution is truly a myth, as Georges Sorel meant the word. It entices imagination and emotion. A harbinger of better times, it leads to action. Besides this revolutionary romanticism it possesses an ideological attraction no less powerful since the French Revolution is an immense effort to establish society on a rational basis.

Let us listen to Tocqueville again: "We saw it, [the Revolution] bring men together or divide them despite laws, traditions, differences, languages, sometimes turning compatriots into enemies and strangers into brothers. Rather it created above all particular nationalities, a common intellectual fatherland of which men of all nations could become citizens."[13]

II

A necessary stage in the transition from feudalism to capitalism, the French Revolution also shaped contemporary history by the solutions it successively devised for the problem of equality of rights. The transformation of the economy through capitalism, concentrated enterprises, multiplied and grouped wage earners, awakened as well as sharpened their class consciousness, and made again the principle of equal rights a primary concern of men. The result was that the principle that the bourgeoisie proclaimed to justify the abolition of aristocratic privileges based on birth led to consequences the members of the Constituent Assembly never foresaw despite the malicious warnings of some clear-sighted adversaries. "The blacks of our colonies and the servants of our homes," says Rivard in the Journal politique national, "can drive us from our inheritance, the Declaration of Rights in hand. How can an assembly of legislators pretend to ignore that the natural rights cannot exist for any length of time along with property rights?"[14] This stated the problem of content of rights: theoretical

---

[13]"Comment la Révolution française a été une révolution politique qui a procédé à la manière des révolution religieuses, et pourquoi," Book I, ch. III, in L'Ancien Régime et la Révolution, 87.

[14]Journal politique national, no. 19 (August, 1789). The members of the Constituent Assembly declared to the whole world

equality or real equality.   On March 13, 1793 Vergniaud affirmed: "Equality for men in society can be only equality of rights." But on the 20th of August of the same year Félix Lepeletier made the suggestion to "eradicate inequality of property" and in the Year IV Babeuf preached "the community of property and work" so as to reach at last "perfect equality." The French Revolution opened the three paths which the contemporary world followed successively.

1.--For bourgeois liberalism, the liberalism of the members of the Constituent Assembly in 1789 and of the Anglo-Saxons, equality is only equality of rights. All citizens are free to use their rights, but not all have the means. The Declaration of the Rights of Man linked equality and liberty but that statement of principle was intended to justify the downfall of the aristocracy and the abolition of noble privileges rather than to encourage popular hopes. By putting property rights among inalienable natural rights, the Constituent Assembly introduced an insurmountable contradiction among its accomplishments.   That contradiction was exposed by the preservation of slavery and the setting of property qualifications. The exercise of voting rights was prescribed according to the payment of certain taxes, in other words, according to the level of wealth. Thus the rights that the bourgeois of the Constituent Assembly recognized as the rights of men and citizens were in fact only the rights of bourgeois and remained theoretical rights, abstract rights, for the masses of passive citizens.

The revolutionary bourgeoisie always stopped there, clearly restating its principles each time popular movements threatened the new edifice. "Are we going to end the Revolution or are we going to start all over?" asked Barnave in a vehement speech delivered July 15, 1791, after Varennes. "You made men equal before the law, you established civil and political equality.... One more step would be a dangerous and culpable action, one step farther along the path of liberty would mean the destruction of monarchy, along the path of equality the destruction of property. If one wants to destroy more when all that should be destroyed has been eradicated, if one believes that more should be done for equality when equality has been secured, where would anyone find

that men were born and remained free, that no man could be more than another, and many other such new ideas. They poked philosophical fun at the English who had been incapable of beginning like them when they gave themselves a constitution in 1688.

an aristocracy to destroy but among property owners?[15] Along the same lines, Vergniaud stated in his speech to the Convention on March 13, 1793, at the time when the pressure from the sections became stronger: "For man in society, equality is equality of rights. It is not equality of fortune anymore than it is equality of size, force, mind, activities, industry and labor.[16] After Thermidor, the bourgeoisie hardened. It no longer hid the fact that it considered the rights of men to be the rights of property owners. "You must guarantee the rich man's property," says Boissy d'Anglas in his preliminary speech to the constitution project, "Civil equality is all that an honorable man can demand.... We must be governed by the best men and the best men are the best educated and the most concerned with the preservation of the laws. With few exceptions, you will find such men only among those who own property, who are attached to the country where that property is, to the laws which protect it and to the tranquility which preserves it, and who owe something to that property and the comfort it brings them.... A country ruled by property owners exists in a state of society; one where non-property owners rule, exists in a state of nature."[17] Since property could be inherited, it could be said that in that sense, the privilege of birth survived.

The path of bourgeois liberalism triumphed in the nineteenth century, having lost none of its value because of its reassuring conservative compromise.

2. --For those who believe in social democracy as it was sketched in the Year II, the right to life predominated over property rights, and equality should mean social equality. In his speech of December 2, 1792, concerning the grain riots of Eure-et-Loire, Robespierre subordinated the rights of property to the right of life and laid the basis for an egalitarian nation. "The authors of the theory considered the products most necessary to life as if they were ordinary products. They saw no difference between trade in grain and trade in indigo. They spoke more of grain trade than of the

---

[15]Le Moniteur, July 17, 1791, 818.

[16]Ibid., March 16, 1793, 341.

[17]Ibid., June 30, 1795. "Complete equality is a chimera," says Boissy d'Anglas. "For it to exist, one would need complete equality of intelligence, virtue, physical force, education and fortune among all men." The continuity of views from the Girondins to the Thermidorians is quite singular.

feeding of the people.... They considered highly the profits of wholesalers and landowners, almost not at all the subsistence of men.... The first right is the right to life; all others are subordinate."[18] Robespierre eventually reached, in his speech of April 24, 1793, a new statement of property rights: "Property is the right every citizen has to enjoy the property guaranteed to him by law and to dispose of it." It is no longer an inalienable, natural right which antedates any social organization, as the Declaration of 1789 claimed. It is now a right fitted within a social and historic framework; it is defined by law.

That is the way the masses understood it. They had always been hostile to economic freedom which paved the way for capitalism and the concentration of industry, hence for their being proletarianized. Not only did the rights of men and citizens remain for them illusory, but also private ownership of land and workshops placed them under the rule of those who, in fact, could alone enjoy them. They therefore invoked the right to life and put forward, against the property-owning bourgeoisie, the principle of equality of property. After August 10, 1792, the revolutionary bourgeoisie allied itself with the people in order to win the war. Universal manhood suffrage was instituted; a democratic and social republic was drafted. The national community, invested with right of control over private property, intervened to maintain a relative equality by reconstructing small properties as economic evolution tended to destroy it so as to avoid the reconstruction of a monopoly of wealth as well as the formation of a dependent proletariat. Laws were therefore passed by the Mountain to encourage small landowners, the economy was directed so as to bring prices and wages into balance, and a school system open to all was instituted. It was, in a word, national welfare. Thus would be realized the purpose assigned to society by the Declaration of the Rights of Man of June 24, 1793, namely, the happiness of all. Thus would become a reality this ideal for an egalitarian society that Saint-Just emphasized in his Institutions républicaines: "to give all Frenchmen the means of earning the necessities of life without being a subject to anything but the laws and without subjugation within the civil state." Or, as he said elsewhere: "Man must live independently."

---

[18]Le Moniteur, December 4, 1792, 1436. See Lefebvre, "Sur la pensée politique de Robespierre," in Etudes sur la Révolution française, 95-98, from a speech delivered for the unveiling of a bust of Robespierre in the Arras city-hall, published in Annales historiques de la Révolution française, X (1933), 492-510.

The attempt at social democracy of the Year II not only frightened the bourgeoisie, but also became a model after 1830 when the Republican party reappeared and even more after 1848 when the reestablishment of universal suffrage gave a new impetus to its principles. The attempt of the Year II nourished the social thought of the nineteenth century; its memory weighed heavily on the political struggle. The reforms drafted by the Mountain were slowly developed under the Third Republic, most of all the establishment of public schools open to all which the sans-culottes had vainly demanded as a necessary condition of social democracy.

At the same time, economic liberty and capitalistic concentration increased social distances and reinforced antagonisms so that equality of property moved farther and farther out of reach. Holding tightly to their condition, the artisans and shopkeepers descended from the sans-culottes of 1793 remained attached to small property founded on personal labor and vacillated between utopia and revolt. The attempt to realize social democracy was weighed down by the same contradiction between the requirements of equality of rights proclaimed in principle and the consequences of property rights and economic freedom and by the same impotence. The tragedy of June 1848 testifies to both contradictions and impotence as do the ups and downs of the Third Republic. Ernest Labrousse called the Year II "the period of expectation." Would it be not the period of utopias? In the fourth fragment of Institutions républicaines, Saint-Just wrote: "There must be neither rich nor poor." But he also notes on his agenda: "There must be no division of property." The egalitarian republic of the Year II remains in the realm of expectations, an Icaria unreachable but always sought.

3.--Yet, as early as the Revolution itself, Babeuf had solved the contradiction and opened a third path to the future by giving the principle of equal rights an extraordinary breadth and strength.[19] Like the sans-culottes, like the Jacobins, Babeuf proclaimed the purpose of society to be "the happiness of all." The Revolution is

---

[19]The present state of Babeuf studies was summed up in Babeuf(1760-1797), Buonarrotti (1761-1837): Pour le deuxième cen - tenaire de leur naissance (Nancy, 1961); Claude Mazauric, Babeuf et la Conspiration pour l'égalité (Paris, 1962); Babeuf et les problèmes du babouvisme, ed. by Albert Soboul (Paris, 1963); V. M. Daline, Gracchus Babeuf avant et pendant la Révolution française (1785-1794) (Moscow, 1963), in Russian, reviewed by Albert Soboul, Revue d'histoire moderne et contemporaine, XIII (1966),

to secure for all equality of property. Since private property necessarily introduces inequality, and since an agrarian law would work but for a day ("on its very morrow, inequality would reappear"),the only way to achieve "actual equality" and to secure for every man and his progeny, however numerous, a sufficiency but only a sufficiency, is to "set up a common administration, to abolish private property, to bind every man to the talent he has, the trade he knows, force him to bring the product to the common store and to establish a simple system of distribution as well as an administration of subsistence which would keep a register of all people and all goods and thereby distribute the goods with a scrupulous equality. "

This program, presented in the <u>Manifeste</u> des <u>plébéiens</u> published by <u>Le</u> <u>Tribun</u> <u>du</u> <u>peuple</u> of the 9th Frimaire, Year IV (November 30, 1795), showed a profound renewal or rather a sudden shift from the <u>sans-culottes</u> and Jacobin ideologies both characterized by a deep attachment to private property derived from personal labor. "The community of goods and labor" preached by Babeuf was the earliest form of the revolutionary ideology of the new society born from the Revolution itself. In other words, Babeuf considered abolishing private ownership of the means of production and establishing a communist democracy as the only means for realizing fully the equality of rights. Babouvism finally turned communism, until then utopian dream, into a coherent ideological system. With the <u>Conjuration</u> des <u>Egaux</u> he entered the history of social and political struggles.

The importance of the <u>Conjuration</u> and of Babouvism can be measured only in the nineteenth century. In the history of the Revolution and the Directory they are but an episode which undoubtedly modified the political balance at the time but had no deep echoes. In his letter of Messidor 25, Year IV (July 14, 1796), which is a veritable political testament, Babeuf recommended to Felix Lepeletier that he gather all his "projects, notes, and drafts of democratic and revolutionary writings, all relevant to the vast purpose, " namely perfect equality, happiness for all. "When one can again think of securing for the human race the happiness we dreamed about, you will be able to look into those papers and present to the disciples of Equality... what today's corrupt men call my dreams. "

166-167; V. Daline, Armando Saitta, Albert Soboul, <u>Inventaire</u> <u>des</u> <u>manuscrits</u> <u>et</u> <u>imprimés</u> <u>de</u> <u>Babeuf</u> (Paris, 1966).

In answer to that wish, Buanorrotti published in Brussels in 1828 the <u>Conspiration pour l'egalite, dite de Babeuf</u>.[20] Owing to it, Babouvism became a link in the chain of communist thought. Thus were born the French Revolution ideas which led, as Marx said, "beyond the ideas of former time," the ideas of a new social order which would be a bourgeois order.

*

Thus the French Revolution is situated at the very heart of the history of the contemporary world, at the crossroad of various social and political currents which divided nations and still divide them. A classical bourgeois revolution, it abolished uncompromisingly the feudal system and the seignorial regime, thereby marking the beginning in France of capitalist society and of the liberal representative system. A peasant and popular revolution, it tried twice to go beyond its bourgeois limits: a first time in the Year II, an attempt which necessarily failed but long remained a prophetic example, a second time during the <u>conspiration des égaux</u>, an episode situated at the very source of contemporary revolutionary thought and action. We can understand those vain efforts to deny the French Revolution--a dangerous precedent-- its historic reality and its specific character, both national and social. We can thus understand also the shock felt by the world and the resounding cry the French Revolution made in the consciousness of men in our century. This memory alone is revolutionary. It still exhilerates us.

---

[20]Last edition, Paris, 1957, preface by Georges Lefebvre.

THE MEANING OF THE FRENCH REVOLUTION:
A PANEL DISCUSSION

<u>Professor Laurent</u>

The French Revolution, as far as I am concerned, completely overturned social structures. Strong opposition developed to feudalism, but the bourgeoisie which emerged and declared itself in opposition tried to retain certain privileges. At the beginning, it was not a true revolution, for while this bourgeoisie in the Declaration of the Rights of Man--that is at the time of the Constituent Assembly--demanded the overthrow of social barriers, and demanded freedom of speech, thought, and action, and proclaimed that all men are free and equal in rights, this same bourgeoisie accepted compromises such as the Colonial Pact which is nothing more, after all, than the exploitation of the colonies for the profit of the mother country. The Constituent Assembly, besides, recognized, accepted, and permitted slavery. Frenchmen declared that man was free and proclaimed the dignity, later the equality, of all men, yet in Santo Domingo the slave trade was tolerated and slavery was perpetuated.

Looking at both aspects of the question, we see that at first the French bourgeoisie did not want a revolution. The bourgeoisie wanted to serve certain interests and make some changes concerning abuses, feudalism, and monarchical policies, that is to say, it confronted the nobility, the aristocrats, and the clergy, in an effort to share political power. This makes sense: the Colonial Pact, after all, had the same purpose since it was intended to enrich the bourgeoisie, being primarily a partnership between the state and bourgeois individuals. Not until the Convention did the Revolution take on another aspect, the equalitarian aspect. At this stage a true revolution took place and thus the Montagnard Convention by the decree of February 4, 1794 freed the blacks of the colonies and ended definitely the slave trade, in the name of humanity.

Professor Soboul

Any event as important as the French Revolution has a double significance, one for the country where the event takes place and one for universal history. Such an event has therefore a double significance and a double message.

Let us look at the general significance. First of all, how does the French Revolution fit into the history, not of the western world--for I do not accept the theory of a "western revolution"-- but of the modern world? I think that all nations and all countries followed generally similar historical development--history has a meaning --but each nation follows that development in its own way. The eighteenth and nineteenth centuries thus have an overall significance we can understand better when we view those periods in terms of the French Revolution.

The French Revolution is a stage in the transition from the Ancien Régime with its feudal survivals to modern society, the society we still live in, a bourgeois society, or, from the economic viewpoint, a capitalistic society. More precisely, what is the meaning of the French Revolution for general history, for what might be called "the law of transition from feudalism to capitalism?" (I use "law" as an historian to mean "tendency," not as the word might be used in the sciences.) The transition from a society with feudal survivals to a modern society theoretically defined by capitalism, history shows us, can be accomplished in two ways. The French way was the revolutionary way, par excellence, which completely destroyed feudal survivals. In 1789, those anachronisms were very much alive and no one who denies their reality can understand the peasant revolts. Masses do not revolt because they enjoy violence and thirst for blood. That was Taine's explanation, but it is not an historical explanation.

The other way, from the point of view of comparative history (and I think historians have to resort to comparative methods) is "the way of compromise," sometimes called "the Prussian way." It is also the Italian way, that of the Risorgimento. It was the way of Italian unification, the way of the Japanese Meiji, which during the transition from old to new society, integrates elements of the old into the new. Thus we have the survival of great landed property of East Prussia or Southern Italy, the persisting structures of which still cause many problems. Thus we have the case of Japan where the agrarian question was not solved by the Meiji but by

MacArthur as late as 1945. This evolution by compromise with its long range consequences weighed heavily on the evolution of those countries in the twentieth century. Prussia chose the way of compromise in going from old to new society. You know the consequences: Hitler and the Nazi regime. As for the Italy born of the Risorgimento, its evolution ended in Mussolini and Fascism.

There is a second aspect, no less important. There I agree with my friend Richard Cobb who believes that specificity alone matters in history. I will insert, therefore, on the specific significance and the original character of the French Revolution, both of which evidently resulted from the social structures of the Ancien Régime. This revolution was a revolution of the Third Estate. The aristocracy was powerful enough to oppose the revolution and reject the compromise offered by the the Constituent Assembly during the summer of 1789. The French Revolution was thus more or less pushed along her specific path: anti-feudal and anti-aristocratic.

This revolution of the Third Estate is more easily defined negatively than affirmatively. Anti-feudal, it destroyed the feudal system completely, uncompromisingly, without compensation for feudal rights as in Italy. It abolished serfdom, freed the peasant and gave him land while in other countries serfdom was abolished, but the peasant received no land: in Southern Italy, in Poland in 1807, and later in Russia. That is the French specificity: anti-feudal and anti-aristocratic revolution.

If we want now to define the Revolution more precisely in its social aspects, to define it positively, not negatively, we will say that it is a bourgeois revolution. There is no doubt that the members of the bourgeois led the revolution. Of course, we cannot use bourgeoisie here in its narrow capitalistic meaning, but the men of 1789--the future Girondins and Montagnards--were in many ways bourgeois. One cannot deny the link between those men, even when they belonged to the liberal professions, and the commercial bourgeoisie. Barnave was tied to the great planters of Santo Domingo; the Girondists were linked to the great harbor bourgeoisie. Let us not forget that slavery was not abolished in the colonies and that political rights were withheld from the free men of color. There was a colonial lobby in Paris, formed particularly by the representatives of the great planters and of the chambers of commerce of the ports. Capitalistic interests were well defined. Let us note also that one need not be a capitalist to defend the interests of capitalism. Beginning with the Directory and even more with the Consulate, the notables, namely those differentiated from the people by wealth and property, led France even if the country did not enter the age of capitalistic development only in the middle of the nineteenth century. In that sense, the French Revolution was indeed bourgeoisie and, in the long run, capitalist.

It is important, however, to introduce some distinctions. It was a revolution of the Third Estate, a revolution led by the bourgeoisie, but also, to answer Miss Hyslop's question, it was a revolution supported by the masses. The people destroyed the old system because the people could no longer bear the burden. Hence, a bourgeois revolution supported by the masses. But one must be more precise. The French Revolution was also a peasant revolution. For the last twenty years we have paid too much attention to the urban masses--the sans-culottes of July 14 and the October Days of 1789, of the overthrow of the monarchy on August 10, 1792, of the elimination of the Girondins on May 31, 1793. Was the Revolution carried out by that urban minority? Most certainly not. One should not forget the peasant insurrection, the Jacquerie everpresent from 1789-1792, which has not been sufficiently studied by French historians. In 1789, peasants and townsmen together pushed the revolution forward--we cannot forget the Great Fear. But in 1791, and until the spring of 1792, the townspeople intervened little or not at all; the masses of countrymen pushed the revolution forward.

French historians have never written the general history of the peasant uprisings and of the Jacquerie from 1789 to 1792, that is until the townspeople took over. There are monographs, the best known being Georges Lefebvre's work on the peasants of the north, but no synthesis, no general work. Recently a Soviet historian, Professor Ado, after spending several years in the French archives, published a work on the subject. I can therefore now answer Miss Hyslop: in 1789, the French Revolution was carried out by the country people and the urban minority, but from 1789 to 1792, it is the peasant Jacquerie which pushed the revolution forward.

Thus I can define that revolution as bourgeois and peasant, and thereby enrich the meaning of the French Revolution.

Questions

Professor Soboul

The French Revolution was antifeminist. The Jacobins, in particular, were quite hostile to the idea of women participating in political life. The sans-culottes, no.

- - - - - - - - - -

Professor Soboul

I will answer first that it was not Napoleon, or rather Bonaparte, who crushed freedom and equality as the sans-culottes understood those terms; it was the Thermidorians and the Directorians. The Directory was not a government of the people. The Brumairians brought Bonaparte to power, but this action followed Thermidor quite logically: Thermidorians, Directorians, Brumairians were the same men. When Bonaparte seized power by the Brumaire coup d'état, the main part of the task was done. From 1795 onward, the people were no longer concerned with politics; freedom no longer existed and equality even less. The Constitution of the Year III set up property qualifications while Bonaparte was clever enough to reestablish universal suffrage in the Constitution of the Year VIII--though he weighed it in favor of the notables.

Yet, Napoleon held on to certain revolutionary principles. He did create a new nobility, it is true, but those new titles carried no privilege, equality before the law and the tax collector was preserved. Napoleon never reestablished nobiliary privileges, never went back on two essential conquests of 1789, civil equality and disestablishment. Napoleon did not touch those two bases of modern French society. The Ancien Régime powers understood it well and till the end opposed in Napoleon the soldier of the Revolution.

What did a liberty the masses would not enjoy mean to that people? Since 1795, the people had been pushed out from the political system. Moreover, the masses enjoyed a real prosperity under the Empire. I do not agree with the economic historians who deny the existence of prosperity and argue that the revolution interrupted French economic growth. One should ask, who benefits from growth? The Revolution by suppressing feudal taxation, by abolishing seignorial rights and tithes, by permitting the peasants who already owned land to acquire more, made a real prosperity possible among the peasants. It is only necessary to read the reports of prefects to realise it. In the cities, starting at the end of the Directory, in 1798, there was a real economic revival. Salaries climbed until the great crisis of 1811-1812 so that the town laborers were grateful to Napoleon, even if that economic tendency was reversed after 1812.

Napoleon was nicknamed "l'Empereur des Faubourgs." If he was Emperor of the faubourgs, it is because from the point of view of the masses he never went back on the essential conquests of the Revolution and that, to some extent, he brought prosperity to the masses.

THE RELATIONS OF THE FRENCH REVOLUTION AND THAT OF SANTO DOMINGO

Gérard Laurent

At the same time a revolution exploded in France, dismantling the monarchical arsenal, abolishing feudal privileges, opening political and administrative careers to a revolutionary bourgeoisie, lightening the burden of a people weary of their fetters, 1800 leagues away, in Santo Domingo, three subversively oriented movements burst through the worm-eaten framework of colonialism and freed a nation of blacks gasping for the breath of liberty.

In many quarters, the French Revolution is held responsible for the upheaval which took place in the propserous colony of Santo Domingo. Some writers have opined that the colonial revolution was the offspring of the mainland event. To hold such a view, however, is to maintain, contrary to the principles of modern history, that revolutions are exportable. A revolution is born of local causes, often from the contradictions within the milieu. A revolution lacks spontaneity and evolves gradually toward a final outburst. An analysis of society leads to the conclusion that a revolution is the logical consequence of social conflict, unequal distribution of wealth, and explosive situations created by a spirit of exploitation and inequity. I am inclined to think that the French Revolution would have left intact the economic and social framework of Santo Domingo had it not been that basic factors disturbed a colonial society already threatened with dislocation.

Before studying the possible influence of the French Revolution on Santo Domingo, or before explaining the relations between the two upheavals, one must investigate the attitude of various

245

social categories: the blacks, the freedmen, the whites, all of them partly responsible for the colonial unrest.

*

A revolution has been prepared by the very act of colonizing the island of Santo Domingo as laborers were drawn from Africa and condemned to serve the cupidity of the colony and the mainland. The single-crop economy had made that importation of workers necessary: sugarcane required a large work force and equally large plantations of at least 300 carreaux. European workers were not anxious to migrate to the Antilles; those who had come as free laborers had found themselves enslaved and, though white, had experienced the shame of the "fleur-de-lys" brand, the whipping post and mutilation. The planters of Santo Domingo had to look elsewhere for labor and found in Africa, because of its tribal wars, an ideal supplier since war prisoners were sold into slavery. The 1685 edict, the Black Code, in article 44 legalized the exploitation of blacks considered as "things" and declared to be such. The colonists then found themselves owning human equipment over which they enjoyed unlimited rights and, eager for wealth, turned to the whip to get the maximum production from their slaves. The uprooted slaves became the object of a double exploitation since the mainland bourgeoisie entered into partnership with the colonists. The work demanded of the slaves was intensive and unceasing, as exhausting as it was brutalizing. To insure continuity of the regime, moral constraint was added to corporal punishment and forced labor, moral constraint with all its implications: dehumanization, isolation in a decadent society, and ignorance perpetuated by the withholding of education. This system sufficed to provide the spark of hatred and anger which would destroy the colony. The discontent of the slaves, subhuman beings immersed in abject conditions of life, and their stored-up grievances led the blacks, as soon as their consciousness awoke, to destroy the regime and to gain human rights. But the slaves were not the only malcontents.

Despite their pride and their prejudices, the Santo Domingo planters could not remain indifferent to the physical beauty of the black girls who were their slaves. From their intimate relations citizens were born whose nuance épidermique approached that of the white. As sons and daughters of colonists, those illegitimate children were emancipated at birth. These freedmen, allowed to inherit from good-natured fathers, found themselves quite wealthy upon coming of age. Some, privileged because of their white parentage, were able to go to France to pursue their studies and complete their education. When they finished school and returned to Santo Domingo, a spirit of solidarity impelled them to found schools for their less fortunate brethren. Generally, those freedmen were hard workers who settled in the lonely southern regions which they transformed by courageously cultivating the land they had improved. On the eve of the French Revolution there were 28,000 such freedmen who owned one-third of the land and a quarter of the 500,000 slaves in the colony. Their wealth, their culture, their large families aroused a fierce jealousy among the poorer whites and a profound concern among the colonists and wealthy merchants. To gratify and soothe those fears, in a spirit of prudence as well as of vengeance, the whites erected barriers against the people of mixed blood who were forced into a humiliating social position. These freedmen within administration, army, or politics encountered degrading abuse in their social life and professional activities. Second-class citizens, they had to accept the insolent arrogance of the poorer whites and the insulting pride of the planters. They dreamed of rebelling against a crushing situation and demanded, in the name of justice, their civil and political rights. They were ready to fight for racial equality.

The lowest class among the whites were the workers and artisans, noisy, impetuous, resentful. Victims of the sugar cane revolution, they found themselves held down in a strongly hierarchical society. Colonists and planters oppressed them economically and excluded them socially. These dispossessed whites, dreaming of vengeance, coveted the economic position of the colonists.

The colonists, in turn, raged at the mother country which subjected them to the colonial pact, this formula devised by Colbert to rescue France from the economic stagnation caused by Mazarin's mistakes of statesmanship and by Louis XIV's thirst for glory. Actually Colbertism, as the system was called, greatly helped France to improve its economic situation, reduce its unemployment rate (through the creation of new industries and the development of coastal cities), and to accumulate capital while enriching the bourgeoisie. On the other hand the pact subordinated the welfare of the colonies to the welfare of the mainland. Under mercantilism the inhabitants of the islands, Santo Domingo especially, were forced to accept situations which were but thinly veiled servitude: commerce with any country besides France was strictly forbidden; the mercantile, slave trading bourgeoisie alone could supply Santo Domingo with goods and black ivory; moreover, the mother country determined the price of tropical products; manufacturing was not allowed; and even the choice of tropical products grown was strictly limited, some being allowed, others not, according to mainland interests. This systematic strangling extended to political affairs so that the colonists found themselves existing only for the well-being of the French bourgeoisie and nobility. They too yearned for a change which would soften this strict control.

Thus in every social component of Santo Domingo--blacks, colored citizens, poor whites, planters--were embittered malcontents who, in the darkness, watched for a chance to overthrow the colonial regime. The planters wished no changes for the other classes, but wanted to abolish the colonial pact to gain the right to administer the colony and legislate in the name of the mother country. The poor whites wanted to turn the colony upside down, to ruin the planters, and to replace them as leaders. The freedmen demanded social reforms though, like the whites, they favored slavery. Not one of those movements, all of which excluded the most numerous class, could be termed revolutionary since revolution implies above all changes in a social structure and an attempt to secure the welfare of the oppressed, degraded, exploited, and humiliated masses. The workshop movement alone had a truly revolutionary character. It would be called upon to sweep away the system, to change the vicious outlook, to tear down the barriers which immobilized a whole group of men, and finally, to bring slaves to the level of human dignity.

Considering the contradictions which permeated the social body, one can easily understand why astute observers compared Santo Domingo to a powder keg ready to explode at the first spark. This explosion, however, could have been delayed, and would have been delayed, had it not been for sparks from the pyre destroying feudal regime in France. From that point of view, it is difficult to deny a close relationship between the events in Santo Domingo and those which rent French society.

Undoubtedly, the French Revolution created a volatile climate in Santo Domingo. It introduced an age of violence and demands. The calling of the Estates General encouraged the reactionary agitation of the planters. Spurred by that first attack on the monarchical regime, the planters attacked governmental authority by defying the governor. Despite his orders, they organized clandestine elections and, with the full knowledge of the authorities, sent to France a delegation entrusted with their grievances. Moreover, the Declaration of the Rights of Man, a charter of social liberation calling for justice and affirming the principles of liberty and equality for all men, aroused the hopes of the freedmen in their desperate struggle for social liberation. Their action was spurred by the humanitarian campaign of the Société des Amis des Noirs which pleaded their cause. Opposed to the Societe were the members of the Club Massiac who, as friends and protectors of the planters, upheld a policy of discrimination. From the first, with the calling of the Estates General, the Declaration of the Rights of Man, and the actions of antagonistic clubs, the French Revolution encouraged a confrontation between planters and administrators, between freedmen and whites. The whites, like the royal officials, tried in vain to dam the torrent with angry reactionary measures. The behavior of the protesting groups (behavior which was a plea for violence) and the rumors circulated among freedmen within earshot of household slaves and artisan slaves awakened the brighter blacks. They finally understood that freedom would not be given to 500,000 slaves; it would have to be wrested from oppressing forces. For such a stake, one might well risk his life. Men weary from centuries of servitude, opprobrium, and misery, had to put an end to these conditions even by bloody revolution. This was the message of the French Revolution which was transmitted through the agitation of planters and freedmen.

The French Revolution did not only give several classes the eagerly awaited chance to manifest their grievances. It went farther and precipitated events by its colonial policy, another aspect which underlines its influence on the several groups of Santo Domingo.

The study of that policy leads us to analyze the decrees of March 8, 1790; May 15, 1791; September 24, 1791; April 4, 1792; February 4, 1794 and to examine the actions of French officials whether in the exercise of their function or under the impact of circumstances.

The Constituent Assembly seriously disturbed Santo Domingo with its indecisions, contradictions, and gropings. Essentially bourgeois, this assembly reached its high point with the Declaration of the Rights of Man, but oriented its colonial policy toward the preservation of slavery. This policy demanded a coalition of landowners: planters and freedmen, those interested in preserving a regime of exploitation had to present a united front. The assembly inclined toward political regrouping when it offered the freedmen civil and political rights with the decree of March 8, 1790, a policy which ran counter to the intransigence of the prejudiced planters and provoked a bloody encounter between planters and freedmen (Ogé affair). Fearing a revolt in the workshops, which threatened slavery, the Assembly passed the decree of May 15, 1791 which gave landowning freedmen, born to free fathers and mothers, full rights of citizenship. This law also provoked an armed clash between planters and freedmen (Affair of the Western Confederates). Fearing a wave of violence which could jeopardize slavery, the Constituent Assembly did an about face and passed the law of September 24, 1791. The whites now controlled the fate of colored people who accepted the decision despite their hatred for the planters and the poor white. Like their leader Julien Raimond, the blacks hoped their submissive behavior would gain them the good graces of the mother country.

In France, the Legislative Assembly (1791-1792), which replaced the National Assembly, included such men as Brissot, Pétion, Condorcet, Abbé Grégoire, Mirabeau. The Assembly legislated for the benefit of freedmen whom it used as the cornerstone of its colonial policy. The April 4, 1792 decree restored their rights: a powerful force was needed to maintain slavery so that planters and freedmen had to be reconciled to safeguard the regime.

This law, however, only served to disturb the political climate in Santo Domingo. The planters in particular, but the whites in general, used the most brutal means to paralyze the Commissaires Civils sent to carry out the decree. This assembly, typical of the liberal bourgeoisie, opposed the French feudal aristocracy which organized the counterrevolution and attacked the royalist colonial planters who were already negotiating with the London government. The Girondin-dominated Convention wanted to safeguard its material interests, particularly the Colonial Pact and feared the separatist policy of the Santo Domingo planters. The Convention wanted to maintain both slavery and the slave trade. "The sweat and blood of the Santo Domingo slaves financed the luxury of Bordeaux negociants." In the Girondin Convention, the bourgeoisie from the great ports defended its rights, and the struggle which opposed its representatives--the Commissaires Civils Sonthonax, Polverel, Ailhaud--to the planters would eventually benefit the slaves. After each maneuver of the planters, the commissaires reacted with fresh violence, seeking help from the freedmen, the citizens of April 4. But when the weakened freedmen proved incapable of holding at bay the united whites, Sonthonax, desperately determined to save the colony, called on the blacks who proved a worthy strike force. The war between France and the monarchical block further emphasized the importance of the blacks for the Santo Domingo leaders.

To resist the Anglo-Spanish aggression and reorganize the plantations, Sonthonax, though his mission had not authorized him to do so, had to liberate the blacks drafted into the republican armies. He could not do otherwise since the slaves were escaping in large numbers from the plantation and joining the Spanish armies as free soldiers. It was thus that the Montagnard Convention on February 4, 1791 ratified Sonthonax's decisions. The concatenation of events continued in France as well as in Santo Domingo.

While the mother country, in defense of its interests, turned first to the whites (September 24, 1791), then to the freedmen (April 4, 1792) and finally to the blacks (February 4, 1794), the slaves helped the freedmen against the whites (the Swiss affair), the royalists against the planters (August 1791), the planters against the Commissaires Civils (Borel affair), the Commissaires Civils against the planters (Galbaud affair), and once they were appreciated as a strike force, the republic against the Anglo-Spaniards (Toussaint L'Ouverture's reversal). In France, the revolution brought about by the grievances of a pro-monarchical bourgeoisie moved toward a popular dictatorship based on terror. The agitation in Santo Domingo evolved in the same direction. The colony was overturned by the landowning colonists who gave way to slave-owning freedmen before being destroyed by the rebellious slaves. Led by an extraordinary leader, Toussaint L'Ouverture, who knew how to exploit local and international contradictions, the former slaves marched from conquest to conquest toward a consecration of the freedom guaranteed them by the Constitution of 1801.

The Directory (1795-1799) slowed the pace of revolution in France. This bourgeois republic adopted a colonial policy as reactionary as that of earlier governments, proclaiming as a necessity the regime which had prevailed in Santo Domingo before 1789. Toussaint L'Ouverture took a strong position against this return to slavery and, to gain a free hand, sent away the French agents whose presence hampered him. Sonthonax who had returned with a second mission was sent back to France in 1797; General Hédouville followed a year later; and the agent Roume returned home in 1801.

Then France experienced the coup d'état of 18 Brumaire which ended revolutionary gains. Napoleon Bonaparte, as First Consul, intended also to put an end to the black revolution and to suppress the natives who, under the leadership of Toussaint L'Ouverture, wanted liberty based on independence. To destroy them and proclaim the return of slavery, a fleet commanded by Bonaparte's own brother-in-law sailed for Santo Domingo. Owing to the new awareness aroused by the teaching of their leader, owing also to their fanaticism, their conviction, their courage, the Santo Domingo blacks overcame all obstacles. On the bodies of that powerful and prestigious European army, the Haitian nation was built. The revolution of the masses begun on August 22, 1791, triumphed on January 1, 1804.

Thus we can conclude that, independently of the contradictions which foreshadowed serious troubles for Santo Domingo, the French Revolution influenced its development by its principles and its colonial policy. From the Constituent Assembly to the Convention, from the Directory to the Consulate, the revolution disturbed the climate of Santo Domingo by its decrees as well as by the acts of its agents, the Commissaires Civils. This influence was such that the blacks, breaking the chains of bondage, occupied the lime-light from 1793 to 1804. The results did indeed go beyond the wishes of the French revolutionaries. They believed that by freeing the slaves they had secured so valuable a colony: this gesture, they believed, definitely tied Santo Domingo to the mother country. They even tried to assimilate the blacks by cutting off their roots and would have succeeded had not circumstances decided otherwise. The counterrevolution safely ensconced in France aroused distrust among the blacks who became aware of threatening statements directed against them. The fear of returning slavery awoke them: they chose to live with dignity or die.

Grateful, the former slaves never disowned the France of the Declaration of the Rights of Man which opened their eyes, nor the France of the Convention which officially made them free men. They remained attached to Laveaux, to Sonthonax, men who showed them the worth of education as a civilizing factor. Some considered an independence which would retain some ties with France, but the policy of the reactionaries harbored by the Directory and especially the Consulate burned the bridges between France and the irreductible blacks. Proud of their dignity, those former slaves, now proselytes of the Declaration of the Rights of Man, could not abdicate this beautiful social gain. It is under that banner that they marched against the armies of Leclerc, last hope of the former colonials.

INDEX

DATE DUE			

Symposium   168612